LAND JUSTICE

Re-imagining Land, Food, and the Commons in the United States

LAND JUSTICE

Re-imagining Land, Food, and the Commons in the United States

Edited by
Justine M. Williams and Eric Holt-Giménez

With Prefaces by:
Winona LaDuke
LaDonna Redmond
George Naylor

Published by Food First Books/Institute for Food and Development Policy

Food First Books
Institute for Food and Development Policy
398 60th Street, Oakland, CA 94618 USA
Tel (510) 654-4400
foodfirst@foodfirst.org
www.foodfirst.org

Cover and interior design by *Marites D. Bautista*
Copyedit and proofreading by *William Wroblewski and Martha Katigbak-Fernandez*
Cover art by *Jonathan Green*

Library of Congress Cataloging-in-Publication Data

Names: Williams, Justine M., 1985- editor. | Holt-Giménez, Eric, editor.
Title: Land justice : re-imagining land, food, and the commons in the United
    States / edited by Justine M. Williams and Eric Holt-Giménez ; with
    prefaces by: Winona LaDuke, LaDonna Redmond, George Naylor.
Description: Oakland, CA : Food First Books, Institute for Food and
    Development Policy, 2017. | Includes bibliographical references.
Identifiers: LCCN 2016058790 (print) | LCCN 2017004590 (ebook) | ISBN
    9780935028041 | ISBN 9780935028195 ()
Subjects: LCSH: Land tenure--United States. | Commons--United States.
Classification: LCC HD1289.U6 L36 2017 (print) | LCC HD1289.U6 (ebook) | DDC
    333.30973--dc23
LC record available at https://lccn.loc.gov/ 2016058790

Food First Books are distributed by:
Ingram Publisher Services - Perseus Distribution
210 American Drive
Jackson, TN 38301
1-800-343-4499
www.perseusdistribution.com

Printed in Canada. First printing 2017.

TABLE OF CONTENTS

LAMENTING A LOST VOICE

Today, we lament a lost voice for human and economic justice: the passing of Kathy Ozer, a person who advocated for family farmers in all the American states from her unique platform in the turbulence of Washington, D.C. Kathy embraced life and goodness but never feared to lead in a political universe of dark and roiling soils.

In decades of directing the NFFC, Kathy did not have the means to cure all the maladies that plague small and new farmers in the brutal corporate realm that now afflicts American agriculture. Her tools were battered farm organizations and nascent groups of healthy food growers in communities everywhere. Her mission was akin to turning the Great Plains with a pair of willful mules.

Across the nation, the foreclosure crisis of the 1980s was fought by desperate farmers; men and women turned organizers for wont of outside help. In these people, Kathy saw potential and greatness. In her they recognized a friend who could be trusted, who always sought victory over injustice. She was their organizer in Washington and across the nation they were her leaders. With infinite thanks owed to Kathy, the organizing and advocacy by family farmers continues across the sweep of our nation. Through them the practical quest for economic and environmental justice lives today.

Kathy's life was an investment in the love of people, their advocacy and their democracy. The continuance of NFFC and Farm Aid are proof of that. Her trust in humanity is still sung by Farm Aid. Her shared faith inspires determined groups across our land. As Kathy might have said, we still want to hug the America of our dreams and to share the virtues of those dreams in the nation's healing. The testament to the human truths in Kathy's persistence is our own determination to see those dreams realized.

ACKNOWLEDGEMENTS

This book has not just been a simple publication project, but a generative and collaborative effort between many activists, scholars, farmers, and organizers to discuss the problem of land in this country, and to imagine how things might be different. The volume that emerges is powerful because of the tremendous enthusiasm and vision of the many contributors who shared, elaborated on, and augmented our ideas about the stories and issues that should fill its pages. We thank them for their dedication to writing and rewriting these chapters—often under short deadlines—and most importantly, for trusting us with the incredible responsibility of publishing their work.

We are grateful for the collaborations that have developed or expanded through the development of this book, and are particularly awed by the collective that came together, under the steadfast guidance of Tracy McCurty along with Gail Myers, to create the section on Black Agrarianism. Their dedication to collective processes of creativity and activism is both instructive and inspirational.

The idea for this book was originally developed with Zoe Brent, through her work with the Land and Sovereignty in the Americas collective of Food First and the Land and Resources Working Group of the U.S. Food Sovereignty Alliance, and we thank her for her instrumental efforts.

Joe Brooks, Nick Estes, Hank Herrera, Gerald Horne, Ahna Kruzic, Annie Shattuck, and Caridad Souza provided indispensable review of and perspective on various pieces included in the book. William Wroblewski copy-edited with a sharp eye for detail and clarity, as did Martha Katigbak-Fernandez during proofreading. Her knowledge of the book production process, too, was essential. Ahna Kruzic helped to bring these chapters to more audiences through backgrounder publications and communications work. Food First interns Eva Perroni and Tasnim Elboute meticulously transcribed interviews, and Ilja van Lammeren provided valuable research support. Coline Charasse, McKenna Jacquemet, Ilja van Lammeren, Matthew Rose-Stark, Erik Hazard, and Hartman Deetz carefully indexed. Other members of the Food First family—Leonor Hurtado, Marilyn Borchardt, Rowena Garcia, and Alyshia Silva—provided institutional support, administrative assistance, home-cooked lunches, and general inspiration.

We are also thankful to Jonathan Green for the generous gift of his artwork (featured on the cover and opening of the Black Agrarianism section), which celebrates the importance of land in Lowcountry life and culture, and to Richard Weedman for facilitating it.

Finally, this book has been made possible by very generous contributions from the Ralph Ogden Foundation, the Jessie Smith Noyes Foundation, WhyHunger, Grassroots International, the Haas Institute for a Fair and Inclusive Society, as well as from individuals including Neil Thapar, Val Voorheis, Gail B. Thomas, Alastair Iles, Adrienne Hirt and Jeffrey Rodman, Thomas Caffrey, Thomas M. Bosserman, Neil A. Holtzman, and Judith Buechner. We are grateful.

This book is dedicated to all those who have lost their access to the land, and to those who continue to fight for land justice.

- The Editors

PREFACE

Recovering our Land to Decolonize our Food

Winona LaDuke

There are 60,000 Native farmers in the United States. Some are farming within large structures, like the Navajo Agricultural Product Industry, Gila River Enterprises, and Tanka Bar. Some are part of smaller organizations, like Tohono O'odam Community Action or the White Earth Land Recovery Project. Many are individual, family farmers. Some have adopted corporate models, but others operate sustainably, nurturing the soil, water, and the people. Many produce food at a scale that feeds both local people and their nations. There would be more of these farmers, but various allotment acts have resulted in "checker boarding" within reservations. This means that many tribal agricultural lands have been sold or leased to non-native interests. This has caused long-term problems for local food security.

I live in what is called Minnesota. It is here where Norman Borlaug, "the father of the Green Revolution," made his plans and carried out his work. The University of Minnesota has a Borlaug Hall, and receives funding from industrial giants, including Cargill and Monsanto. Together, they promote the practice of growing single crops intensively on large scales. It is a war on the land, and has wrought destruction across it.

In some areas in Minnesota, more than 90 percent of the original wetlands have been drained.[1] The western third of the state, including the portions that were ceded to the Ojibwe tribe in an 1855 treaty, were once covered with wetlands. But this is no longer the case. The Minnesota Pollution Control Agency released a daunting report stating that one-fourth of southern Minnesota's lakes and rivers are too polluted to use

---

[1] As reported by the Minnesota Board of Water and Soil Resources. Undated. "Wetlands Regulations in Minnesota." Accessed November 11, 2016, http://www.bwsr.state.mn.us/wetlands/publications/wetland-regulation2.html.

as drinking water.[2] Moreover, the Minnesota Pollution Control Agency (MPCA) reported that 41 percent of all the state's streams and lakes have excessive nitrogen, which can be toxic to fish and other forms of aquatic life. Most of this pollution is caused by industrial agriculture: the mono-cropping of corn and soybeans. The effects are far-reaching: nitrogen pollution from agricultural runoff travels downstream, where it is the primary contributor to the dead zone in the Gulf of Mexico.

Industrialized agriculture is toxic, and it is also unsustainable. The fossil fuel use of agriculture (from seed to table) results in up to one quarter of all carbon dioxide emissions, which in turn contribute to global warming.[3] It is said that if we were to transition our world to an organic agricultural system, we could sequester one quarter of this carbon.

And yet, the USDA wants us, as Native people, to adopt industrial-style agriculture. They want this despite the fact that it is destroying the environment, and that such practices counter what we know to be true: that you cannot treat a plant like a machine—it is a living being. You cannot create a condition where there are more antibiotics served and injected into healthy animals than given to sick humans. These practices will not work out over the long term for any of us living on this land.

Indigenous agriculture—based on biodiversity and the use of multiple locally adapted crops—is the real future for agriculture. Already, indigenous food producers and farmers are adapting crops in the face of climate change, utilizing knowledge of seeds selection and cropping systems that have been passed down through the millennia. On a global scale, indigenous farmers using traditional and innovative techniques and resisting the corporate model are producing up to 70 percent of the world's food.

The food we produce in this way is special. Plants, simply stated, are magical beings. They provide complex nutrients, medicinal values, cultural and spiritual connections, and they feed the soil. "Corn, beans, squash, and tobacco grew from the body of Sky Woman, the daughter of the mother of the Creator of the world," said Teena Delormier, a Mohawk and professor of Public Health at the University of Hawaii in Mano. The foods we grow and harvest have a combination of special powers. As nutritionist Harriet Kuhnlein explains: "Singularly, tortillas are at 62 on the glycemic index, and beans are at 22. Put together into a meal, they are at 32." The magic of foods is a real medicine. Daphne Miller from San Francisco State explains

---

[2] See Minnestoa Pollution Control Agency. 2013. "Report on nitrogen in surface water." Accessed November 1, 2016, https://www.pca.state.mn.us/news/report-nitrogen-surface-water.

[3] As reported by a variety of sources including GRACE Communications Foundation. 2016. "Taking a Bite out of Climate Change." Food Program: Agriculture, Energy, and Climate Change. Accessed November 11, 2016, http://www.sustainabletable.org/982/agriculture-energy-climate-change.

that there are 300 natural medicines found in indigenously grown plants that serve to reduce blood sugar.[4]

To continue and expand on our production of these healthful and medicinal foods, we must have control over lands and our seeds. Projects like the White Earth Land Recovery Project work toward this by, for instance, creating seed libraries that help us to increase the diversity of vegetables grown on the reservation, and to cultivate varieties that are best suited to our ecological conditions. One farmer, Ronnie Chilton, described an indigenous corn variety to me that even the deer prefer to the field corn grown by industrial farmers.

Indigenous farming is essential to our people. It helps us to revalorize traditional roles for women, to establish community relationships, and to recover from historic traumas. As my friend Sugar Bear Smith once explained to me, "You cannot talk about being sovereign if you can't feed yourself."

When we practice indigenous farming we can create restorative, sustainable landscapes and contribute to national foodsheds. But to do this we must reclaim our land. We have lost a great deal. For decades, the US government deprived Native farmers of access to the resources necessary to capitalize and expand their production. As a result, their farms have declined, and many have been forced off the land. At the same time, the US Department of Agriculture has made loans available to non-Indians, who are able to take advantage of the cheap land left behind by Indians, and to build farms up in their place.

In 1999, a class action lawsuit known as *Keepseagle v. Vilsack* was filed. The lead plaintiffs, George and Marilyn Keepseagle, explained that they had been unfairly denied operating loans. As a result, they were required to sell off portions of their large farm on the Standing Rock Reservation in North Dakota. They contended that this was part of a persistent pattern of discrimination that was undermining Native land ownership and moving it into non-Native hands. The suit, following the model of a similar lawsuit filed by Black Farmers, resulted in an award of $680 million to Native farmers and the organizations that support them.

The impacts of this suit remain to be seen. What is clear is that we are in the midst of an important moment in Indigenous agriculture in North America. There is a resurgence and recovery of Indigenous farming, harvesting, food security, sovereignty, and chefs. Seed savers like Rowen White, Carolyn Chartrand, and Dream of Wild Health are part of a movement to

---

[4] All of these quotes from the Indigenous Terra Madre Conference, 2015, held in Shillong, Meghalaya, India November 3-7.

restore our seeds and bring them back to the land and people; groups like the Grand Ronde Food Sovereignty Project, Hopi Permaculture Project, Oneida Nation Farms, and the White Earth Land Recovery Project are engaging in tribal food work; and a growing number of Native farmers are gardening for their families and communities. Harvesters are also working together to collect fish, wild rice, and maple syrup. Stories are being told and shared, and international work is underway.

Our food systems have been colonized and deconstructed, and our wealth taken by others. But now is the time to begin decolonization. As we re-establish our relationships with them, the seeds, our foods, are coming home. This year, I held some rice in my hand from Onamia Lake in Minnesota. The seed had been dormant for 17 years, but seeds dormant for centuries can return and flourish. This year, I used a horse to plow and plant my cornfield, tilled in fish fertilizer from the lakes, and had a bountiful harvest. The seeds I plant, like other old seeds, flourish in a pre-industrial, and now post-industrial world. Those seeds, our communities, and our prayers, are not only the future of our food, but the future of food for all in this world. To bring them back to the earth, we will need to restore our access to and relationships with the land.

The struggle over land in our nation begins and ends with recognizing our spiritual relationship with our seeds, our food, the air we breathe, the water we drink, and the earth we walk upon.

The Land is Contested

LaDonna Redmond

This land is contested.

The arrival of the first Europeans on Western soil set a course of events that reverberates throughout history and continues today. This pattern of exploitation is still unfolding in urban and rural communities all over the United States.

At the founding of the United States of America, Indian removal policies of the newly formed government made it possible to push indigenous people off land they had inhabited for centuries. The trails of tears, from south to west, continued during the harshest of weather. Many died. Others that fought back were killed. No longer sovereign, indigenous people were considered hostile enemies on their own land. Killing off the buffalo along the way made sure that their survival was unlikely.

This land is contested.

The holocaust of the indigenous set the stage in the United States for the rise of capitalism. However, the quest for wealth would not be complete without the enslavement of Africans. It is estimated that 10 to 12 million African men, women, and children were kidnapped from their homes. Forced to march as many as 1,000 miles to the sea, they were then often held in underground dungeons for up to a year. It is documented that 54,000 slave ship voyages were made to the Americas. Free labor built on stolen land is what built the wealth of the so-called New World.

The Homestead Act, signed on May 18, 1862, allowed immigrants to homestead on public land for a small fee. This "public land" was actually land that belonged to the indigenous. In August of 1862, the Dakota War began, and ended on December 26th of the same year with the order to execute the 38 captured warriors, known as the Dakota 38 + 2. It was Abraham Lincoln who sanctioned the largest mass execution in the United States. A few days later, the Emancipation Proclamation was issued on January 1, 1863.

However, Emancipation did not guarantee freedom for the Africans. Lynching became the way that the newly freed realized that they were not free. At the same time, free Africans generally could not take advantage of the Homestead Act; the Act simultaneously allowed arriving immigrants the opportunity to settle on indigenous land while preventing freed Africans from even considering freedom west of the Mississippi. Black codes or vagrancy laws enacted at the time meant Black men that were arrested for minor infractions and convicted were then committed to involuntary labor. In essence, these laws were used to maintain a steady supply of free labor.

This Land is contested.

The turn of the nineteenth century and the industrialization of agriculture did not minimize exploitation. The theme of exploitation along race, class, and gender lines continued with the 13th Amendment, ensuring that prisoners could be forced back into slavery; for minor infractions, thousands of African American men were sold as free labor to build railroads, dig in coalmines, and slave other industries.

It is at this point where the food movement typically chooses to begin the timeline of agricultural injustice: with the industrialization and increasing urbanization of America.

Native Americans were forced into reservations. Black folks were terrorized out of the south to the north. This "Great Migration" was undertaken with promise of an escape from Jim Crow. But the reality was a great disappointment. Racism was alive and well in the North.

This Land is contested.

My family migrated to Chicago in the early 1920's, leaving behind the land and all their knowledge of it in Brookhaven, Mississippi. Urban agriculture came to me out of my DNA. I could see unused land in my community, and I imagined a food system that would feed me, and that my family could feed a community. But I did not realize that the "vacant" land was contested.

Growing food is not just about the food. Food production is tied to resistance: resistance to injustice, and by default a place of refuge. The theft of land and its underlying water, oil, and mineral resources, is a crime against humanity. On the surface, it's the land that is up for grabs, but what is truly at stake is the dignity of those that live on the land and the destiny of those generations that come after.

The nineteenth-century narrative used by the food movement, for all the good that it has done, has ignored history. To change the trajectory of exploitation that emerges in communities of color and tribal nations, it must acknowledge that this country is founded on contested land. This contested land is rooted in genocide.

Protectors, rather than protestors, are emerging as tribal nations band together to protect the land and all its natural resources. We stand in solidarity with them. The implication of this movement is monumental. Women of color and people of all gender identities are at the forefront of land and water liberation in Chicago, Detroit, Portland, and Oakland.

As protectors, we must protect the planet and all its inhabitants. We are required to stand strong against corporate oligarchy and federal imperialism.

This land is contested, but not for long.

Agricultural Parity for Land De-commodification

George Naylor

I've been a farmer and farm activist for 40 years, and have raised exclusively non-GMO corn and soybeans on my family farm near Churdan, Iowa. Now I am transitioning half of my home farm to organic and starting an organic cider orchard with the help of my partner, Patti Edwardson, a food and farm activist who focuses on garden and orchard production.

I believe we need to transform our food system. To do this, we need everybody to be a piece in the same puzzle—a puzzle for democratic, egalitarian social change that respects our ecological limits, not a puzzle that supports the status quo and creates more problems for our democracy, our health, our society, and our environment.

Land—and how we steward it—is a fundamental part of this transformation.

The typical farmer in the Midwest owns probably only 10 percent of the land they farm; the rest is cash rented. Landlords often take the highest rent bid from the biggest, most industrialized farmer. Through the years, farmers have invested in bigger and bigger livestock facilities, only to lose money, watch their facilities become "obsolete," and abandon their beneficial crop rotations. Today, almost all the pigs, chickens and even market cattle in the United States are owned by corporations and fed in giant feedlots and concentrated animal feeding operations (CAFOs). The millions of gallons of CAFO manure, along with the remaining farmers' fencerow-to-fencerow corn and soybeans rotation, pollute our lakes and waterways. Getting bigger is clearly not the answer to our problems.

When a big farmer is going broke, I often hear, "Well, do you really feel sorry for them? They brought it on themselves." My answer to that is, "We should all feel sorry for ourselves for losing one of our most precious institutions, the family farm." Farm depressions do not reverse farm consolidation; the land will continue to be farmed, but by some other farmer who pursues the inevitable call to "get big or get out." In some cases, corporations are already doing the farming. We are headed to a time of "farming without farmers," where the bottom line drives every decision.

I take my hat off to all the farmers we still have, small or large, and to those many young people who seek a place on the land producing healthy food while taking care of Mother Earth.

Sentimentality or political campaign lines like "I love farmers" won't remedy our food and agriculture problems. Agribusiness and other wolves in sheep's clothing use the same devices. Fortunately, some farmers who defy the odds by farming agroecologically or organically are preserving inherited wisdom and developing new methods and techniques. We will all need these practices when our society recognizes that we *can* provide healthy food and leave a beautiful planet for future generations. And likewise, simply voting with our fork won't do the trick. We need to recognize how market forces affect farmers, the land, and consumer behavior, and demand policy solutions to achieve a sustainable future.

What is driving the lack of access to healthy food and affordable land? What is decimating our rural communities? It's our widely held beliefs about commodities in this capitalist agricultural system: more is better, cheaper is better, and farmers should do whatever it takes to fill our supermarkets.

We need to de-commoditize food and land. Unless we recognize that industrialized agriculture depends on the production, consumption, and sale of commodities (often speculatively), and that our most basic assumptions and economic behavior actually reinforce the industrial status quo, we can't begin to address the problems of land concentration, unhealthy food, and the degradation of rural environments.

The industrial agrifood complex tell us only big, industrial agriculture with more and more technologies (including those that are needed to fix the problems caused by current technologies) are the only way to feed a global population predicted to reach 10 billion people by 2050. This "Golden Fact" is actually a "Big Lie." We produce one and a half times more than enough food for everyone on the planet—already enough to feed 10 billion people. But more than one billion people are still going hungry because they are too poor to buy the food being produced. Just producing more commodities won't help them. No matter, corporate salesmen tell farmers to increase production with GMOs and chemicals. My co-op even tries to demonstrate how farmers' yield will increase by throwing everything in the spray tank except the kitchen sink. Why not the kitchen sink? Because Monsanto doesn't sell kitchen sinks.

The Golden Fact/Big Lie also claims that by increasing yields on existing farmland, we can avoid the need to convert virgin land—like the rainforest, marshland, or the savanna—to commodity production. The opposite is actually true; any time you increase yields, you cut the cost of production, making cultivation on marginal land even more likely.

The biggest market for chemical and biotech products is the production of storable commodities: feed grains, mostly corn; food grains, mostly wheat and rice; and oilseeds, mostly soybeans. There are approximately 250 million acres of these storable commodities, versus only about 12 million acres of fruits and vegetables in the US. The feed grains and oilseeds comprise most of the feed for producing industrial milk, meat, and eggs—not food that hungry people can afford when shipped from thousands of miles away. Much of the corn and soybeans are used to produce biofuels and biochemicals—again nothing that will relieve anyone's hunger.

Farmers are going broke growing these commodities and spending big bucks on inputs. Why do they do this? Another big lie is that farmers produce commodities because they are subsidized. Almost everyone in the food movement, people that I love and respect, repeats this lie *ad infinitum*.

The truth is, commodities like grains and oilseeds are storable—not perishable—and can be converted to cash throughout the year. Raised on the vast motherlode of arable soils we have in the US, much of it far from city populations, these commodities were traditionally stored and fed to livestock. If just 10 percent of these commodity acres were converted to fruits and vegetables, the production of these foods would triple, and you'd see those farmers going broke as perishable food rotted in the fields. We can use a lot more produce raised locally, but to think that a corn and soybean farmer could convert their land to fruits and vegetables is unrealistic. Midwestern farmers plant corn and soybeans fencerow-to-fencerow because there are really no alternatives in the capitalist commodity system.

The subsidies paid to commodity farmers from the US Department of the Treasury only partially make up for low grain prices. It is important to understand that these subsidy programs weren't designed to make farmers rich or create the economic framework for diversified family farms; on the contrary, these payments are only intended to keep the commodity system itself from self-destructing.

In addition, cheap grain policy makes it very easy for industrial livestock companies to order all the feed they need over the phone. They don't need to grow the feed or take any responsibility for the environmental and social damage involved in producing mountains of corn and soybeans using chemicals and genetically modified crops. It's simply not true that most of the subsidies go to big farmers, and even mid-sized family farms need subsidies to stay afloat. Diversified farms that raise their own feed with sustainable crop rotations—including hay and pasture along with responsible use of manure—can't compete with this bifurcated system. The subsidy system is an agribusiness scheme to have our citizens pay for the destruction of the very kind of sustainable farm we all want.

To effectively address the commodities problem, we must look back to the lessons from the Dust Bowl, the Great Depression, and the New Deal.

New Deal farm programs involved conservation-supply management to avoid wasteful, polluting over-production; a price support that actually set a floor under the market prices rather than sending out government payments; grain reserves to avoid food shortages and food price spikes; and a quota system that was fair to all farmers and changed the incentives of production. "Parity" was the name associated with these programs because it meant the farmer would be treated with economic equality and prices would be adjusted for inflation to remove the destructive cost-price squeeze and the need for farmers to over-produce their way out of poverty and debt. It was understood that the farmer's individual "freedom" to do whatever he or she wished with the land would be tempered for the good of all farmers and society. A social contract was established.

Under the current laissez-faire policy of planting fencerow-to-fencerow, a farmer is always going to try to produce more bushels to sell—either out of greed or fear of going broke. If a chemical input can seemingly increase income over the cost, they'll use it. But when all farmers follow suit, overproduction results in low prices and our land and water are degraded.

What if each farm had a quota based on their history of production and an assessment of how a good crop rotation along with conservation plantings could regenerate the soil and biodiversity? What if farmers were compensated with a price that stabilized his or her income? Their thinking and practices would be the opposite of the laissez-faire, free market straightjacket. If a farm has a quota of 10,000 bushels of corn, that farmer would think, "How can I produce 10,000 bushels of corn with the *least* amount of chemicals and fertilizer and the most amount of conservation? Maybe I could use some of the other land for soil-saving hay and pasture to feed a new herd for grass-fed beef or dairy." That farmer would be well on the way to becoming organic.

We citizens of the United States, with a heritage of democratic ideals, and today's food movement that values farmers, well paid farm workers, properly labeled healthy food, and ecological food production, have a great responsibility to make "Parity" our national policy. With "Parity" we can achieve the kind of nutrition, farm communities, and conservation within the agrarian traditions we desire. What we all need for a well-nourished, democratic, and peaceful world is food sovereignty. This will go a long way to establishing a rational food system and to providing land access to those who truly want to live a good life farming sustainably.

As my dad once told me, "Farming is the best occupation anybody can choose." Yet in our efforts to transform the food system, we can learn from noted author Edward Abbey, who wrote, "Do not burn yourselves out. Be as I am—a reluctant enthusiast. . . a part-time crusader, a half-hearted fanatic. Save the other half of yourselves and your lives for pleasure and adventure. It is not enough to fight for the land; it is even more important to enjoy it.

Agrarian Questions and the Struggle for Land Justice in the United States

Eric Holt-Giménez

> *Afterwards they (as many as were able) began to plant their corn, in which service Squanto [Tisquantum] stood them in great stead, showing them both the manner how to set it, and after how to dress and tend it. Also he told them except they got fish and set with it (in these old grounds) it would come to nothing, and he showed them that in the middle of April they should have store enough come up the brook, by which they began to build, and taught them how to take it, and where to get other provisions necessary for them; all which they found true by trial and experience.*
>
> *- Of Plymouth Plantation,* 1604-1627 (Bradford 1621)

The Structural Roots of Land Justice

Tisquantum's[1] act of solidarity is an emblematic preface to 500 years of agrarian transformation in North America. How did a starving, inept band of pilgrims manage to introduce the explosive process of colonization and nation-building that would set the stage for the globe's most powerful food regime in history?

The short answer is: they didn't.

It wasn't the original colonists who transformed North America; it was *wave upon wave* of dispossessed British, Nordic, and European peasants.

---

[1] Tisquantum, aka "Squanto," was captured by explorers, taken to Europe, and held for 16 years. In his absence his tribe was decimated by disease. When he returned to his homeland, he worked as translator and mediator between settlers, and the Massasoit and Wampanoag peoples. Some historians suggest he was poisoned by the Wampanoag, who considered him a traitor.

The Old World's "agrarian transition" privatized the rural commons, destroyed village life, and subsumed agriculture to the needs of industry. It also uprooted millions of peasants. This provided a cheap, reserve army of labor to fuel the Industrial Revolution. It also threw masses of desperate villagers—willing to risk all for a new life—into the colonial cauldron of the Americas. These pioneers were part of a western demographic shift that included a quarter million indentured servants and over ten million enslaved Africans. Millions of immigrants from other parts of the world would follow, as variations of this massive transition blazed a trail of dreams and fortune; of genocide and empire; and of destruction, trauma—and, also, resistance. Contemporary agrarian transitions continue to this day, fueling social movements for an alternative agrarian future.

Racial injustice and the stark inequities in property and wealth in the US countryside aren't just a quirk of history, but a structural feature of capitalist agriculture. This means that in order to succeed in building an alternative agrarian future, today's social movements will have to dismantle those structures. It is the relationships in the food system, and how we govern them, that really matter.

The rural landscape of the United States has been thousands of years in the making. The transformation of indigenously-managed gardens, woodlands, marshes, drylands and prairies into industrial farms of globally-traded commodity crops and concentrated animal feeding operations (CAFOs) has been dramatic. However, the forms of private land ownership at the core of our food and farming systems have changed surprisingly little since early colonization.

On one hand, this dichotomy reflects the amazing ability of people to remake farming as a response to capitalism's need for constant growth, concentration, and standardization. In doing so, they develop what are called agriculture's "forces of production," i.e., the resources, technologies, tools, and skills used to produce our food. On the other hand, it also reflects the steady expansion of a dominant system of private ownership and market exchange. This constitutes the "relations of production," or interactions between all the owners, workers, and consumers that make up our food system. The association between the forces and relations of production has been far from peaceful, but over the last few hundred years, they have evolved in tandem, turning the US into the global center of a powerful, multi-trillion dollar food regime.

The forces of production and the relations of production in our food system are not working together very well, anymore.

Even as the pressures of industrialization and financialization drive medium-sized farmers out of agriculture, there is a contingent of farmers that are increasingly avoiding the destructive inputs pushed on them by the seed and chemical industries. Moreover, a growing number of consumers are rejecting the poisonous, processed food sold by the agrifoods industry; rural and indigenous communities are rising up to resist fracking, pipelines, and CAFOs; and farmworkers and foodworkers are organizing strikes and boycotts against starvation wages and inhumane working conditions. Across the entire country, there are instances of older and beginning farmers ushering in agroecology, permaculture, and organic and urban agriculture; they are working with consumers to get fresh, healthy food to the people who need it most. There are counter-movements for food justice and food sovereignty growing in rural and urban communities all over the US, and people from all walks of life are looking to return to farming. Historic forms of agrarian relations, like the commons (which was never a significant part of the relations of production in the US) are being revived and resituated to address the needs of communities in the present food system (Bollier 2014). It is an exciting time of innovation and solidarity as the food movement stretches its imagination across rural and urban areas, and from farm to fork. Paradigms, practices and politics are all changing, but facing resistance from the agencies and corporations of the existing food regime. Unlike the past, in which struggles for land and territory defined people's resistance, today the entire food system makes up the terrain of agrarian struggle.

But the farmers on the front lines of this new agrarian struggle are finding that efforts to build healthy, equitable food systems that provide jobs and keep the food dollar in the community are inevitably limited by the lack of access to one essential resource: land.

Good agricultural land—rural or urban—is unaffordable for all but the top one percent of our society. The new forces of production being advanced by food movements—like agroecology, permaculture, and agroforestry—are being held back by the old relations of production and ownership, which serve the interests of the corporate food regime (McMichael 2009). Historically, when the forces of production and the relations of production enter into contradiction, deep reforms—or revolutions—happen.

The politics of food is never far from the politics of land, water, or labor. Changing the food system without changing the systems of land access, land tenure, and land use is not only unlikely, it may well be impossible. But to change the politics of land is to change the politics of property—a historically daunting proposition in the US.

Changing the politics of property is precisely what the authors of this book propose. From the *acequias* of the greater Southwest, to the centers of Black agrarianism in the Deep South, and to new farmers, women farmers, and urban farmers, communities on the front lines of food justice and food sovereignty are calling for *land justice*. At its core, the demands for equitable land access revive an age-old issue: the Agrarian Question.

The original Agrarian Question—the role of smallholder agriculture in the development of nineteenth century capitalism—was thought to have been resolved long ago in the United States. After all, agriculture had become highly industrialized, changing it from a way of life into a business. Over the last half century, corporate capital appeared to absorb all aspects of agriculture… until it didn't. To understand why the Agrarian Question is still relevant today, we need to take a walk down the furrows of our agrarian history.

A (Very) Short Agrarian History of the United States

When mercantile magnates and emerging industrialists forced Europe's excess agricultural population to colonize the Atlantic coast of North America, the first pilgrims perished by the hundreds until the indigenous inhabitants—who were farmers and lived in towns—taught them to farm, fish, and hunt. These Native Americans would come to regret this humanitarian gesture: they lost nearly 1.5 billion acres of land to white settlers (Dunbar-Ortiz 2014). After the first wave of genocide and dispossession, enslaved African farmers were brought to work the tobacco and cotton plantations. The tremendous profits of slave agriculture filled bank coffers in London, Boston, and New York. Slavery became central to the construction of US capitalism:

> "[It] was not the small farmers of the rough New England countryside who established the United States' economic position. It was the backbreaking labor of unremunerated American slaves in places like South Carolina, Mississippi, and Alabama… After the Civil War, a new kind of capitalism arose, in the United States and elsewhere. Yet that new capitalism… had been enabled by the profits, institutions, networks, technologies, and innovations that emerged from slavery, colonialism, and land expropriation." (Beckert 2014)

Slavery, indentured servitude, and genocidal dispossession laid the foundation for the emergence of capitalist agriculture—a new form of production and consumption that emerged in the transition from agrarian to industrial society. Beginning with the enclosure of the commons in Britain and the forced migration of the peasantry to urban factories and the colonies, from as early as the sixteenth century, the agrarian transition has always entailed a violent restructuring of environment, production, and society. This occurred sometimes through reforms and sometimes through markets, but always by coercion—a point usually missed in triumphal narratives of agrarian greatness.

The agrarian transition in the US mobilized poor peasants and former indentured servants westward to displace indigenous populations. The "agrarian reforms" that were implemented at the colonial frontiers drew hundreds of thousands of poor settlers, many of whom were quickly displaced by large landowners. The only agrarian reform that could be considered redistributive (rather than genocidal) was declared in 1865 at the end of the Civil War when General William Tecumseh Sherman distributed 400,000 acres to African-Americans who had fought for the Union. President Andrew Johnson rescinded the reform a year later. The South wanted cheap labor, not more independent, yeomen farmers. Freedmen and freedwomen became sharecroppers and tenant farmers, or were imprisoned and forced into chain gangs. This turned out to be more lucrative for plantation owners: now they did not have to bear the costs of reproducing the labor force.

But the North had other ideas. Even before the war, northern states sought to outflank big southern planters with smaller, yeomen farmers, by giving indigenous land away to settlers. The Homestead Acts, starting in 1862, opened up 270 million acres of land west of the Mississippi River to 1.6 million homesteaders. Settlers bust the sod of the Great Plains and established the mid-western breadbasket. Further west, they established rangelands and raised livestock. Over time, the massive expansion of agriculture led to a sustained boom in production, eventually saturating markets and dropping prices paid to farmers below the costs of production. This led to widespread bankruptcies in the early half of the twentieth century. The spread of agriculture to southwestern soils for dryland farming eventually destroyed the region's fragile layers of topsoil, leading to the Dust Bowl (Holleman 2016). As homesteads failed, many farmers went to work for cattle and timber barons, or were forced out of farming altogether.

But the stolen dreams of Europe's surplus labor led to resistance.[2] In the Midwest, farmers organized into strong agrarian populist movements that fought against banks and railroad monopolies. They organized the Farmers' Alliance that in 1890 called for land reform and even formed a populist political party. Despite resistance, the US's agrarian question

---

[2] Thanks to Annie Shattuck for this brilliant phrase.

was resolved in favor of the landed bourgeoisie, thanks to the power of the banks, the military, the railroad, and the steady mercantilization of agriculture. The new agrarian territories were structured by the logic of international capital over a century before today's so-called globalization.

Since World War I, the tendency of capitalist agriculture toward overproduction and concentration has steadily erased smallholders from the agrarian map of the United States. African-American farmers were the exception: despite racism and exploitation, by 1910 they had accumulated over 15 million acres of farmland—without benefitting from any land reform. Thanks to Jim Crow laws and discrimination by banks, traders, and the United States Department of Agriculture, over the next 100 years, they would lose most of this land (Mittal and Powell 2000).

With World War II, North American agriculture changed radically. While the US work force was enlisted in the military, thousands of Mexican peasants were brought in to work the fields. Without them, the US could not have fought the war. Mexican workers were so productive that after the war the US government implemented the Bracero Program to bring 4 million more. To this day, peasants and indigenous peoples of Mexico, Central America, and the Caribbean pick our crops, process our meat, and cook and serve our food. They are also at the core of farm and food labor struggles.

After the war, US agricultural production experienced a boom, thanks to a combination of chemicals, hybrid seeds, heavy machinery, and the lack of European competition. Farmers quickly saturated the market with their products and prices dropped again. They cut back on buying new inputs. Grain and new tractors piled up, unsold. In an effort to resolve a crisis of overproduction, the US extended its new technologies to the "Third World" through credit in a campaign called the Green Revolution. It also implemented food assistance programs to off-load excess production and establish new markets overseas.[3] This was called "development," and it often included changes to established systems of land tenure.

Land reforms accompanying the US development project were conducted in countries where there were perceived threats of communism— which is to say, far from the United States. The US State Department and the US Agency for International Development applied a variety of models, including distributive reforms guided by the state, counter-insurgency

---

[3] Public Law 480, which created the Office of Food for Peace, is usually thought of as a beneficent program to donate excess food to poor countries to end hunger. In reality, it was a market expansion program: "To increase the consumption of United States agricultural commodities in foreign countries, to improve the foreign relations of the United States, and for other purposes." Agricultural Trade Development and Assistance Act of 1954.

reforms managed by the army, and regressive reforms led by the market. These reforms were tailored to reproduce Northern forms of production offered by the Green Revolution.

North American farmers were recruited into the development project under the pretext of saving the world from hunger. Farmers were lent easy money to buy more land and larger machinery, and to export more and more food. Given the possibility of high export profits, the price of agricultural land began to climb rapidly—faster than the rate of inflation. Banks offered big loans on inflated farmland values to buy more farmland and bigger machinery. This is precisely what Third World governments did with their development loans, as well. Industrial agriculture boomed in Asia and the Americas, concentrating production in fewer and fewer hands—and dropping prices paid to farmers. By the late '70s global overproduction and falling prices prevented Third World governments from repaying the foreign debt incurred for development. Third World governments signed austere structural adjustment programs with the International Monetary Fund (IMF) in order to receive emergency loans from the World Bank— just so they could make their debt payments to Northern banks. Northern farmers just went bankrupt. The US lost *half* of its farm families in this crisis (Strange 1988). This was nothing more than a new iteration of the agrarian transition begun in the 1600s.

The US's agrarian transition has concentrated production in huge agro-industrial areas: the endless prairies of transgenic maize and gigantic hog farms in the Midwest and the Carolinas; the feudal model of poultry production in the Southeast; the massive CAFOs of the West... Slaughterhouses and processing plants are everywhere, worked mostly by peasants uprooted from Mexico and Central America. Agrarian capitalism has devastated rural life in the US, turning the countryside into a vast green desert of toxic monocultures crisscrossed by pipelines, trembling with fracking, and riddled with illegal methamphetamine labs. The middle-class family farmer is steadily being eliminated, gobbled up by mega-farms owned by corporations, banks, or insurance companies. The social breakdown in the countryside is palpable in the rural towns with boarded-up shops around empty town squares.

Throughout these transitions, resistance has also flourished. Those who are today demanding fair wages and humane working conditions, healthy food, sustainable agriculture, and access to farmland are part of a long tradition of this struggle.

An emblematic case is that of the Southern Tenant Farmers Union. During the Great Depression, poor farmers violated entrenched segregation and formed the Union with Black and White tenant farmers joining forces. This movement spread west throughout the cotton territory, reaching California for the Great Cotton Strike of 1933. Six-year-old Cesar Chavez participated in the strike. Thirty years later, following the unionizing work of Filipino farmworkers, he would organize the United Farm Workers union (UFW). In the 1960s, through boycotts and strikes, the UFW managed to paralyze the California vegetable industry, gaining the right to organize, better working conditions and better wages. Today, veterans of *La Unión* continue to organize against Driscoll's, the largest berry corporation in the world. They replicate and improve upon the strategies of the United Farm Workers, forging alliances with students and the church and extending their ties across borders with berry workers in Mexico.

There is a long tradition of agrarian populism among family farmers in the Midwest, starting with the Farmers Alliance (1890), and later The National Farmers Union (1902) and the National Farmers Organization (1955). The tradition was revived with the American Agriculture Movement, whose struggle against farm debt in 1979 brought thousands of farmers to Washington DC in "tractorcades" that closed off the offices of the Department of Agriculture. The current Rural Coalition (1978) and National Family Farm Coalition (1986) are a testament to more than a century of agrarian struggles.

In 2016, after centuries of genocide, dispossession and indignity, Indigenous peoples from across the US gathered by the thousands in Standing Rock, North Dakota to protect their burial and ceremonial sites from the Dakota Access Pipeline project. In doing so, they were also leading a national movement to protect our water from industrial contamination.

The US countryside has a long history of resistance movements that rise against each crisis and each structural adjustment. However, there has been a steady consolidation of agricultural land and loss of farmers, who now represent less than 1.5 percent of the national population. Today, the US has more people in prison than farmers working the land.

Today's Agrarian Question

Contrary to what many might think, most of the US farm industry—97 percent—is in family hands. Nearly 90 percent of these farms depend on family labor. But over 90 percent of all farm households depend on non-farm income. These statistics reflect deep inequities: farms with more than $1 million in annual sales make up four percent of farms, while 80 percent of farms sell less than $100,000 annually. Large farms have a yearly average of nearly $600,000 in net income. Small farms average $2000 per year in losses (USDA Economic Research Service 2014).

This differentiation has racial, age, and gender biases:

As of 2012, farmers numbered only 3.2 million people. Of these farmers, only eight percent are Indigenous or of Asian, Latino, or African descent (although the numbers are growing, particularly among Latinos). Women make up 14 percent of producers, but three quarters of them sold less than $10,000 annually (USDA NASS 2013).

Between 2007 and 2012, 90,000 farmers left agriculture, while only 1,200 entered. The dominant trend is that of huge farms cultivated by a few older, white men, and a lot of small farms cultivated by minorities, women, and young farmers. The medium-sized family farmer is disappearing. The bad joke among farmers is that today the average age of farmers is 59 years old... In ten years the average "age" will be dead.

The contradictions of the capitalist food regime have exacerbated vulnerabilities and historical injustices. This country produces more food than any other, yet one in seven people are food insecure. There are epidemics of diabetes, hypertension, and other diseases related to unhealthy food. People of color, children, women, and those working in the food sector are most affected.

These injustices have given rise to a food movement promoting agroecology, food justice, food sovereignty, and land justice. Urban gardens have multiplied, as have consumer cooperatives, organic farms, food workers' unions, organic restaurant chefs, consumer groups, and farmers markets. In the past 20 years agricultural land trusts have bought and preserved 6 million acres of farmland.

The food movement is gaining strength amongst young people and many conventional farmers tired of the corporate food regime. The media is full of positive stories about permaculture, organic agriculture, Slow Food, and also about the growing protests against mines and pipelines, fracking, and GMOs. While regulatory victories are few, there are those who speak of a "food revolution."

But a revolution does not just stop pipelines or change production practices and consumer habits. A revolution also transforms power structures. A food revolution would have to reverse the corporate agrarian transition currently bearing down on us.

Meet the New Agrarian Transition

From seed to fork, the food system is being primed for further intensification. Nanotechnology and synthetic biology have surpassed the inefficient technologies of genetically modified seeds by light years, allowing direct manipulation of DNA without having to resort to inaccurate and expensive genetic transfer (Specter 2016). Now, you can download a "genetic map" from the Internet and directly manipulate DNA, changing its metabolic pathway to express any phenotypic characteristic, not only to produce seeds, but also to make any kind of being. What we could only dream of doing with DNA, can now be realized with DNA (Mooney 2016). New technologies collapse and shorten the innovation time between conception and commercialization. And they are accessible to any molecular biologist. The big monopolies now have to resort to mass data and corporate concentration to ensure their dominance.

Corporations are investing in "digital agriculture," in which massive amounts of information about the environment, climate, soil, and cultivars are carefully recorded by satellite, then analyzed and sold to farmers, supposedly to reduce their exposure to climate change and apply inputs with infinitesimal precision. All major corporations in the food chain, from Monsanto, John Deere, and Cargill, to Walmart and Amazon are using these big data information systems.

The integrated control of genetic and environmental information increases the tendency of land consolidation in every way: among the six monopolies that control 51 percent of seed and 72 percent of the pesticides in the international market there is strong pressure towards corporate mergers. Syngenta, ChemChina, Monsanto, Bayer, Dow and DuPont are all in frantic negotiations. When two merge, the others have no choice but to merge, as well. Vertical consolidation is also underway. Amazon, in open war with the Walmart model, is planning to sell food through huge supply centers to be delivered by food taxis and drones. Don't doubt the seriousness of this for agriculture: Amazon today employs more agronomists that the Consultative Group on International Agricultural Research (CGIAR), the scientific flagship of the Green Revolution.

All the financial and structural pressure of this multi-trillion dollar sector leads to even larger forms of production. Seeds, inputs, machinery, financing, insurance, and mass information are made to deliver larger and larger batches of uniform products to retailers—the monopolies that are even bigger and more concentrated. To participate in the new food value chains, producers will have to massively refinance. Where will they get the money?

The land.

Banks now hold workshops to advise producers about the sale and financialization of the land as a business measure to recapitalize its operation. Since the financial crisis of 2007-2008, speculative investments in agricultural land have risen substantially-now covering perhaps 25 percent of all acquisitions. The exchange value of agricultural land in the US is outpacing its use value, becoming "like gold with yield" (Fairbairn 2014). Institutional investors have bought about $40 billion of agricultural land—which in a market of $8.4 trillion still can't be considered a bubble, but is a growing form of "neo-rentism" (Edelman 2016). They would buy more if they could, but farmers are not selling. Even in the US—corporate territory par excellence—farmland is largely in the hands of family farmers who resist selling their land. In five years, however, 63 percent of agricultural land will likely be inherited or sold. The question is, "Who will take over"? Corporations or trusts? Banks or family farmers? Right now, the front line of resistance to the financialization of agricultural land in the United States is made up of aging, white family farmers, the producers of genetically modified corn and soybeans who are still stuck on the fertilizer and pesticide treadmill.

While it is not a radical or transformative struggle—yet—the US food movement is an expression of both everyday survival and resistance to business as usual. It has a social base of almost three million rural and urban producers, 800,000 agricultural workers and 46,000 workers in processing plants. If we add up all those working in the food industry—including immigrants working in restaurants—they approach 12 percent of the national workforce.

Why does this calculation matter?

It should be very clear that US farmers are a small social force that alone have no chance of advancing reforms. Without a broad convergence between producers, consumers, and related workers—with strategic alliances with other key social movements for climate justice, indigenous rights, immigrants, and other human rights movements—there will not be enough social force to influence the current agrarian transition to corporate-owned mega-farms. Capitalism will proceed to its liking, implementing its destructive forms of production, consumption, hoarding, and speculation.

The original agrarian question dealt with the role of the peasantry in a class struggle in which this same class would have to disappear with the industrial revolution—be it capitalist or socialist. But, peasants, indigenous people, and small farmers refused to disappear.

They live. Badly, perhaps, but they live. With 25 percent of the world's agricultural land, they produce 70 percent of the food we eat, virtually with little or no government support (GRAIN 2014). The 2.5 billion peasants and small farmers make up a third of the world's population. If rural communities are displaced, they will be pushed to the city slums. Samir Amin (2011) points out that the global economy would have to grow at a rate of seven percent over 50 years to absorb just a third all this labor. This is impossible. The current agrarian transition—and the American path projected for the rest of the world—not only condemns a third of humanity to dispossession, unemployment, and misery, but most likely means global chaos.

We must repopulate the countryside, not empty it. We have to invest to improve the quality of rural life, not just extract its wealth. We must break up and redistribute large plantations and implement agroecology on a small and medium scale in order to restore the environment, cool the planet, and ensure a decent income to rural people. We need to open up farming in the city, instead of paving over farmland. We must advance a transformative agenda of land sovereignty to block the capitalist agrarian transition. For this, we must implement social and structural changes beyond land reform, beyond farmers and beyond the countryside itself. Put simply, we have to change everything.

But how can this be achieved if the majority of small farmers are struggling for their own survival?

Land, a Vision and a Call

Karl Polanyi (1944) wrote, "The fate of classes is determined more by the needs of society than the needs of classes." In the US, the future of the struggles for agrarian reform, food sovereignty, environmental justice, human rights, and racial and gender equity will be determined by the combination of these struggles, rather than by any single struggle. This position does not invalidate the importance of class, race, gender, climate, or land issues in and of themselves. It recognizes that alliances *between* these struggles are fundamental for social transformation.

This book is divided into six sections, although the themes in each are overlapping and interdependent. The first section, "Black Agrarianism," deals with the deep roots of agrarianism in Black communities and liberation struggles in the US, using the Gullah Geechee people of South Carolina and Georgia as a central focus. It details the long and intentional history of dispossession, as well as the many visionary struggles to resist and regenerate by cooperatively building land access and sustainable farming traditions. The next section turns to women's work on the land, highlighting both long-term discrimination against women in making decisions about land, and means through which women – in very different contexts – are building alterative pathways through their use of the land.

The third section considers how privilege shapes the creation and protection of land-use niches, as well as the rise of indigenous leadership to protect them. One chapter looks at the problems associated with renting for young farmers, and the challenges of creating systems of access that do not replicate structures of privilege. Another chapter tells the chilling story of how poor, mostly white, rural refugees of neoliberalism are threatening the traditional *acequia* systems of water management and farming in Latino communities of Colorado. The final chapter addresses native identity and struggles to defend sovereignty and land.

The fourth section continues the theme of migration and transnational implications of food regimes and land use with a poignant life history interview with farmworker activist Rosalinda Guillen and then, an analysis of forces pushing some young farmers from the US to move to Brazil.

The fifth section turns to the urban context, examining histories of land-based racism and dispossession in both Oakland and Detroit. Both cases reveal how food access patterns can be cemented through urban land policy, and how communities are mobilizing to reshape them. Finally, the sixth section focuses on instances and opportunities for activism. Here, an analysis of Occupy the Farm (near Berkeley, California), a history of the National Land for the People movement of the 1970s, and a look at opportunities for convergence between Black and Indigenous land struggles point toward the need for collaboration between movements.

The authors of these accounts make it clear they are not just in an agrarian struggle, but in a struggle to remake society. For them, land justice, the premise of this book, is both a vison and a clarion call.

References

Amin, Samir. 2011. "Food Sovereignty: A Struggle for convergence in diversity." In *Food Movements Unite! Strategies to Transform Our Food Systems*, edited by Eric Holt-Giménez, xi–xviii. Oakland: Food First Books.

Beckert, Sven. 2014. "Slavery and Capitalism." *The Chronicle of Higher Education*, December 12. Accessed 11/19/2016. http://chronicle.com/article/SlaveryCapitalism/150787/.

Bollier, David. 2014. "Regional Food Commons as a Systemic Answer." *News and Perspectives on the Commons*. March 18. Accessed 11/19/2016. http://www.thefoodcommons.org/project/article-regional-food-commons-as-a-systemic-answer/.

Bradford, William. 1656. "Surviving the First Winter of the Plymouth Colony, 1620-1621." Excerpt. Washington, DC. Accessed 11/19/2016. https://nationalhumanities center.org/pds/amerbegin/settlement/text1/BradfordPlymouthPlantation.pdf.

Dunbar-Ortiz, Roxanne. 2014. *An Indigenous People's History of the United States*. Boston: Beacon Press.

Edelman, Mark. 2016. "Land and Territory in the Americas." Keynote, Bogota, Colombia, August 23.

Fairbairn, Madeleine. 2014. "Farmland Meets Finance: Is Land the New Economic Bubble?" *Food First Policy Brief,* Land & Sovereignty in the Americas, no. 5 (May).

GRAIN. 2014. "Hungry for Land: Small farmers feed the world with less than a quarter of all farmland." Barcelona: GRAIN. Accessed 11/19/2016. http://www.grain.org/article/entries/4929-hungry-for-land-small-farmers-feed-the-world-with-less-than-a-quarter-of-all-farmland.

Holleman, Hannah. 2017. "De-naturalizing ecological disaster: colonialism, racism and the global Dust Bowl of the 1930s." *The Journal of Peasant Studies,* July, vol. 44:1, p. 234-260.

Holt-Giménez, Eric, and Yi Wang. 2011. "Reform or Transformation? The Pivotal Role of Food Justice in the U.S. Food Movement." *Race/Ethnicity: Multidisciplinary Global Contexts* 5 (1): 83–102.

Mooney, Pat. 2016. The Corporate Strategy to Control the Food System. Interview. August 13. World Social Forum.

McMichael, Philip. 2009. "A Food Regime Genealogy." *Journal of Peasant Studies* 36:139–69.

Mittal, Anuradha, with Joan Powell. 2000. "The Last Plantation." Backgrounder, Winter vol. 6:1. Oakland: Food First.

Polanyi, Karl. 1944. *The Great Transformation: The Political and Economic Origins of Our Time.* Boston: Beacon Press.

Specter, Michael. 2016. "How the DNA Revolution Is Changing Us." *National Geographic,* August. Accessed 11/19/2016. http://www.nationalgeographic.com/magazine/2016/08/dna-crispr-gene-editing-science-ethics/.

Strange, Marty. 1988. *Family Farming: A New Economic Vision.* San Francisco: Food First.

USDA Economic Research Service. "Key Statistics & Graphics." 2014. Accessed 11/19/2016. http://www.ers.usda.gov/topics/food-nutrition-assistance/food-security-in-the-us/key-statistics-graphics.aspx#.Uz72wsfY-TV.

USDA NASS. 2013. "2012 Census Highlights: Farm Demographics - U.S. Farmers by Gender, Age, Race, Ethnicity, and More." 2012 Census of Agriculture. https://www.agcensus.usda.gov/Publications/2012/Online_Resources/Highlights/Farm_Demographics/#how_many. Accessed 11/19/2016.

SECTION 1:

Black Agrarianism

Africa's Dream
Gail Myers

We are the pride of our Ancestors!
From their souls
from earth's soil
we have emerged victorious children of
Angola Sierra Leone Senegal Gambia Mali Congo
we were engineers basket weavers botanists
blacksmiths griots healers
taken from the heart of our mother Africa
half-ways stowed away
Middle Passage stolen
runaways moving forward
circling back
This time we want to remember
to discuss – to ancestralize our
Roots of Resistance a Regeneration of the
Reclamation of our Promised Land

By our own hands
this is the land of our mothers too
our fathers paid with their backs and bruises
when we reconstructed our families
we reconstructed our communities
we had land
as loss became more – land less
as we talked from our mother tongue
they kept us boxed out of our dowry
soil matters
but possessing the song we danced in the Sun
one by one
two by two ten by ten
we danced in communion
we danced to Africa
even in death
the voices speak
"children grow"
They say "children go
fly back to Africa"
Fear not we live in the memory
we live in the land
we live in the trees
we live in the waters of Yemoja's spirit
for our dreams united there
harmonies planted flowed together there
for dreams united
for Africa's Dream
We are the pride of our Ancestors!

Clam Diggers by Jonathan Green

Preface for Black Agrarianism
Monica M. White

> Collective black self-recovery takes place when we begin to re-
> new our relationship to the earth, when we remember the way
> of our ancestors. Living in modern society without history, it
> has been easy to forget that Black people were first and foremost
> people of the land, farmers.
>
> - bell hooks[1]

We are returning to our roots, we are renewing our relationship to the
earth, and we are remembering the ways of our ancestors. An example of
this are the Gullah Geechee, currently engaged in a struggle to retain land
passed down by our ancestors. Much research has characterized Southern
land as a location of oppression. The agrarian lifestyle is complicated for
Black Americans. It comes with the historical traumas of slavery, sharecropping, and tenant farming. It also comes with the constant struggle
to hold onto the land—often against overwhelming odds fueled by racism and discrimination. We fled oppressive economic systems in the South
during the Great Migration to Northern and Western parts of the United
States; but we are returning. Black families, who once left the South as a
statement against racial, economic, and social oppression, are now working to reclaim the land—much of which is heir property—left by parents
and grandparents. From our African roots and connections to the land, we
are once again, at this historical moment, re-connecting with our agrarian
origins in order to build and rebuild sustainable communities.

In forging these connections, those engaged in reverse migration, from
north to south, are not alone. The practices of connecting land, food, and
freedom have a rich and complex history. From bringing seeds through the
Middle Passage, to cultivating provision grounds during slavery, to establishing Maroon communities with self-reliant food systems; agricultural
and environmental knowledge were the cornerstone of Black Liberation.
In the late 1960s, the Southern Cooperative Movement, which included former sharecroppers, tenant farmers, and farmers who owned land,
formed a bridge between the Civil Rights Movement and the Black Power
Movement by offering a way to stay in the South, live on the land, and
build sustainable, autonomous communities with agriculture at their base.
Today, in response to increasing racism resulting in unemployment and

---

[1] From: hooks, bell. 1993. *Sisters of the Yam: Black Women and Self-recovery*. Boston: South End Press.

economic dislocation, Black families and communities are once again realizing and taking advantage of opportunities inherent in the land by growing food in cities, building community gardens, and creating alternative food systems for community health and well-being, as well as economic empowerment.

The following chapters, with their emphasis on Roots, Resistance, and Regeneration, show the relevance of the past to contemporary food movements and demonstrate agriculture as the basis of self-provisioning, but also beautification, social responsibility, and resistance. The richness of these pieces reveals the importance of our relationship to the land in constructing collective and cooperative relationships and in providing new narratives of self-determined agrarian community. Confronting their own fears, struggles, and hard work, many of these farmers are reconnecting to these collective traditions, and to the agricultural knowledge of our ancestors, as they create alternative pathways to freedom.

The following chapters profile the socio-political landscapes of land loss and retention and the agrarian struggle for Black rural communities— including the Gullah Geechee—in the South, as well as the perennial work of Black Liberation movements to advance the regeneration of Black agrarianism. This remembrance of the Black agrarian experience on the land in the United States is shared through the polyphonic voices of an "UpSouth/DownSouth" *griot*[2] collective of authors comprising the ancestors, returning generation farmers, activist agroecologists, land rights advocates, and attorneys. With this intentionality, the chapters are organized in three non-linear patchwork frames of consciousness: Roots, Resistance, and Regeneration.

---

[2] The word griot comes from the West African term for a travelling storyteller, musician, historian, poet, and bearer of oral tradition.

CHAPTER 1
Roots!

Owusu Bandele and Gail Myers (Equal Authorship)

"Ah wakuh muh monuh kambay
yah lee luh lay kambay yah lee luh lay tambay."

"Everyone come together, let us work hard;
The grave is not yet finished; let his heart be perfectly at peace."

- Amelia's Song (California Newsreel 2016, 1)

This song, of African origin, is performed by Mende women at cer-emonial burials in southern Sierra Leone. Of the cargo of African women transplanted into America that ended up in Georgia dur-ing the slave trade, one woman retained her memory of this traditional song. Growing up on the Sea Islands of Georgia generations later, a woman named Mary Moran learned it from her grandmother, Amelia. "Amelia's Song," spoken in the Mende native language, was preserved for perhaps more than ten generations. The film *The Language You Cry In* tells this re-markable story. It is a testament to the power of memory and the potential for language and culture to survive over space and time. In the film, the Moran family makes an historic trip back to Sierra Leone to connect with the women there who still perform the song for ceremonies. When asked why Amelia's great grandmother would preserve the song and pass it down generations, a Mende elder had this to say:

> That song would be the most valuable thing she could take. It could connect her to all of her ancestors and to their continued blessing. You know who a person really is by the language they cry in (California Newsreel, 2016,1).

"Amelia's Song" bonded African women from two continents who otherwise would not have known each other. Much like the Mende song, African agrarian roots have survived through the memory and practice of a deep enduring connectedness to the land. Today, there are Africans in America who have been rooted on family land for over 150 years. Like "Amelia's Song," they are still surviving, struggling to retain their land, agrarian roots, and memory of communal beliefs about land ownership and caring for nature. They are threatened by a food and agricultural system supported by discriminatory government policies, and further challenged by the swiftly moving tide of massive urban and rural development.

We dedicate this chapter—an analysis of African agrarian roots in the US and efforts across the generations to ground them in the land—to the Gullah Geechee people of coastal South Carolina and Georgia, whose wisdom and skills built the rice industry in the South. It is that same wisdom and spiritual awareness that keeps Gullah Geechee people living close to, and in harmony with, nature. Though thousands of miles away from the Motherland, the connection to their roots was always as close as the seeds that were carried across the Middle Passage. The offspring of some of those same seeds are held in hands today: seeds of knowledge, like an ecological wherewithal rooted in love for people and spirit. These agrarian roots continue today and will for generations moving forward. We also dedicate this chapter in memory of our close friend Cynthia Hayes, cofounder of the Southeastern African American Farmers Organic Network (SAAFON).

African Seeds, Wisdom, and Knowledge

African agrarian wisdom is an acknowledgment of the link between the natural and the spiritual. In African societies, one finds a strict adherence to preserving, conserving, and regenerating soil, water, and the local eco-culture of life (Burnham 2000; Mbiti 1992). African societies have created cultural narratives by preserving natural elements so that humans and other life can exist symbiotically. This ecological belief system endured in the Americas, even under the most exploitive conditions of chattel slavery. Europeans document examples of the reverence for nature among enslaved Africans as far back as Stedman's (1796) work in Suriname and MacFadyen (1837) in Jamaica. Grimé's review of Stedman and MacFadyen's work reveals similar practices of African rootedness in nature among enslaved Africans. Asking a village elder in Suriname why they paid such reverence to a tree, and why the people bring offerings to the wild cotton tree, it is explained:

Having no churches, no places built for public worship as you have on the coast of Guinea, and this tree being the largest and most beautiful growing here, our people assembling under its branches when they are to be instructed and defended by it from the heavy rains and scorching sun. Under this tree our *gadoman*, or priest, delivers his lectures and for this reason our common people will not cut it down upon any account whatever. . . and account it sacrilege to injure it with an axe; so that even the fear of punishment will not induce them to cut it down (Grimé 1976, 95).

African mythology, origin myths, and spiritual practices all revere the centrality of nature. Stories of trees, animals, birds, flora, and natural elements all had their origins in preserving and conserving the fragile relationship between humans and their environment. Moreover, African ecological thought utilizes land as part of the ritual of how to honor spirit. These ritualistic expressions of an eco-spiritual worldview were imprinted on the daily lives of those enslaved Africans and impacted their beliefs about food, farming, family, and forest (Grimé 1976, Vlach 1994). Land was the quintessential ingredient for maintaining these traditions. As noted by John Mbiti in *Introduction to African Religion*:

African peoples have through the centuries lived by farming, stock keeping, hunting and fishing, as well as by food gathering in some cases. Many rituals have been evolved to cover all these means of livelihood, incorporating what people believe, the values they attach to those activities and the right procedures or behavior required for making them run smoothly (Mbiti 1991, 134).

The African connection to food crops and herbal remedies is evident throughout the Gullah Geechee regions, where descendants of West and Central African peoples live and maintain cultural practices. Although rice is no longer a major crop here, crops of African origin are found throughout the region today, including okra, watermelon, cowpeas, and black-eyed peas. Other less known crops of African origin are also grown in the region. Joseph Fields, for instance, a farmer from the Gullah Geechee community in South Carolina, grows all of these crops plus the less-common pigeon pea (Fields 2016).

Wilson Moran recollected that his grandfather, Robert, Amelia's husband, planted a variety of crops including sweet potatoes, collards, corn peanuts, and speckled lima beans. He remembered that his grandmother was both "midwife and doctor," and prescribed a mixture of plant-based medicines, which were administered "according to phases of the moon" (Moran 2016). He attributes the fact that he rarely needed a doctor's care to his grandmother's care and wisdom.

Crops of African origin, as well as the technology used by Africans to produce them, have had a profound effect on food and agriculture throughout the world. For example, several important fruits, vegetables, and herbs that are popular in the Western Hemisphere have their origin in Africa. Both enslaved Africans and their captors transported indigenous seeds and crops from Africa. A summary of those crops is found in Table 1.

In addition to these crops, which are the traditional legacy foods of Africans in the Americas, Robert Grimé has documented other plants that accompanied Africans on their forced exodus: *Cannabis sativa*, senna, cucumber, and calabash nutmeg. According to oral history, enslaved African women brought okra and rice seeds to the Americas by hiding them in their braided hair. These crops were essential to people of African descent. In fact, cowpeas, okra, and, especially, rice all have had profound culinary and cultural effects in the Americas.

TABLE 1. Selected Food Crops of African Origin

Crop	Scientific Name	Crop	Scientific Name
Ackee	*Blighia sapida*	Muskmelon	*Cucumis melo*
African rice	*Oryza glaberrima*	Okra	*Hibicus esculentus*
African yam	*Dioscorea rotundata*	Pigeon Pea	*Cajunus Cajun*
Bambara groundnut	*Vigna subterranean*	Roselle, hibisicus	*Hibiscus sabdariffa*
Bitter melon	*Momordica charantia*	Sesame	*Sesamum alatum*
Black eye pea, cowpea	*Vigna inguiculata*	Sorghum, Guinea corn	*Sorghum bicolor*
Coffee (arabica)	*Coffee Arabica*	Tamarind	*Tamarindus indica*
Cola nut	*Cola nitida*	Vegetable amaranth	*Amaranthus spp.*
Melegueta pepper	*Aframonum melegueta*	Watermelon	*Citrullus lanatus*

Source: (Bandele 2015a, 407)

Not only were the plants essential to the development of the Americas, seen today in places like the Sea Islands of South Carolina, but African agrarians, fisher folk, and engineers transformed the landscape of the waterways. Even today these changes contribute to more environmentally sustainable waterways, enhancing the ecological landscape and the state tourist economy. In an interview with Jonathan Green, an international artist from the Gullah Geechee region, he paints this picture:

> Imagine being brought here in chains. They could not imagine where they were. The entire state was covered in plantations at one time. There were moccasins, rattlesnakes, alligators and the forest was thick. They could not see sunlight. Now you see the beauty of the Lowcountry rice culture that built the economy. The money from rice. . . Africans transformed and created an eco-culture for bird watchers. The bird hunting and watching people come from everywhere to watch birds here. This was not able to be traversed at one point because the islands were a very thick forest, with cypress trees. The Gullah Geechee people preserved the fields and formed the hunting and bird watching habitats. Blacks were not given credit for creating those ecosystems (Green 2016).

That Black-labor-built wealth in the Americas has been widely documented. However, too often, Africa's contributions to agricultural technology are greatly minimalized. Africans were the original plant and animal scientists. Plant domestication likely first started in the highlands of Ethiopia. Agricultural technology enabled the ancient Egyptians to develop a civilization along the Nile River with their expertise in irrigation, including the first use of hydraulic engineering (Bandele 2015b). Ancient Egyptians also invented the axe, hoe, and plow, and had extensive knowledge of the medicinal properties of plants.

African agricultural technology was by no means limited to Ancient Egypt or northern Africa. Tropical farmers demonstrated a deep appreciation and respect for the environment while raising crops. Tropical African farmers showed their agricultural expertise in a myriad of ways, including:

- planting on raised mounds, thereby avoiding excess moisture in wet areas;
- planting on terraces to reduce erosion;
- flattening and planting on top of termite mounds, which were fertile sites;

- using both compost, manures, and ashes to enhance soil fertility;
- using live trees as support for vining crops;
- pruning trees to allow adequate light for crops planted under them;
- identifying shade tolerant crops which could be planted under trees;
- adjusting plant spacing to reduce competition among intercropped plants;
- preserving useful trees when land was cleared for agricultural uses;
- identifying which crops could tolerate excessive moisture, as well as those that could tolerate drought;
- obtaining proper canopy to reduce soil erosion;
- using legumes to increase nitrogen in soils; and
- using rotational cropping systems to maximize land and nutrient use (Ibid.).

African crops and agrarian wisdom were the basis for wealth not only in the United States, but also in Brazil. Even though the introduction of rice into the Western Hemisphere is most often associated with its arrival in South Carolina shortly after the founding of that colony in 1670, rice was grown in Brazil approximately one century earlier (Carney 2004). In fact, other crops of African origin were found in Brazil as early as 1560, including okra, pigeon peas, black-eyed peas, millet, sorghum, yams, and African oil palm. But rice had the greatest agricultural and cultural impact. In fact, French historian Jean Suret-Canale stated that the importation of crops and food-processing technology and nutritional practices from Africa to Brazil laid the cornerstone for civilization in Brazil; as one Brazilian official stated, "It is Africa that civilised (sic) Brazil" (Carney 2001). Three quarters of enslaved Africans brought to Brazil between 1548-1560 came from the rice-growing region of Senegambia. Rice was grown both as a plantation and subsistence crop in Brazil. It was an important source of food for the maroons who escaped slavery.

The enslaved Africans' knowledge base related to rice production was an extensive one that spanned the diaspora. Enslaved Africans farmers in South Carolina knew much more about rice production than did the plantation owners. In 1670, approximately 100 enslaved Africans were brought by the first white settlers to reach South Carolina (Carney 2001). There is evidence that rice was grown there from the beginning of the colony's existence. Their technology and labor created a multimillion-dollar industry that eventually provided the revenue for the Industrial Revolution. African seeds and knowledge also supported the development of rice production in Louisiana. According to historian Gwendolyn Hall, two slave ships from

Senegambia arrived in Louisiana in 1719 carrying several barrels of rice seed that probably came from that region (Carney 2001).

Jonathan Green conveys the ingenuity of Africans coming into South Carolina. "All the earth was moved by people only using sweetgrass baskets. They moved earth larger than the Great Wall of China… larger in volume than the pyramids." (Green 2016; Ferguson 1992). However, once the enslavement of Africans by Europeans began, Europeans erroneously took credit for introducing both rice and the technology for growing it. The Portuguese were said to have introduced rice from Asia into Africa. Not until the 20th century was this misinterpretation corrected (Carney 2001). Several indigenous wild rice varieties were found throughout Africa (Littlefield 1981). The main improved variety of rice grown in Africa was *Oryza glaberrima*, which was of a different species than the main variety that developed in Asia, *Oryza sativa*.

Indeed, these agrarian roots made Africans valuable to the development of white supremacist capitalism in the Americas. Today, those same agrarian roots remain the essence of the survival for African land-based communities. The traditional Gullah Geechee farmers and other Black landowners are struggling desperately to hold on to their land and, consequently, the last vestiges of an indigenous African agrarian culture and lifestyle. The Gullah Geechee communities represent the hopes of our connection between reclaiming our African agrarian roots and preserving African-based culture and food ways.

Building Community Through Land-Based Values

The same land worked by enslaved folks provided the platform for the creation of community infrastructure in the coastal South. Schools, businesses, churches, and praise houses each evolved within the context of traditional, agrarian values. Africans were able to survive the harsh realities of plantation life because they came from agrarian tribes and grew food and medicinal herbs to nourish themselves (Blassingame 1972).

From Richard Westmacott's (1992) interviews with 47 gardeners in three locations—the Lowcountry of South Carolina, the southern Piedmont of Georgia, and the Back Belt of Alabama—as well as his analysis of 200 years of records, we have a window into the survival strategies of Africans on the plantation. Enslaved Africans kept flourishing "slave gardens" on the plantation for daily survival (Vlach 1993; Westmacott 1994; Raper 1936), and continued to maintain gardens after emancipation. Raper (1936) notes that between 1927 and 1934, years of economic crises and depression, the average annual income of Black farm owners in Greene County, Georgia halved from $494.92 to $236.85. Yet, during the same period, the food produced in gardens doubled. Farm-owning families produced "practically all their foods," but others who were sharecroppers or wage laborers either did not have gardens at all or had gardens inadequate for providing for their food needs (Raper 1936). The "slave gardens" were places of power and resistance that were vital during enslavement and remained a source of food, pride, and community after emancipation. Findings from interviews with African American in these communities reveal that many still grow their own vegetables (Westmacott 1992).

Amelia's grandson holds in his memory from childhood another African carryover—the swept yards. On the historic trip to Sierra Leone, depicted in the previously mentioned film, he saw how the women in the villages stressed cleanliness by sweeping the compound yards clean. He noticed the same characteristic with his grandmother, who would sweep the yard each night. "In this way, she could observe what creatures (including humans) were doing there in the night by the footprints and other evidence that they left behind" (Moran 2016). During enslavement, gardens and swept yards were a function of survival. Later, those gardens and yards were also maintained for aesthetic value. The vernacular yard landscapes provided a visual platform for an artistic expression highlighting cultural design patterns around recycling materials. Swept yards also commonly practiced in West Africa and in parts of the South were used for family gatherings, religious and ritual celebrations, and daily tasks (Westmacott 1992).

One other distinctly Southern community institution that aided the land-based community in surviving hostile environments was the praise house. These were situated throughout the Gullah Geechee communities, usually placed in the woods (Visit to Coffin Point Praise House, St Helena, SC). Jonathan Green shares his memory of those praise houses:

> They were hidden in the woods. Praise houses were not in full view. Praise houses were places people aired and settled their disputes under the guidance of elders. All community business was taken care of in the praise house. Friday night praise house and Sunday church" (Green 2016).

Praise houses, like the one at Coffin Point, operated outside the purview of the mainstream white community. Unmistakably African, people blended traditional spiritual practices with European religious ideology. These ritualistic expressions of a worldview were imprinted on the daily lives of farmers and their beliefs about food, farming, family, and the world. Women needed the forest and woods to forage for medicinal herbs for midwifery and healing diseases. The woods and forest were important, and the people maintained biological diversity and ecological balance so that the herbs flourished. Community institutions, like the praise houses situated throughout the Gullah Geechee communities, were placed in the woods because of the protection the isolation provided, and also for the ability to access the outdoors as part of the ritual of honoring spirit.

On his trip to Sierra Leone, Moran also noted that fishing techniques found today among Gullah fisher folk had a strong connection to those he saw in West Africa. This included the use of the same type of netting used by their African counterparts. Their African ancestors also harvested oysters, as practiced today in the Lowcountry along the coasts (Moran 2016).

That Africans in the Americas are a people rooted in land, even after generations of torture on the plantations and so much ongoing land loss, may not be surprising. After enslavement, Africans acquired land on former plantations and claimed it as their home (Joyner 1984). According to a 1971 report on the state of Black land tenure on the South Carolina Sea Islands, 10 to 15 years prior to the publication of the report, "almost all of the Sea Islands largely in Beaufort and Charleston Counties, with a few in Jasper and Colleton, were owned by blacks" (Black Economic Research Center, Appendix E 1973). However, by 1960 most of the large Black landholdings of 100 acres or more were lost. The historical significance of these five counties is that they comprised part of the freed people territory authorized by General Sherman's Field Order No. 15. Although the possessory titles were never confirmed by Congress, small parcels were purchased by Africans when abandoned plantations were sold by federal tax commissioners during the latter part of the Civil War and during Reconstruction (Ibid.).

In Joyner's *Down by the Riverside: A South Carolina Slave Community*, he shares information about Elder Morris, a formerly enslaved African, who was being thrown off the plantation by its owner. Elder Morris went to the plantation owner and had this to say:

> I was born on dis place before freedom. My Mammy and Daddy worked de rice fields. Day's buried here. De fust ting I remember are dose rice banks. I growed up in dem from dat high. . . De strength of dese arms and dese legs and of dis old back. . . in your rice banks. It won't be long before de good Lord take de rest of pore old Morris away too. An' de rest of dis body want

to be with de strength of de arms and de legs and de back dat is already buried in your rice banks. No. . . you ain't agoin' to run old Morris off dis place (Joyner 1984, 42-43).

Elder Morris expresses his rootedness in a place and sense of claim to the land, even in its pain-filled memory. Joyner's passage speaks volumes about the meaning of freedom. For even after his "freedom," Elder Morris remains rooted in that soil, in those riverbanks. His parents are there, and generations like him recognize that they had a claim to the land they worked without payment. Rooted in the seeds of African agrarian principles of water and soil conservation and preservation, African American farmers have an uninterrupted cord of environmental and land-based knowledge guiding them in their land steward practices. Root medicines survived, and iron casting, fishing techniques unique to West Africa, are still practiced in the Gullah Geechee communities (Goodwine 2006; Jones-Jackson 1987). The isolation of the Sea Islands and the skills needed to negotiate the terrain, the similarities in the languages of those Africans coming together to inhabit those Islands after enslavement: these uninterrupted agrarian roots and linguistic patterns facilitated the survival of "Amelia's Song."

Given all the phases of modernism and development that have come since the Gullah Geechee communities set roots in the Carolinas, Florida, and Georgia, it is no wonder that the culture is being lost.

> The culture is dissipating though. It will be dissipated if not nurtured. We have an abundance of land, we can travel anywhere, so much activities of choice... But we have not realized the importance of nurturing. Nurturing the activities back is the key. Food is culture. More than putting hands in the ground... There is culture. We lost the importance of the activities related to farming. . .The visual importance of planting and harvesting are gone (Green 2016).

Life in Gullah Geechee communities was by no means idyllic or without racial threats and challenges. Moran recalled that his family members would often sell blue crabs to white entrepreneurs. When his father tried to go into the crab business for himself, the Ku Klux Klan tried to kill him. His father was able to escape because of his knowledge of the wooded pathways. It is quite understandable why his father kept a gun in practically every room and vehicle (Moran 2016).

The Harris Neck Conflict

Historically, Black landowners have faced threats from white racists groups and individuals; but too often, governmental policies are the root of the problem, as in the case of the Harris Neck land dispute. The history of the Harris Neck land dispute stretches back to 1863, when the Emancipation Proclamation was announced, and 1865, when General Sherman issued Field Order No. 15, designating nearly 400,000 acres of land along the southern coast (in the Gullah Geechee region) to be parceled out to formerly enslaved persons. The field order was later rescinded, but plantation owner Margaret Harris willed her land, located within this area, to formerly enslaved persons, including Robert Dellegall, an ancestor of Wilson Moran. The area became known as "Harris Neck," and the 75 families living there became the legal landholders (Harris Neck Land Trust website).

However, years later they were uprooted from their land. During World War II, the federal government used eminent domain to seize the Harris Neck land for construction of a federal airstrip, displacing 75 families from over 2,600 acres of land. According to Reverend Robert Thorpe, who was there at the time:

> Many families saw their homes bulldozed and their crops burned. My family was able to hurriedly disassemble our house before the bulldozers got it. . . We were promised that we could return to our land when the war was over. Now people say, 'There's no record of that promise' (Thorpe 2012,1).

Eventually, the land was given to the Department of Interior, which converted it to a National Wildlife Refuge in 1962. Residents have been waging an ongoing battle to regain their land since. No one has struggled longer more consistently on behalf of the Harris Neck community than Reverend Edgar Timmons Jr.. Reverend Timmons used all forms of resistance to the federal land takeover, including press conferences, court petitions, and direct action (Dickson 2007). In 1979, Timmons, along with Wilson Moran and others, occupied part of the disputed area by establishing a village of tents, and "at the end of two weeks, we decided it was time to start building our homes" (Dickson 2007). Subsequently, Timmons, Chris MacIntosh Jr., and Hercules Anderson were arrested and sentenced to 30 days in jail; they served half of their sentences (Ibid.).

In 2006, community residents formed the Harris Neck Land Trust to reclaim the land. In 2013, the trust, acting on the political realities, decided to request a long-term lease on a portion of the land, rather than request the return of the entire acreage taken.

The Deep Roots of Centennial Farms

The Harris Neck families have lost much of their land but, like so many other Black landowning communities throughout the country, they continue to fight courageously for their land and dignity. In spite of serious obstacles and challenges, many African American farm families across the diaspora continue to manifest a respect for agrarian practices deeply rooted in values that are in harmony with nature and with creating and maintaining a sustainable lifestyle. They strive to keep their agrarian roots by holding on to hard-earned family farmland or tribal lands.

Some are succeeding. For instance, the Joseph Fields Farm on John's Island, South Carolina has been family-owned for over one hundred years. The same is true for what is currently known as the Marshview Community Organic Farm, owned and operated by Sará Reynolds Green and her husband Bill on Saint Helena Island, South Carolina. Both of these families come from Gullah Geechee heritage. The Greens also have operated the Gullah Grub Restaurant in St. Helena, South Carolina for over 15 years.

As Jonathan Green, whose family has been on their 300 acres since 1870, describes, "It's in heir property. Land is still in the family. There were the agrarian roots where the work was done through kinetic energy (everyone worked together). We all worked together to do all things like the annual planting, clearing, turning soil, all done in unison. . . Now the elders continue the tradition working together and the churches work together to keep the agrarian activities going" (Green 2016).

Green and others interviewed for this chapter all speak of the disappearance of culture, yet they all agree that solutions rest in maintaining an agrarian rootedness, especially within a communally owned, land-based system.

On Sapelo Island, Georgia two other Gullah Geechee communities are struggling to hold on to their land. Purchased in the 1860's, Hogg Hummock and Raccoon Bluff are two of 12 remaining settlements. Sapelo Island residents are also working hard to bring back Behavior Cemetery. Due in large part to the leadership of Reginald Hall, a descendant of Hogg Hummock and four volunteers—Pamela Flores, Al Bartell, Alexander Henderson, and Kelly Brown—the residents are reclaiming their sustainable life ways by reclaiming their family land. Hall, who had been living in Cape Cod, Massachusetts, went back to his family land in 2009 after he received a call from his father late one night. His father asked him to research why the family was losing their land on Sapelo Island. Hall and his team are pressing for legislation to reclaim the original 5,176 acres of land owned by the Gullah Geechee people.

> Most of these original 44 families on Sapelo Island are descendants of the seven daughters of Bilali Mohammed, one of the most educated men to enter the United States as a slave. Ancestor Bilali Muhammed was taken from Sierra Leone to the Bahamas to be seasoned as a slave. . . The first Masjid was built on Sapelo Island in 1802. The Raccoon Bluff church built in 1866 still stands erected from the driftwood from a hurricane. . . . If we look at the 12 communities. . . these communities were not the ones where land was given to them. From the 1860's the ancestors paid American currency to get the whole title and deeds (Hall Interview 2016).

Since 2009, Reginald Hall and his team of volunteers have been working tirelessly and fearlessly to preserve what remains of Sapelo Island's Gullah Geechee communities, and reclaim land taken illegally by the State of Georgia.

> We now have proven within this new resort development, the people who claim they own the land, don't own the land and the titles show it. One of the title researches was of my grandfather's land, which sits right next door to the land I've been willed, and it has two resort-style developments built on this land that now proves this is my land. Well, each one of those two acres was sold for $500,000 per acre between the developers. In December 2009 they took this land and transferred it. . . You tax the poor Black people out, and you come back and now you have taken their land illegally (Hall Interview 2016).

Mr. Hall compares their land reclamation effort to a movement, and he has been successful in organizing others in the community:

> We fight for those people who are not on the face of this earth yet. If not, when they come, they will have nothing left. What do we do when they come and none of their rights have to be followed because we didn't stand up for the rights our ancestors put in place for us (Hall Interview 2016).

The African agrarian roots in the South are not confined to the Gullah Geechee corridor. Sandra Simone, for instance, owns and operates Huckleberry Hills Farm, located in Talladega, Alabama, which her family has owned for 140 years. Simone's great grandfather on her mother's side,

John Easley, who she affectionately called "The African," acquired the land during the 1860s (Simone 2016). Easley, originally from Mozambique, was not an enslaved person. He worked on passage ships and eventually found his way to Alabama. According to Simone's great uncle, Sippe Easley, John Easley's son, his father acquired over 2,000 acres, some of which was prime land located along a lake. John Easley prospered. "They had everything there," reports Sandra Simone. "A general store, blacksmith shop, sawmill, cows, goats, hogs, and a variety of crops. I was told that because so much was there it was called 'Nigger Town' by envious whites in the area."

A few family members continued to farm, but most sold the land (often much too cheaply) and moved away. Today, the family owns less than 300 acres, of which Sandra Simone owns about 100 acres, which she purchased from other family members. She is the only one still farming the land. Simone had moved away from Alabama, and did not plan to return. However, when attending a family function there, her late husband, Harold Burke, encouraged her to do otherwise. "I know it was never a plan of mine to return and live in Alabama, and certainly not in the country," she says. "But my husband started talking to me, almost preaching to me about the value of the land, the value of my great grandfather's accomplishments, and what it meant for Black folks to hold on to the land, to stop selling the land. . . That woke it up." Sandra Simone is now an organic grower and a founding member of the Southeastern African American Farmers Organic Network (SAAFON). She has conducted numerous workshops involving youth, and her vision is to establish a youth camp connecting young people to the land and agriculture. Her view of, and connection to, the land has changed drastically over the years. She says, "Now I know I love it, and I am so grateful to be here. I thank the Creator and I thank my ancestors, and I hope they are guiding me to what I think I'm supposed to do."

Carver and Whatley: The Seeds of Their Wisdom Are Still Taking Root

As African Americans work to maintain land and knowledge, they draw inspiration from two leaders who have developed new roots for African-American agrarian traditions: Drs. George Washington Carver and Booker T. Whatley. The ideas and research of these two men represent the legacy of an African/African-American agricultural knowledge base that continues to contribute to the world agricultural landscape. The two scientists had much in common; both started from humble beginnings and had to overcome tremendous obstacles in a racist, oppressive country. Dr. Carver was born to an enslaved mother around 1864. Dr. Whatley was born in 1915 and raised on a farm in Anniston, Alabama during the Jim Crow era, and was the oldest of 12 children. Education was important to both men. Dr. Carver earned a master's degree from Iowa State College in 1896 (and received several honorary doctorate degrees). Dr. Whatley earned his Bachelor of Science from Alabama A&M University, a predominantly Black 1890 land grant university, and a doctorate degree from Rutgers University. However, their real-world agricultural education started outside of formal education. According to Ferrell (2009, 12) Carver learned a lot as a boy while staying with a Black family, led by Mariah and Andrew Watkins:

> Carver received an education of a different sort. Mariah was a nurse and midwife with knowledge of medicinal plants. By passing on her herbal knowledge to Carver, Watkins may have sown the seeds of her pupil's future fascination with the unrealized potential for plant-based products.

Dr. Whatley once told a class at Tuskegee Institute (now Tuskegee University) that his grandfather taught him that it was time to plant cotton when "the leaves on a pecan tree were about as big as a squirrel's ear" (Bandele, personal observation, 1983). Whatley explained that there was a scientific basis for this, because frosts are rare once the pecan leaves reach that stage.

Both professors achieved greatness by dedicating their lives to work on behalf of African American farmers who were discriminated against by a racist American agricultural system. African American farmers, primarily from Macon County, Alabama came to Carver's lectures or visited him at Tuskegee Institute's agricultural experiment station. Dr. Whatley lectured throughout the state and country. With his credentials he could have obtained a position at a "mainstream" university with a higher salary, yet he chose to dedicate his talents to Southern and Tuskegee Universities.

Dr. Carver was known as the "peanut man" because he discovered over 300 uses of the crop, including milk, cheese, coffee, plastics, soap, cooking oil, and medicinal massage oil. He also developed several sweet potato products, including synthetic rubber, starch, livestock feed, dyes, vinegar and ink, and soy-derived products including ice cream, soup mixtures, cheese, coffee, flour, and bisque. Carver recommended these crops as alternatives to the monoculture production of cotton that he recognized would seriously deplete the soil over time (Bandele 2009).

Carver's recommended agricultural practices helped lay the foundation for today's sustainable and organic agricultural movements. Initially, due to his mainstream agricultural training at Iowa State College, Carver advocated for the use of commercial fertilizers. However, the price of the products precluded poor African American farmers from utilizing them. According to Hershey:

> . . . it was his concern for the South's Black farmers that served as a catalyst in fostering his unique conservation ethic, an ethic that became increasingly pronounced over the course of his first two decades at Tuskegee Institute (2009 57).

Dr. Carver was an advocate of "doing more with less." He came to recognize that the over reliance on commercial fertilizers without adding humus would deplete the soil and render it unproductive (Hershey 2009). Many of the practices that he advocated are today the cornerstones of organic production (Ibid.), including:

- crop rotation to prevent disease and insect buildup;
- leguminous cover crops to build soil fertility (especially nitrogen);
- animal manure as a natural fertilizer;
- compost from crop debris and leaves; and
- soil and water testing.

Dr. Whatley was often referred to as the "small farm guru," and is most often discussed in association with his plan for small-scale farms—often referred to as his "Tuskegee Plan." Whatley also had close ties to the predominantly Black 1890 land grant universities. His collegiate teaching and research career began at Southern University, a predominantly Black land grant institution in Baton Rouge, Louisiana.

Dr. Leodrey Williams, now Chancellor Emeritus of the Southern University Agricultural Research and Extension Center, was in Dr. Whatley's first class at Southern University in 1957 (Williams, 2016). He recalls:

> [Dr. Whatley] was one of my very favorite professors. He would always show up for class and really teach. His concern for the students was obvious. Dr. Whatley was a staunch believer in being practical. He believed that if you knew it, you should be able to duplicate it and put it into practice. And if he said 'you birds better get this,' you knew it would be on the next exam! (2016).

After spending over ten years at Southern University, Whatley arrived at Tuskegee:

Well, I've always wanted to work at Tuskegee. After all, George Washington Carver had worked there. . . and then Booker T. Washington, the man I was named after, was the founder and first administrator of the school (Mother Earth Editors 1982).

Like Carver, Whatley advocated a diversification of cropping systems, which were more ecologically sound than planting without rotations. His ideas were summed up in his book, *How to Make $100,00 Farming 25 Acres* (Whatley 1987). These ideas included:

- diverse planting systems, including greens, sweet potatoes, southern peas, blueberries, muscadine grapes, and strawberries;
- establishment of apiaries for both enhanced pollination of fruits as well value-added bee products; and
- utilization of a U-Pick system to reduce labor costs during harvests, coupled with a "clientele fee" that U-Pick customers paid in addition to the cost of produce picked.

Whatley's 25-acre plan was an ambitious one, and many agriculturists criticized it for not being realistic. However, he often stated that he did not expect farmers to adopt the whole plan, but to choose what was workable for them, and indeed, many small farmers, both Black and white, throughout the South put parts of his plan into action.

Whatley was also a plant breeder, and was very thoughtful in the names that he chose for the varieties that he established. He released a muscadine grape variety, "Foxy Lottie," named after his wife. He named one of his sweet potato varieties "Carver" and another "1890," in tribute to the predominantly Black 1890 land grant institutions (Bonsi 2016).

Shortly after Whatley's death, J. Helms had this to say:

Almost 20 years ago, Whatley was writing about U-Pick operations, community supported agriculture (CSA), drip irrigation, rabbit production, farmer-owned hunting preserves, kiwi vines, shiitake mushrooms, veneer-grade hardwood stands, on-the-farm bed and breakfasts, direct marketing, organic gardening and goat cheese production. What's even more astounding is that he was advocating many of these ideas in the 1960s and '70s (Alabama Federation of Farmers 2005).

As George DeVault similarly wrote, "He was way ahead of his time. . . He was one of the heroes of 20th century agriculture" (Bandele 2009).

Doctors Carver and Whatley each helped propel the 1890 Land Grant Universities, along with Tuskegee University, to the forefront of educating African American agricultural teachers and professionals, and they both provided assistance to African American farmers who had been—and continue to be—marginalized by the predominantly white 1862 land grant institutions and the United States Department of Agriculture. There is no telling how many professors and other agricultural professionals were students of Dr. Whatley and Dr. Carver, or of their students. Together, the two developed a network of disciples that continue to spread their mutual vision of a sustainable agricultural system that is inclusive, equitable, and rooted in African agrarianism.

Conclusion

African American farmers throughout the South continue to maintain and enrich a deep-rooted agricultural heritage. Gullah Geechee landowners and farmers, who might be the last surviving roots of their intact African agrarianism, are particularly emblematic of this struggle. These deeply rooted communities have preserved Africanisms such as the Mende song, net fishing, basketry, and love of nature, just to name a few. Reginald Hall truly honors the memory of his ancestor, Bilali Mohammed, by continuing that noble tradition of determination and love of family. So, too, have other current Gullah Geechee farmers: Joseph Fields, Sara Reynolds Green, Bill Green, and a host of others, known and not so well known, who draw on the inspiration not only from their African ancestors, but also from African American predecessors, such as Carver and Whatley, who continue to inspire family farmers. Black farmers from coast to coast embody the branches of these roots, full of hope for a new generation. These agrarian and cultural roots flow directly to Africa. These are, indeed, very deep roots.

References

Bandele, Owusu. 2015a. "Food Crops, Exchange of Between Africa and the Americas." In *The Sage Encyclopedia of African Cultural Heritage in North America*: *Volume 1*, edited by Mwalimu J. Shujaa and Kenya J. Shujaa, 406-409. California: Sage Publications, Inc.

Bandele, Owusu. 2015b. "Food Cultivation." In *The Sage Encyclopedia of African Cultural Heritage in North America*: *Volume 1*, edited by Mwalimu J. Shujaa and Kenya J. Shujaa, 409-413. California: Sage Publications, Inc.

Bandele, Owusu 2009. "The Deep Roots of Our Land-Based Heritage; Cultural, Social, Political and Environmental Implications." In *Land and Power: Sustainable*

Agriculture and African Americans, edited by Jeffrey Jordan, Edward Pennick, Walter Hill and Robert Zabawa, 79-92. Waldolf, MD: SARE publication.

Bandele, Owusu. 1983. Personal Classroom Observation.

Black Economic Research Center. 1973. *Only Six Million Acres: The Decline of Black Owned Land in the Rural South, Appendix E*. Accessed March 7, 2015. http://www.federationsoutherncoop.com/files%20home%20page/Only%20 6%20Million%20Acres/Only%20.

Blassingame, J. W. 1972. *The Slave Community: Plantation Life in the Antebellum South*. New York: Oxford University Press.

Bonsi, Conrad. 2016. Personal Interview by Owusu Bandele. July 11.

Burnham, Owen. 2000. *African Wisdom*. London: Piatkus Publishers.

California Newsreel. 1998. "The Language You Cry In." Accessed February 10, 2016. http://newsreel.org/video/THE-LANGUAGE-YOU-CRY-IN.

Carney, Judith. 2001. *Black Rice: The African Origins of Rice Cultivation in the Americas*. Cambridge: Harvard University Press.

Carney, Judith. 2004. "'With grains in her hair': rice in colonial Brazil." *Slavery and Abolition* 25:1, 1-27. Accessed Feb. 18, 2016. http://www.sscnet.ucla.edu/ geog/downloads/594/33.pdf.

Dickson, Terry. 2007. "Families Join in New Quest for Harris Neck Land." *Florida Times Union*, January 14. Accessed October 22, 2016. http://jackson-ville.com/tu-online/stories/011407/   geo_7329032.shtml#.WAu16OArJVM. Accessed October 22, 2016.

Ferrell, John. 2009. "George Washington Carver: A Blazer of Trails to a Sustainable Future." In *Land and Power: Sustainable Agriculture and African Americans*, edited by Jeffrey Jordan, Edward Pennick, Walter Hill and Robert Zabawa, 11-32. Waldolf, MD: SARE publication.

Ferguson, Leland. 1992. *Uncommon Ground: Archaeology and Early African America*,1650-1800. Washington, DC. Smithsonian Institution Press.

Fields, Helen. 2016. Personal Interview by Owusu Bandele. March 8.

Goodwine, Queen Quet Marquetta L. 2006. *Gullah/Geechee: Africa's Seeds in the Wind of the Diaspora, Volume V Chas'tun an e Islandts*. Charleston, SC: Kinship Publications.

Green, Jonathan. 2016. Personal Interview by Gail Myers. February 24.

Grimé, William Ed. 1976. *Ethno-Botany of the Black Americans*. Algonac, MI: Reference Publications, Inc.

Hall, Reginald. 2016. Personal Interview by Gail Myers, June 7.

Harris Neck Land Trust. "Chronology." accessed February 21, 2016. http://www. harrisnecklandtrust1.xbuild.com/#/chronology/4529751659.

Helms, J. 2005. "Dr. Booker T. Whatley: His Seeds and Ideas are Still Taking Root Today." Alabama Federation. Accessed April 2007 www.alfafarmers.org/ neighbors/neighborsStory.phtm?id=4311.

Hershey, Mark. 2009. "The Transformation of George Washington Carver's Environmental Vision, 1896-1918." In *Land and Power: Sustainable Agriculture and African Americans*, edited by Jeffrey Jordan, Edward Pennick, Walter Hill and Robert Zabawa, 57-77. Waldolf, MD: SARE publication.

Iliffe, John. 1995. *Africans: The History of a Continent*. Cambridge. Cambridge University Press.

Jones-Jackson, Patricia. 1987. When Roots Die: Endangered Traditions of the Sea Islands. Attens: University of Georgia Press.

Joyner, Charles. 1984 *Down by the Riverside: A South Carolina Slave Community*, 42-43. Urbana: University of Illinois Press.

Littlefield, Daniel C. 1991. *Rice and Slaves: Ethnicity and the Slave Trade in Colonial South Carolina*, 199. Champaign: University of Illinois Press.

Macfadyen, James MD. 1837. The Flora of Jamaica: a description of the Plants of that Island arranged according to the natural orders: With an appendix containing an enumeration of the genera according to the Linnean System, and an Essay on the geographical distribution of the species. Volumes 1 and 2. London: Orme, Brown, Green, & Longman.

Mbiti, John. 1991. *Introduction to African Religion*. Long Grove, IL: Waveland Press.

Mother Earth Editors. 1982. "The Small Farm Plan by Booker T. Whatley." Accessed June 27, 2016. www.motherearthnews.com.

Moran, Wilson. 2016. Personal Interview by Owusu Bandele. February 23.

"Niche Farming 'Guru' Dead at 89." *Montgomery Advertiser.* September 9, 2005.

Raper, Arthur. 1936. *Preface to Peasantry: A Tale of Two Black Belt Counties*. Chapel Hill: University of North Carolina Press.

Simone, Sandra. 2016. Personal Interview by Owusu Bandele, February 21.

Stedman, John Gabriel. 1796. NARRATIVE, of a five years' expedition against the *Revolted Negroes of Surinam*, in GUIANA, on the Wild Coast of South America; from the year 1772, to 1777: elucidating the History of that Country and describing its Productions, viz. Quadrupedes, Birds, Fishes, Reptiles, Trees, Shrubs, Fruits, & Roots; with an account of the Indians of Guiana, & Negroes of Guinea. Volumes 1 and 2. London: J. Johnson & J. Edwards.

Thorpe, Robert 2012. "Thorpe: Harris Neck: 70 Years to Justice" *Savannah Morning News*, July 27. Accessed Feb 21, 2016. savannahnow.com/column/2012-07-27/thorpe-harris-neck-70-years-justice#.UDfPCdZlRcQ.

Vlach, John Michael. 1993. *Back of the Big House: The Architecture of Plantation Slavery.* Chapel Hill: The University of North Carolina Press.

Whatley, Booker T. 1987. *How to Make $100,000 Farming 25 Acres.* Emmaus, PA: Rodale Press.

Westmacott, Richard. 1992. *African American Gardens and Yards of the Rural South.* Knoxville: University of Tennessee Press.

Williams, Leodrey. 2016. Personal Interview by Owusu Bandele, June 28.

Appendix: Dr. Booker T. Whatley's: The Guru's 10 Commandments

Thy small farm shalt

1. Provide year-round, daily cash flow.
2. Be a pick-your-own operation.
3. Have a guaranteed market with a Clientele Membership Club.
4. Provide year-round, full-time employment.
5. Be located on a hard-surfaced road within a radius of 40 miles of a population center of at least 50,000, with well-drained soil and an excellent source of water.
6. Produce only what they clients demand—and nothing else!
7. Shun middlemen and middlewomen like the plague, for they are a curse upon thee.
8. Consist of compatible, complementary crop components that earn a minimum of $3,000 per acre annually.
9. Be 'weatherproof,' at least as far as possible with both drip and sprinkler irrigation.
10. Be covered by a minimum of $250,000 worth ($1 million is better) of liability insurance.

- Booker T. Whatley, *How to Make $100,000 Farming 25 Acres*

CHAPTER 2

Resistance

Dãnia C. Davy, Savonala Horne, Tracy Lloyd McCurty,
and Edward "Jerry" Pennick (Equal Authorship)

If you ever find
yourself, some where
lost and surrounded
by enemies
who won't let you
speak in your own language
who destroy your statues
& instruments, who ban
your omm bomm ba boom
then you are in trouble
deep trouble
they ban your
omm boom ba boom
you in deep deep
trouble

humph!

probably take you several hundred years
to get
out!

- Amiri Baraka (1995, 7)

In 1803, seventy-five captured Igbos seized control of a ship headed to St. Simons Island, Georgia, forcing the white abductors to jump overboard and drown (Ciucevich 2009). According to archival evidence, upon arrival on the shores of the island, the Igbos marched together into the creek chanting, "The Water Spirit Omambala brought us here. The Water Spirit Omambala will carry us home" (Ebo [Igbo] Landing Project 2016; Ibid, 151-152). This act of resistance became one of the most heralded examples in the United States of enslaved Africans using mass suicide to free themselves from chattel slavery. The Igbos, who resisted slavery through communal death and transcendence, were canonized as the "Flying Africans" centuries later in Gullah Geechee and African American folklore (Powell 2011). Through African oral tradition and collective memory, the Igbos metamorphosed into supernatural birds that soared above slavery and cultural annihilation.

Though the Igbos resisted slavery through death, millions of African descendants resisted slavery through life, ensuring the transference of *omm boom ba boom* (i.e., ancestral knowledge, regenerative ideologies, and agrarian lifeways) to future generations in efforts to repel the permutations of white supremacist capitalism. Given the fact that the African consciousness and cosmovision are filtered through a kinetic agrarian identity, many of the manifestations of resistance utilized by African descendants in the United States are rooted in this identity (e.g., maroon settlements, self-governing agrarian communities, and collective agrarian land reforms).

This chapter pays homage to the "Flying Africans" of the Black agrarian liberation movement(s) in the United States—our collective triumphs, defeats, and rebirths. We acknowledge that it would be impossible to encompass the breadth of the African American experience of land-based resistance in the United States in a single book chapter. Thus, our intention is to pass on the invaluable historical and contemporary lessons of Black agrarians, advocates, attorneys, and rural organizations who understood that land ownership and access are elemental to the social, political, economic, and spiritual ascension of African descendants in the United States.

* * *

The 400-year Black agrarian liberation struggle in the United States is inextricably bound to the European construction of racial identity, hierarchy, and domination enshrined in American jurisprudence and societal custom. In her seminal work, "Whiteness as Property," Cheryl Harris examines how the origins of property rights in the United States were ingrained in the racial subjugation of Africans and Native Americans through the parallel systems of slavery and colonization (1993, 1716). In *Johnson and Graham's Lessee v.*

M'Intosh (1823), a keystone decision subordinating the land rights of Native Americans to conquest, the United States Supreme Court "established white-ness as a prerequisite to the exercise of enforceable property rights" (Ibid., 1724). The praxis of whiteness as property undergirded federal legislation and policies that formed starkly disparate trajectories to land ownership for whites and African descendants. The Homestead Act of 1862, a massive federal subsidy program, transferred over 50 million acres of Native American lands to mostly white male colonists and land speculators through 160-acre homesteads in exchange for five years of farming or payment of $1.25 an acre (Zinn 1999, 238). In comparison, the federal government abandoned the imperative of large-scale land redistribution efforts aimed to support the 4 million newly emancipated Africans whose bodies and agrarian expertise—as discussed in the previous chapter—supplied unprecedented wealth to the planter, industrial oligarchies, and the nation.

General William T. Sherman's Field Order 15—commonly known as "40 acres and a mule" within African oral history—is the most recognized of the failed federal land redistribution initiatives during the Reconstruction Era. In January 1865, after meeting with a group of African leaders and Secretary of War Edwin Stanton in Savannah, Georgia, General Sherman issued the order, which redistributed abandoned and confiscated lands along coastal South Carolina, Georgia, Florida, and the Sea Islands as (up-to) 40-acre parcels for distribution to African families. Within six months, 40,000 African families held possessory titles to 400,000 acres of land, and thousands more families flooded into the freedpeople territory to claim their land. However, the Africans' blueprint for economic independence through land ownership within an autonomous territory were dashed when President Andrew Johnson restored all abandoned and confiscated lands to the rebel planter oligarchy. Although subsequent legislation was proposed to confirm all possessory titles issued to Africans under Sherman's Field Order 15, Congress failed to marshal the political support needed for the legislation to survive a presidential veto (Oubre 1978).

The Southern Homestead Act provided marginal gains for the millions of African families striving to break free from the impoverishment of tenant farming and sharecropping. Enacted on June 21, 1866, the Act opened up over 46 million acres of unclaimed public lands in five southern states to newly emancipated Africans and white Union loyalists under home-steading provisions congruent to the provisions in the Homestead Act of 1862 (Ibid.). As aptly noted by historian Claude Oubre, a key provision of the Act stipulated that "freedmen would have the right to enter the land without competition from 'disloyal' whites until January 1, 1867, yet most labor contracts did not expire until that date" (Ibid, 186). Effectually, the fallacious statutory construction of the legislation excluded millions of African families from entering homesteads under the Act, because of their inability to breach existing tenant labor contracts. Other precursors of the Act's inevitable failure included the absence of financial assistance and farm supplies to transitioning tenant farmers, the undesirability and degraded soil quality of the majority of the land included in the Act, and the entrenched racial hostility of whites in the local land offices who withheld information from African families regarding the availability of public lands (Ibid., 95, 186-187). Predictably, by the time Congress repealed the Act in 1876, 6,500 African families had entered claims to homesteads, but less than 1,000 received final property certificates (Ibid, 188).

* * *

By 1910, despite perennial neglect of the federal government and anti-Black terrorism condoned by Southern states, Africans owned over 218,000 farms and had amassed over 15 million acres of farmland (Gilbert and Eli 2000, 37). Undeniably, this era of rabid anti-Black physical and economic violence necessitated the creation of resistance strategies to acquire and preserve land for the development of self-sufficient African communities. According to Oubre, from 1865 to 1870, newly emancipated Africans deposited over $16 million with the Freedmen's Savings and Trust Company, a private financial institution established by Congress. Approximately 70 percent of the monies later withdrawn were used to purchase real estate (Oubre 1978, 161). Near Georgetown, South Carolina, 160 African families acquired a former plantation and held the land together in a joint stock company. This demonstrative act of solidarity economics and collective land ownership was commonly used by African agrarian communities throughout South Carolina (Ibid, 167). With the intention of building an autonomous community, another 300 African families purchased 10-15 acre farms at a tax sale on St. Helena Island (Ibid, 168). Over a hundred years before Student Nonviolent Coordinating Committee (SNCC) activist James Forman released the *Black Manifesto*, calling for a $200-million capitalized southern land bank to acquire land and establish farm cooperatives, the celebrated abolitionist and scholar Frederick Douglass put forth a proposal to establish a $100-million capitalized national land bank to acquire and resell land on equitable terms to Africans (Ibid.; Black Economic Research Center 1973).

In addition to acquiring millions of acres of land through collective strategies, Africans boldly rejected European standards of individual property rights and intergenerational wealth transfer by reestablishing the African village in the United States through the creation of collectively owned family land. The profundity of this epic strategy of land-based resistance is captured in the living history of the Ellis' centennial family farm in Vidalia, Georgia:

> As early as 1872, Donald Ellis' great-grandparents began the visionary work of acquiring farmland to create a family estate. Over the course of their lives, they amassed over 500 acres of farmland in Southwest Georgia. At one time, the farm was home to a successful syrup company through which they grew and processed sugar cane to produce and sell syrup. Over the family's century-plus ownership of the land, they have been able to maintain approximately 100 of the originally acquired acres. Ellis was raised in Detroit, but spent much of his childhood with his family on the estate in Georgia. His fond memories created during that time have made him uncompromisingly committed to preserving his ancestors' land. Equipped with a degree in Agriculture, but very little practical experience farming on a large scale, Ellis has worked tirelessly to make a livelihood and honor his family's landowning heritage for the next generation (Ellis 2015).

Within the last century, the remarkable Black land ownership advances achieved during a span of 45 years (1865-1910) have been alarmingly eroded. In fact, the last five decades have signified the nadir of Black land ownership in the Black Belt region. Today, African Americans comprise a mere one percent of all US farmers, and own only 7.8 million acres of land (National Agricultural Statistics Service 2014; Gilbert, Wood, and Sharp 2002, 55). The staggering decline of Black land ownership resulted from a confluence of factors, including institutional discrimination; anti-Black terrorism; domination of the industrial agricultural paradigm; European cultural hegemony; structural dispossession processes and systems (i.e., foreclosures, partition sales, adverse possession, eminent domain, tax sales); lack of access to affordable and trustworthy legal services; and massive rural-to-urban migration. According to historian Pete Daniel in *Dispossession: Discrimination Against African American Farmers in the Age of Civil Rights*, "[In] the quarter century after 1950, over a half million African American farms went bankrupt, leaving only 45,000. In the 1960s alone, the black farm count in ten southern states (minus Florida, Texas, and Kentucky) fell from 132,000 to 16,000, an 88% decline" (2013, xi). Moreover, in *Who Owns the Land?: Agricultural Land Ownership By Race and Ethnicity*, a 2002 report that contextualizes the 1999 United States Department of Agriculture (USDA) Agricultural Economics and Land Ownership Survey, data revealed, "of all private U.S. agricultural land, whites account for 96%

of the owners, 97% of the value, and 98% of the acres" (Gilbert, Wood, and Sharp 2002, 55). The report further revealed that "compared with other races (including whites), a large proportion of Blacks are non-operator owners, who own two-thirds of all Black-held agricultural land" (Ibid, 61).

* * *

Free the land!

   - Salute of the Republic of New Afrika

The 1960s and 70s represented a groundswell of fearless visioning that reflected the full spectrum of Black Liberation ideology and praxis. Ignited by the African Liberation movements dismantling European imperialism and rebuilding self-determined African nations throughout the Continent and Diaspora, in 1968, over five hundred Black Nationalists declared independence from the United States of America in Detroit, Michigan, pledging their allegiance to the newly formed Provisional Government of the Republic of New Afrika (RNA) (Lumumba 1981). Claiming the five Southern states of Alabama, Georgia, Louisiana, Mississippi, and South Carolina as its national territory, the RNA situated their lands within the overwhelming African-majorities in the southern states and Black Belt counties (Obadele 1972). Moreover, citing the international precedent of the 1952 Luxembourg reparations agreement, in which West Germany paid the new state of Israel over $800 million in reparations for crimes committed against Jewish Europeans during the Holocaust, the RNA demanded reparations from the US government for the perpetual economic and violent crimes against African descendants (Ibid.). Upon successful negotiations with the US government, the RNA planned to use reparations to build an "Ujamaa" economy, guided by the principles of African Socialism (e.g., familyhood, cooperative economics, communal landholdings, and self-reliance) articulated by Tanzanian President Julius Nyerere in the Arusha Declaration (Ibid.; Brooks 1971; Nyerere 1968).

The RNA's calls for reparations and independence through the establishment of a sovereign Afrikan republic within the Southern United States threatened the white supremacist status quo in the rural South, but also in "Up South" cities, especially Detroit. Foreshadowed by the historical record, the RNA faced the incarnation of the tyrannical institutional force(s) that criminalized and severely crippled the dauntless mass reparations organizing efforts of freedwoman pioneering activist Callie House and the 300,000+ members of the National Ex-Slave Mutual Relief, Bounty and Pension Association over seventy years prior (Berry 2005). From RNA's inception, the FBI's ignoble COINTELPRO (Counter Intelligence Program) set out to decimate the leadership of the RNA through illegal surveillance, internal sabotage, frame-ups, imprisonment, and armed aggression (Lumumba 1981, 78). A successful Freedom of Information Act (FOIA) suit filed by the RNA exposed the voluminous COINTELPRO file on the movement—over 70,000 pages of surveillance and counterintelligence reports (Ibid.).

In March 1971, RNA citizens entered a land purchase agreement with a Black landowner in Hinds County, Mississippi to establish El Malik, the first Afrikan capitol of the RNA (Ibid, 73). The RNA's highly publicized Land Celebration Day was undermined by the repudiation of the agreement by the Black landowner as a result of undue pressure by the FBI (Ibid.). The state of Mississippi then filed an injunction against the RNA prohibiting the organization from reoccupying the land in Hinds County (Nelson 1978; Umoja 2013).

In the summer of 1971, the FBI and the Jackson police department coordinated two full-scale military attacks on both the RNA government office and residence in Jackson, Mississippi, resulting in unjust criminal charges, criminal trials, and long prison sentences for some of the RNA citizens (Lumumba 1981). Unfortunately, these unrelenting attacks all but destroyed the organization. Still, the RNA's vision to advance land-based power for African-majority communities in the Black Belt region endured as other organizations have taken up the mantel and pursued various incarnations of its aims.

Republic of New Afrika Land Celebration Day, March 1971. Courtesy of the archives of Chokwe Lumumba.

> Our cooperative is like the railroad station in our community. It will be here, even if the trains don't come anymore and somebody far away decides to pull up the track, we will still have our cooperative in our community because we built it ourselves, no matter what happens.
>
> - Eldridge Willie "E.W." Steptoe (Federation of Southern Cooperatives/ Land Assistance Fund 1992, 7)

The legacy of resistance has borne out one inescapable reality: individual efforts to challenge race-based oppression cannot dismantle the ubiquitous system of racism. Identifying institutionalized, discriminatory practices that destabilize economic independence as the basis of wealth disparities, several Black-led initiatives resisted dispossession by implementing solidarity economy models to promote collective Black land ownership and community wealth. Fannie Lou Hamer's visionary challenge to the political status quo, for instance, simultaneously advanced Black political engagement and economic autonomy. Hamer attributed persistent, economic inequities to plantation-style, individual-owner land monopolization. As an alternative, she advocated for cooperative land ownership, which would advance Blacks toward their "ultimate goal of total freedom" (Nembhard 2014, 178). Her revolutionary Freedom Farm Corporation, founded in 1969, acquired over 600 acres of land in Ruleville, Mississippi within its first two years of operation. The Freedom Farm created a shared ownership model, allowing cooperative members to "feed themselves, own their own homes, farm cooperatively, and create small businesses together in order to support a sustainable food system, land ownership, and economic development" (Ibid., 181, 182).

While providing small business incubation services and substantial amounts of food to over 200 financially insecure families locally and in Chicago, Illinois, Hamer acknowledged that the farm was not sustainable because it did not generate capital. By 1974, Freedom Farm lost 640 acres to creditors and ceased operations shortly thereafter. Freedom Farm's vision, impressive accomplishments, and even its shortcomings provide insight into the role cooperative land-based initiatives could play in realizing Black liberation.

In 1967, 22 cooperatives with deep roots in the civil rights movement, including the Freedom Quilting Bee in Alberta, Alabama and the Grand Marie Vegetable Producers Cooperative in Sunset, Louisiana, convened at Atlanta University to form the Federation of Southern Cooperatives (FSC), an umbrella nonprofit cooperative membership organization to address the survival of Black agrarian communities in the rural South through the proliferation of cooperatives as an alternative, democratic economic system (Federation of Southern

Fannie Lou Hamer Standing in the Freedom Farm Field, Mississippi, 1971. Copyright Louis H. Draper Preservation Trust, Courtesy of Steven Kasher Gallery, New York

The Freedom Quilting Bee, June 1974. Courtesy of Patricia Goudvis, FSC/LAF collection at Amistad Research Center, Tulane University

Grand Marie Vegetable Producers Cooperative. May 31, 1966. Courtesy of Ronnie Moore collection at Amistad Research Center, Tulane University

Cooperatives/Land Assistance Fund 2007). Throughout the Black Belt region, there was concern that civil rights did not necessarily mean economic rights. As stated succinctly by Erza Cunningham, a farmer and founding member of FSC, "You can't eat freedom. And a ballot is not to be confused with a dollar bill" (Bethell 1982, 5). At the time, African Americans were still largely dependent on a repressive, white-controlled economic system that tried to stifle any pursuit of their economic independence. This was especially true for Black landowners and farmers; many of whom had openly participated in or provided support to the civil rights movement.

In Sumter County, Alabama, tenant farmers who had been evicted from cotton plantations after registering to vote formed the Panola Land Buyers Association for the purpose of acquiring land (Ibid, 6). Like most emerging Black farmer cooperatives in the rural South, the financial resources of the Panola Land Buyers Association were scarce, and thus the cooperative turned to FSC for assistance. In 1968, FSC cobbled together $50,000 for the down payment on 1,325 acres in Sumter County to establish a rural training and research center, as well as to provide land access to the Panola Land Buyers Association. This was an impressive feat, given the fact that while African Americans accounted for more than 75 percent of the county's population of 17,000, they held no political offices in 1968, and owned less than 10 percent of the land (Ibid, 8). Before the ink could dry on the deal, white local officials descended on Sumter County to challenge the legality of the sale, initiating a litigious process that would drag on for three years before FSC would prevail in court (Ibid.).

By 1979, FSC was providing technical assistance, start-up capital, and mutual aid to 30,000 low-income rural families organized into 130 various cooperatives in 14 states throughout the Black Belt region (Ibid, 2). At this time, FSC was receiving over $2.5 million of funding annually, 85 percent of which was funneled through several federal agencies and programs. In response to the growing Black economic and political power in the county, a coalition of local, state, and federal officials launched a coordinated effort to destroy the organization. That same year, a federal grand jury served a subpoena on FSC, demanding "any and all documents in connection with federal funding of the Federation of Southern Cooperatives and its affiliated cooperatives" (Ibid.). Since FSC relied on both public and private support, a subpoena for a federal criminal investigation had the potential to end or severely limit the organization's effectiveness. This attack lasted nearly eighteen months before the Department of Justice declined prosecution. The justification for the investigation would remain shrouded in secrecy (Ibid.). FSC survived the federal grand jury investigation and the long winter of a tenuous financial future. The enduring historical lesson survived too—the sustainability and effectiveness of community-based organizations that provide pathways to economic autonomy for Black folk should never be determined by the federal government and/or philanthropic organizations. We, the Black community, must sustain ourselves.

More than a century ago, W.E.B. Du Bois published his iconic piece *The Souls of Black Folk*. In the chapter, "Of the Black Belt," Du Bois established the standard for scholarship in the field of modern rural sociology, and provided a critical overview of agriculture and land ownership patterns of the Black community in Dougherty County and Southwest Georgia. Southwest Georgia had the largest concentration of African Americans during and after slavery (Du Bois 1998, 105-107). Through sheer determination and grit, African American families transitioned from sharecropping to farm ownership, in some instances individually owning upwards of 600 acres of productive farmland by the dawn of the twentieth century (Ibid., 124). Du Bois noted that in Dougherty County, evidence of "systematic modern land grabbing and money getting" on the part of the "Plantocracy" was readily buttressed by the use of state police power and discriminatory financial institutions (Ibid. 123). The continuous seizures of Black-owned land ignited the movement against racial oppression, shepherding in the 1960s Southwest Georgia Movement with its ancillary programs promoting land retention and economic autonomy.

The Southwest Georgia Movement, under the strategic leadership of Charles Sherrod, a revered champion in SNCC, developed its comprehensive societal transformation platform through the instrument of the ballot box, enshrining voting rights as the fulcrum from which all human and economic rights flowed. However, the obstructions of the white political establishment were relentless in their opposition to the desegregation of Southwest Georgia. Realizing more sufferable defeats than sustained victories from their steadfast organizing efforts to elect African American farmers onto the influential and racially oppressive Agricultural Stabilization and Conservation Service committees (USDA local loan and subsidy governance bodies), the Southwest Georgia Movement adopted a more radical land-based resistance strategy through the establishment of New Communities, Inc. (NCI), which centered collective practices in their unyielding determination to achieve community sovereignty (Sherrod 2012, 92). As poignantly articulated by civil and land rights advocate Shirley Sherrod in her autobiography, *The Courage to Hope: How I Stood Up to the Politics of Fear*, the NCI vision was "a land trust operation that would boost economic sustainability while also helping individual families maintain their own residences" (Ibid, 84).

In order to find effective pathways toward "a brighter future" for African Americans throughout the country, NCI representatives from numerous civil rights organizations researched agricultural cooperative development models across the United States, India, and Israel (Sherrod and Sherrod 2016). In 1968, Charles Sherrod, C.B. King, Slater King, Robert Swann, and several others travelled to Israel to study Moshavim and Kibbutzim, collective farming land ownership models where shared-equity and land tenure rights were secured by a community-controlled entity (Ibid; Sherrod and Sherrod 2016). Profoundly impacted by these models, the community members returned to Southwest Georgia determined to implement a hybrid of these models, which entailed both individual homestead leases and community farming leases. The NCI's development plans were anchored in cooperative ownership and marketing as the basis for evolving into a self-sustaining agricultural community that would have all of the infrastructure associated with a small town (e.g. schools, utilities, small-scale industry, a childcare center, a retreat center, and local self-government). The vision was reminiscent of triumphant Reconstruction and post-Reconstruction Black town developments like Promised Land, South Carolina (1870); Nicodemus, Kansas (1877); and Mound Bayou, Mississippi (1887) (Sherrod and Sherrod 2016). At the outset of the planning process, over 500 families expressed a desire to move to New Communities (Sherrod et al. 2000, 6).

In 1969, over 50 African American families formed the nascent NCI with a vision of a "perpetual trust for the permanent use of rural communities" (Sherrod and Sherrod 2016). Battling racial discriminatory practices in the federal farm loan programs, the NCI purchased 5,736 acres of farm and forest land in Lee County, Georgia. In the luminous history of the Southwest Georgia Movement, Lee County was a key battleground site where Black landowners such as the lionhearted farmer and midwife Mama Dolly Raines provided armed protection and respite to hundreds of SNCC workers during long nights of racial terrorism (Sherrod 2012, 85; Sherrod et al. 2000, 15). This unprecedented land acquisition by African Americans in the midst of civil rights struggle has no historical antecedent, and irrefutably spawned the community land trust movement in the United States.

The NCI received a planning grant from the federal Office of Equal Opportunity (OEO) and submitted a comprehensive economic development plan for operating funds. Their land struggle intensified when Georgia Governor Lester Maddox, an avowed racist, blocked the OEO funds and thus the economic and structural advancement of NCI's programs (Ibid., 86-87). According to Charles Sherrod, "many of the original 50 families became disillusioned and lost faith in the vision;" but a faithful cohort of the founding families remained undeterred. As Sherrod stated, "we have never had our hands on this much land before and we will fight to hold on to it" (2016). Responding to OEO's cowardly acquiesces to Governor

Maddox, NCI secured private funding from foundations and churches, and long-term financing from Prudential Insurance.

For nearly ten years, NCI prospered with the help of a former Tuskegee Institute extension agent who employed many of the agrarian techniques and production processes championed by Carver and Whatley, including diversification, value added production, and a direct marketing system (Sherrod and Sherrod 2016). Specifically, NCI cultivated over 2,200 acres, growing varied vegetables and fruits—including muscadine grapes—and built an impressive "pick-your-own" operation. NCI also developed a sugarcane mill for syrup production, a 2.5-mile farmers' market, and an on-site smokehouse for fresh sausage production (Sherrod 2012, 88).

A combination of market downturns, extensive droughts, and political pressures eventually resulted in the collapse of NCI landholdings. Undeniably, the USDA Farmers Home Administration's overt racial discrimination provided the crushing blow to NCI when it refused to provide timely emergency disaster assistance, while at the same time providing loans to white farmers of large plantations throughout the area. The NCI fought USDA mightily for over three years with assistance from a variety of community-based organizations. Unfortunately, these collective efforts were not enough to sustain NCI, and in 1985 Prudential Insurance foreclosed, selling the property for $1.1 million, one-fifth of its value (Sherrod et al. 2000, 6). The new owner demolished and bulldozed all buildings and destroyed all crops, as if to wipe NCI from both memory and history (Sherrod and Sherrod 2016). However, the visionary work and legacy of NCI, the nation's first cooperative community land trust, could never be razed, and remains in the hearts and souls of the pioneering families of NCI.

* * *

Although the conventional wisdom has been to favor and encourage a rural-to-urban migration pattern, the recent deterioration of the large cities of America; the realization that some 75% of our U.S. population is crowded onto less than 2% of the land; the alarming size and density of these megalopolises, the newly discovered interest in environmental factors and in simpler life styles; together with some questioning of the social desirability of permitting the unchecked acquisition of title to the national territory by the corporate giants, have combined to force some discreet questioning of whether continuation of the unchecked human abandonment of the countryside is indeed in the national interest.

- Black Economic Research Center (1973, 1-2).

The Emergency Land Fund (ELF) was created out of the same rebellious spirit as the Freedom Farm, FSC, and NCI—the desire to realize autonomous self-sufficiency for the Black rural community. ELF's history can be traced back to the Black economic development conference held in Detroit, Michigan in 1969, where James Forman released his impassioned *Black Manifesto* calling for a southern land bank to stimulate cooperative development and economic autonomy for Black rural communities (Ibid, 5). Although several follow-up meetings were held, there was a lack of consensus on how to address the demands in the manifesto. Robert S. Browne, an economist and founder of the Black Economic Research Center (BERC), obtained funding from Clark College to study how the land bank concept might best be implemented (Pennick 2016). In 1971, a cadre of Black attorneys and land rights advocates convened at Clark College to further examine the land question and generate viable land retention strategies (Black Economic Research Center 1973). During the vigorous discourse numerous proposals were presented, including the development of a fund to pay delinquent taxes and to bid up the selling price of auctioned land that could not be saved; exploration of obtaining church or publicly owned land; and the development of a for-profit entity that would sell shares in a land tract to investors while retaining the management and land use responsibilities (Ibid., 8, 11).

In 1973, the BERC published *Only Six Million Acres: The Decline of Black Owned Land in the Rural South*, the first comprehensive report on the state of Black land tenure in the Black Belt region (Pennick 2016). The publication and subsequent wide circulation of the report was a defining moment in the enduring struggle of African Americans to hold onto their land and launched the formal organization of the Emergency Land Fund to develop and implement land retention strategies.[1] In many ways, ELF would address many of the issues expressed in the *Black Manifesto* and championed by the RNA. Under the guidance of Executive Director Joe Brooks, former National Minister for Economic Planning and Development for the RNA, ELF launched a three-pronged resistance strategy to stymie the sweeping tide of Black land loss: a regional attorney network to provide legal representation to Black landowners; a revolving loan fund to assist Black landowners in various land loss proceedings; and a local grassroots advocacy and political education network to defend the rights of Black landowners (Ibid.).

---

[1] In 1979, the USDA commissioned a study by the Emergency Land Fund out of concern for "increasing the marketability and productivity of rural land, particularly that of minority landowners." Purportedly, the USDA was concerned that a significant number of Black landowners were unable to access USDA resources because they were heir property owners and therefore did not have clear title to the land as required. Based on extensive research, ELF proposed 19 solutions to the problem. Although this was the most scientific and comprehensive study on problems related to heir property, the USDA adopted none of the solutions and the problem still persists (Emergency Land Fund 1980).

In order to strengthen the grassroots land retention efforts of ELF, Black farmers and rural landowners formed the National Association of Landowners (NAL) in 1977, a movement led and controlled by African Americans organized to build power and resist the takeover of Black-owned land (Brooks 2016). Through the leadership of Fred Bennett, a farmer whose family owned a 400-acre farm in Greeneville, Alabama, NAL negotiated a low interest loan of $1 million with Equitable Life & Casualty Insurance Company to save Black-owned land in Alabama (Pennick 2016). NAL saved hundreds of acres by thwarting tax sales and through forced, below market value partition sales.

At its zenith, NAL had a paying membership base of over 4,000 Black farmers and landowners, mostly from the South, but including a significant number of "Up South" members (Ibid.). Unfortunately, Equitable's infusion of capital was a one-time investment, and NAL could neither attract significant public or private funds nor generate enough funds internally to sustain the emergency loan fund. Still, over a ten-year period, ELF and NAL handled over 1,000 land cases and saved over 50,000 acres (Ibid.). Moreover, in over 60 counties throughout the Black Belt region, a stalwart grassroots county contact network monitored and confronted efforts to dispossess Black landowners of their land (e.g., pooled financial resources to bid at tax sales in order to restore land to either the original landowner or a landless farmer; conducted title searches; and kept landowners informed of local land-related issues). This formidable network of Black land rights advocates still exists informally today. In 1985, the leadership of FSC and ELF combined programs to maximize impact and self-sufficiency, officially becoming the Federation of Southern Cooperatives/Land Assistance Fund (Brooks and Prejean 1982, 74).

* * *

For the master's tools will never dismantle the master's house. They may allow us to temporarily beat him at his own game, but they will never enable us to bring about genuine change.

- Audre Lorde, (1984, 112)

The groundbreaking civil rights case, *Brown v. Board of Education Topeka Kansas* (1954), marshaled in an era of using litigation as a resistance strategy. However, the litigation-based model has had significant shortcomings in addressing systematic discrimination in preserving Black land ownership rights. A glaring example of the limitations of litigation as a land preservation resistance strategy is the now well-known *Pigford v. Glickman* case. *Pigford* was an attempt to use class-action litigation to address the well-documented pattern of discriminatory lending practices employed by the USDA against Black farmers.

In 1997, the Civil Rights Action Team, established by the USDA, reported that "minority farmers have lost significant amounts of land and potential farm income as a result of discrimination by [Farm Service Agency of the United States Department of Agriculture] programs and the programs of its predecessor agencies" (Civil Rights Action Team 1997, 30). That same year, the Office of the Inspector General found that the discrimination complaint process at the FSA lacked "integrity, direction, and accountability," making it so grossly inadequate as to be functionally nonexistent (Viadero 1997). These reports emphatically corroborated the personal accounts of discrimination shared by Black farmers across the country throughout the 1980s and 1990s.

In 1997, attorneys filed the *Pigford* lawsuit arguing that the USDA had institutionalized a practice of race-based discrimination by, among other things, unfairly denying, restricting, and severely underfunding Black farmers who applied for loans and other financial assistance from the Department throughout the eighties and nineties. Further, since the Reagan Administration had shut down the investigation of these discrimination complaints, Black farmers had no recourse for addressing their discrimination other than litigation.

The 1999 *Pigford* settlement created two tracks by which Black farmers who believed they had been discriminated against by the USDA could either file a complicated claim form and submit substantiating evidence of their discrimination to receive a $50,000 cash settlement (Track A), or individually litigate their discrimination claim (Track B). Of the 22,552 Track A claims that were filed, approximately two-thirds were approved and roughly one-third were denied (Office of the Pigford Monitor 2016). However, considerably more individuals were denied because they missed the deadline; roughly 73,800 claims were filed after the close of the filing period (Cowan and Feder 2012, 5). If the significant success rate of the timely filers validated the claims that they had previously faced institutionalized discrimination, the exclusion of the late filers from the process emphasized the continuing failure of the process to reach affected Black farmers.

As a result of the shamefully insufficient claims resolution process, Congress re-opened the filing period for certain class members in the 2008 Farm Bill. In the resulting *Pigford II* claims process, notice was distributed to over 80,000 individuals who had reasonably missed the filing deadline or never received an adjudication of their claim. While providing over $2 billion in cash settlements and other limited remedies to the victims of race-based discrimination, *Pigford I* and *II* did not restore the land lost during the era of intentional discrimination and complicit governmental actions.

The *Pigford* case revealed the significant shortcomings of employing litigation within an unjust legal system as a stand-alone resistance strategy.

One bright light at the conclusion of the *Pigford* process was the recent re-birth of New Communities, Inc. After 10 years of litigation, NCI prevailed with a $12.5 million settlement, one of the largest settlements resulting from *Pigford*. In 2011, the NCI board reclaimed their 40-year deferred dream by purchasing a 1600-acre former plantation and renaming the lands worked by enslaved African ancestors as 'Resora.' Guided by the NCI's blueprint for community self-determination, Resora will serve as a cultural and leadership development center to train next generation Black agrarians and civil rights advocates, and as a demonstration farm, again employing the agrarian regenerative systems and production methods forged by Carver and Whatley (Sherrod and Sherrod 2016).

Today, in addition to manifesting the legacy of resistance, many nonprofit organizations continue to exemplify the spirit of cooperation to promote Black land ownership. Founded in 2011, the Black Farmers and Agriculturalist Association – Florida Chapter (BFAA-FL) is dedicated to identifying and expanding economic opportunities for Black agribusiness owners. In 2015, BFAA-FL partnered with Florida Agricultural & Mechanical University (FAMU) to steward 3,800 acres of land FAMU acquired from the USDA (Gunn 2015; Kaplan 2015). The property, located in Brooksville, Florida, comprised one of the single largest land transfers to a historically Black land-grant institution (Kaplan 2015). FAMU agreed to share this land resource with BFAA to provide land access and research-based technical assistance for Black farmers in the state (Gunn 2015; Kaplan 2015). By engaging a genuinely collaborative initiative, the BFAA-FAMU partnership could establish a modern, large-scale model for cooperative agricultural production. Accessing the politico-economic resources of an 1890 land-grant institution will help BFAA expand opportunities for Black farmers, laying the foundation for a replicable cooperative model.

History has granted significant insight into the collective creativity required to develop solutions for Black land loss. The legacy of resistance must play a role in the process by which proposed solutions are examined. Recreating individualistic land ownership models, which resettle status quo discrimination from the post-colony culture into the Black consciousness, must be met with scrutiny and critical evaluation.

The evolution of resistance as a cultural practice demands a continued dialogue, readily integrating persistent racial discrimination, intra-community disparities, and on-going political disenfranchisement against the backdrop of the economic reality of the erosion of Black wealth. As Harriet Tubman admonished the resistance-wary travelers, we must advance together toward freedom or face certain death. The collective Black community must engage cooperative economic investment to preserve livelihoods, property, and lives. This is the hope of enslaved African ancestors and the promise to be fulfilled for future generations.

* * *

Take the story of them people what fly back to Africa. That's all true. You just had to possess magic knowledge to be able to accomplish this.

- WPA interview with George W. Little, root doctor from Brownsville, Georgia, circa 1930s (Powell 2011, 254; Georgia Writer's Project 2014, 67)

Appendix: Land is Power: Leaders in the Resistance Movement for Black Agrarian Liberation

With each generation, variations of the strategies discussed above were utilized by the beloved community that comprise the long arc of the Black agrarian liberation movement in the US including: millions of Black agrarians who left their land wealth to their families and future generations via heir property (1865); the Colored Farmers' National Alliance and Cooperative Union (1886); the Student Nonviolent Coordinating Committee (1960); the Rural Advancement Fund of the National Sharecroppers Fund (1966); Muhammad Farm (1966); the Federation of Southern Cooperatives (1967); the National Conference of Black Lawyers (1968); the Republic of New Afrika (1968); the Freedom Farm Corporation (1969); Floyd B McKissick Enterprises, Inc. (1969); the New Communities Community Land Trust (1969); the Emergency Land Fund (1971); the National Association of Landowners (1977); the Arkansas Land and Farm Development Corporation (1980); the North Carolina Association of Black Lawyers: Land Loss Prevention Project (1982); Operation Spring Plant (1987); the Black Farmers and Agriculturalists Association – North Carolina (1997), the Oklahoma Black Historical Research Project (1998); the Southern Rural Black Women's Initiative for Economic and Social Justice (2002); the Center for Heirs' Property Preservation (2005); Southern Rural Regenerative Enterprises for Families (2009); the Black Farmers and Agriculturalist Association – Florida Chapter (2011); and the Black Belt Justice Center (2012). This is by no means a complete or exhaustive list, but merely a sampling of organizations that have been committed to promoting Black land ownership.

References

Baraka, Amiri. 2007. "Wise 1." *Wise, Why's, Y's: The Griot's Song Djeli Ya*. New York: Third World Press.

Berry, Mary Frances. 2005. *My Face Is Black Is True: Callie House and the Struggle for Ex-Slave Reparations*. New York: Alfred A. Knopf.

Bethell, Thomas N. 1982. *Sumter County Blues: The Ordeal of the Federation of Southern Cooperatives*. Washington, DC: National Committee in Support of Community Based Organizations.

Brooks, Joseph. 2016. Interview by Tracy Lloyd McCurty, Esq. January, 18.

Brooks, Joseph. 1971. "Ujamaa for Land and Power." *The Black Scholar* 3: 13-20.

Brooks, Joseph and Charles Prejean. 1982. *A Joint Program of Comprehensive Rural Development Between the Federation of Southern Cooperatives and the Emergency Land Fund*. Atlanta: Federation of Southern Cooperatives.

Black Economic Research Center. 1973. *Only Six Million Acres: The Decline of Black Owned Land in the Rural South*. New York: Black Economic Research Center.

Ciucevich, Robert. 2009. *Glynn County Historic Resources Survey Report*. Brunswick: Glynn County Board of Commissioners.

Civil Rights Action Team. 1997. "Civil Rights at the United States Department of Agriculture." Washington, DC: United States Department of Agriculture. Accessed February 16, 2016. http://www.federationsoutherncoop.com/pigford/research/CRAT%20Report%201997.pdf.

Cowan, Tadlock and Jody Feder. 2012. "The *Pigford* Cases: USDA Settlement of Discrimination Suits by Black Farmers." Washington, DC: Congressional Research Service. Accessed February 16, 2016. http://www.clearinghouse.net/chDocs/resources/caseStudy_TadlockCowenJodyFeder_1361971920.pdf.

Daniel, Pete. 2013. *Dispossession: Discrimination Against African American Farmers in the Age of Civil Rights*. Chapel Hill: University of North Carolina Press.

Du Bois, W.E.B. 1998. *The Souls of Black Folk and Related Readings*. Evanston: McDougal Littell.

Ebo (Igbo) Landing Project. 2016. "About." Accessed January 23, 2016. http://igbolandingproject.com/about/.

Ellis, Donald. 2015. Acres of Ancestry Oral History Project Interview by Dánia C. Davy, Esq. December 28.

Emergency Land Fund. 1980. *The Impact of Heir Property on Black Rural Land Tenure in the Southeastern Region of the United States*. Atlanta: Emergency Land Fund.

Federation of Southern Cooperatives/Land Assistance Fund. 2007. *Four Decades (1967-2007): Historical Review of the Federation of Southern Cooperatives/Land Assistance Fund*. Atlanta: Federation of Southern Cooperatives/Land Assistance Fund.

Federation of Southern Cooperatives/Land Assistance Fund. 1992. *25th Annual Report*. Atlanta: Federation of Southern Cooperatives/Land Assistance Fund.

Georgia Writer's Project. 2014. *Drums and Shadows: Survival Studies Among the Georgia Coastal Negroes*. Self Published: Georgia's Writer's Project.

Gilbert, Charlene and Quinn Eli. 2000. *Homecoming: The Story of African American Farmers*. Boston: Beacon Press.

Gilbert, Jess, Spencer Wood, and Gwen Sharp. 2002. "Who Owns the Land?: Agricultural Land Ownership By Race and Ethnicity." *Rural America* 17:4 55-62.

Gunn, Howard. 2015. "Legislative Update." President's Remarks at the annual board meeting for the Black Farmers and Agriculturalist Association – Florida Chapter. Orlando, Florida. November 21.

Harris, Cheryl I. 1993. "Whiteness As Property." *Harvard Law Review* 106:8 1707-1791.

Order. 2012. *In re Black Farmers Discrimination Litigation*. Case No. 08-mc-0511 (D.D.C.).

Kaplan, Kim. 2015. "USDA Transfers 3,800 Acres in Brooksville to Florida A&M University." USDA. Accessed January 24, 2016. http://www.ars.usda.gov/is/pr/2015/151020.htm.

Lumumba, Chokwe. 1981. "Short History of the U.S. War on the R.N.A." *The Black Scholar* 12:1 72-81.

Lorde, Audre. 2007[1984]. "The Master's Tools Will Never Dismantle the Master's House." *Sister Outsider: Essays and Speeches*. Ed. Berkeley, CA: Crossing Press. 110-114.

National Agricultural Statistics Service. 2014. "2012 Census of Agriculture Highlights: Black Farmers." Accessed February 5, 2016. http://www.agcensus.usda.gov/Publications/2012/Online_Resources/Highlights/Black_Farmers/Highlights_Black_Farmers.pdf.

Nelson, William E. 1978. "Black Political Power and the Decline of Black Land Ownership." *The Review of Black Political Economy* 8:3 253-265.

Nembhard, Jessica Gordon. 2014. *Collective Courage: A History of African American Cooperative Economic Thought and Practice.* University Park: Pennsylvania State University Press.

Nyerere, Julius. 1968. *Ujamaa: Essays on Socialism.* London: Oxford University Press.

Obadele, Imari Abubakari. 1972. "The Struggle is for Land." *The Black Scholar* 3:6 24-36. Taylor & Francis, Ltd.

Office of the Monitor. 2016. "National Statistics Regarding Pigford v. Vilsack Track A Implementation as of February 16, 2012." Accessed February 6, 2016. http://media.dcd.uscourts.gov/pigfordmonitor/stats/.

Oubre, Claude F. 1978. *Forty Acres and a Mule: The Freedmen's Bureau and Black Land Ownership.* Baton Rogue: Louisiana State University Press.

Pennick, Edward "Jerry". 2016. Interview by Tracy Lloyd McCurty, Esq. January, 18.

Powell, Timothy. 2011. "Summoning the Ancestors: The Flying Africans' Story and Its Enduring Legacy." In *African American Life in the Georgia Lowcountry: The Atlantic World and the Gullah Geechee,* edited by Philip Morgan. Athens: University of Georgia Press.

Sherrod, Charles, Shirley Sherrod, Edward "Jerry" Pennick, and Heather Gray, eds. 2000. *Celebrating the Southwest Georgia Movement: Reviewing Our Past to Chart Our Future.* Albany: The Southwest Project for Community Education, Inc.

Sherrod, Shirley and Charles Sherrod. 2016. Interviews by Edward "Jerry" Pennick. June, 17, 20.

Sherrod, Shirley with Catherine Whitney. 2012. *The Courage to Hope: How I Stood Up to the Politics Fear.* New York: Atria Books.

Umoja, Akinyele Omowale. 2013. *We Will Shoot Back: Armed Resistance in the Mississippi Freedom Movement.* New York: New York University Press.

Viadero, Roger C. 1997. *Report for the Secretary on Civil Rights Issues – Phase I.* Washington, DC: Office of the Inspector General. Accessed February 16, 2016. http://www.usda.gov/oig/webdocs/oig.htm.

Zinn, Howard. 1999. *A People's History of the United States (1492 – Present).* New York: HarperCollins.

CHAPTER 3
Regeneration
Leah Penniman and Blain Snipstal (equal authorship)

Afro-ecology: A form of art, movement, practice and process of social and ecological transformation that involves the re-evaluation of our sacred relationships with land, water, air, seeds and food; (re)recognizes humans as co-creators that are an aspect of the planet's life support systems; values the Afro-Indigenous experience of reality and ways of knowing; cherishes ancestral and communal forms of knowledge, experience and lifeways that began in Africa and continue throughout the Diaspora; and is rooted in the agrarian traditions, legacies and struggles of the Black experience in the Americas.

- Black Dirt Farm Collective, Black Dirt Farm, Maryland

In recent years, there has been growing movement to regenerate Black agrarianism in urban and rural spaces, amongst youth, elders, and those in between, domestically and internationally. Within these efforts, there are many commonalities, and one issue in particular is rising to the surface: the struggle for land. From our histories, we have a deep understanding that land is power. It doesn't get much simpler than that. The struggle to "free the land" goes hand in hand with developing organizing methods, practices, and identities. The farmers, rural landowners, and agrarian organizers who are part of the radical black agrarian tradition have historically served as the vanguard and custodians of revolutionary moments for African descendants and people of color. As we raise the banners of agroecology and food sovereignty, in solidarity with our historic banners of struggles—reparations, abolition of the prison industrial complex, self-determination—the moment to return as a vanguard is now.

As part of the historic, diasporic movement of African people across land, water, space, and time, the Black agrarian experience in the Western Hemisphere has always been international. The historic and current experiences of descendants of free, enslaved, and migrated Africans in the US—as depicted in this chapter—are not unique to the US, but are a window into experiences and views on the various exploitative systems of power that exist around the world. Our struggle has been, and will always be, global in scope.

Our historic struggles are intimately linked to our radical agrarian efforts. This connection has been strengthened through the efforts of Black returning generation and established farmers; food sovereignty and agroecology training programs; the re-articulation of the role of cooperatives; and Black and Brown alliances within the food system. These efforts are all based upon one common thread: that land is power, and through organization, our power becomes real.

We are confronted today with two global crises: the rapid transformation of the climate and the aggressive advancement of white supremacy and financial capitalism. The Black agrarian struggle finds itself at the juncture of these two historic forces.

The recent wave of Black folk returning to the land is claiming its agrarian identity as "returning generation farmer," an historic social actor who is class-conscious, in other words, aware of his/her historic agrarian conditions and also of the moment for transformation. Our struggle is material, but it also deals with our identities, assumptions, and values. Bringing value and dignity back to the image of the Black farmer working with the land and nature is fundamental. Revaluing Black agrarian identity and Black agrarianism more broadly is a core task of this "returning generation."

This chapter is organized around four themes: resilience, leadership, activism, and healing. The themes arose out of a series of interviews with Black farmers, elders, landowners, and organizers from "Up South" and "Down South" farms and rural communities. We organized this section around 'regeneration' because of the value it plays in the ecosystem, and to situate regeneration as a conscious and political principle of this current moment of Black agrarianism.

Building Fortitude Towards Resilience

Our trauma is like the grain of sand that gets into a clam. She can't cough, so she keeps producing pearly mucus to cover it up layer upon layer. The pearl looks beautiful, and it's ours because it was passed down through the mothers, but what's inside is a lot of deep trauma. We get to notice the pearl and how important it is for people to hold onto the pearl. That pearl becomes part of the clam and part of our story, too. If we yank it out, we will kill her and we don't want to do that. We've got to recognize our trauma and what is covering it up and what to do with it. I hope that many young people, Black folks, will go out and start growing food. It's about survival, dynamic and creative ways to take care of ourselves—it's connected to our whole sovereignty and our whole liberation.

- Chris Bolden-Newsome, Urban Farmer

There is no crystal staircase ready to guide returning generation farmers back home to the land. Through incredible fortitude and personal sacrifice, Black farmers are healing and garnering necessary training and resources. Not only are returning generation farmers navigating a society that devalues the small agriculturalist, they are also confronting the same oppressive structures that dispossessed Black people of 90 percent of our land over the last century (Rosenburg 2015).

Small farm training in the North often demands that learners give up their bodies and labor freely or cheaply to a landowner who provides instruction, under the title of an apprenticeship or work-exchange. For many Black people, women in particular, the generational trauma of this arrangement is unbearable, and they choose alternate career paths. Jalal Sabur, a farmer, activist, and prison abolitionist with the Freedom Food Alliance, endured his apprenticeship experience and went on to start his own farm.

After studying urban agriculture with the Farm School NYC and at Dig It, his father's urban youth farm in Philadelphia, Sabur headed to upstate New York to apprentice on the 1000-acre McEnroe's organic farm. For three seasons, he barely broke even economically and struggled with the isolation of being a Black person in the rural, white landscape of the cold North. He expected more of his farm mentors, explaining, "The apprenticeship program was just 'do what I tell you to do' and not teaching you anything—basically slave labor. You got minimum wage and had to pay rent out of that. We were just scraping by" (Sabur 2016).

Finding the resources to purchase the necessary land and infrastructure presents an additional hurdle to returning generation farmers. Even today, Black farmers receive 50 percent less government support in terms of loans, conservation programs, subsidies for crop production, and disaster insurance than the average farmer of any race (USDA 2012). Frederick

Wellington, elder herb and vegetable farmer in Schoharie, NY explains, "For years I applied for seed money and got nothing."

The Wellingtons liquidated their savings and retirement to buy the land and build the infrastructure for their 45-acre farm, which employs four people. Wellington shares:

> Statistics show that most farmers other than the very big ones still rely on some outside income from members of family. It's hard to make a living from farming. I was able to do it in the sense that I used my pension, but I'm not sure it was the best decision, so I squandered my savings to provide the irrigation ponds, barns, roads, tractors, and fencing. I had to use my own resource to do that (2016).

The wealth of this nation was built, and continues to be constructed on, the backs of our people, and this has left us with deep, inheritable scars. Returning to the land requires that we address emotional and spiritual healing with at least as much intention as we invest in training and material resources.

Yonette Fleming, a farmer, healer, and organizer with Hattie Carthan Community Garden, was raised in Guyana by a family and society that cherished sustainable agriculture. When she moved to the US, she was swept up by a corporate culture that demanded that she sacrifice her body and spirit to advance capitalism. Fleming shares, "I learned to be a 'white male' and put money above every other interest. I worked for 12-14 hours daily with mandatory overtime. I became grossly overweight" (Fleming 2016).

On September 11, 2001 Fleming emerged from the subway on Chamber St., Manhattan and witnessed her office towers fall, and with them, everything inside of her. With dust on her pressed suit and patent leather heels, she walked all the way back to Brooklyn and began to examine how she had lost herself in the money structure and artificial constructs of success. She deconstructed her false life and built it again on integrity and ancestral wisdom. She became a "servant to this planet."

"I came to the earth with an open heart and said 'teach me, mold me, shape me, inform me with a new intelligence.'"

Similar to how our ancestors amassed 15 million acres of farmland despite the Reconstructionist lie of "40 acres and a mule," Sabur, Wellington, Fleming, and 46,000 other Black farmers in the US are holding fast to their commitment to work the soil and feed their communities in the face of steep obstacles (Gilbert and Eli 2000).

Still, an untold number of Black farmers in the US remain landless and uncounted. Migrant, seasonal farmworkers from Jamaica, Haiti, and other parts of the Caribbean pick the nation's apples and cherries for low wages and without a pathway to land sovereignty. Urban farmers remediate and coax life into the exploited soils of vacant lots that they do not own and that can be seized at any time in the name of capitalist development.

The returning generation has the necessary fortitude to make it on the land, but policy change is imperative. As Wellington, who was the first Black person on the USDA Farm Service Agency Committee in New York, advises, "If we don't know the system, they will keep robbing us. We've got to claim our share."

Regenerative Leadership

> When I'm talking about leadership, I'm not talking about [how] I need somebody to tell me how to farm. I'm talking about, we have the land but how do we get the power—the economic force to create political change for things to become more favorable for us. So that's the kind of leadership piece that I see is missing in the movement, or there isn't enough of in the movement.
>
> - Matthew Raiford, Gillard Farms, Brunswick, GA

Within the agricultural tradition, the intergenerational formation of relationships and the transmission of knowledge and wisdom are critical. This is so, not just for the transmission of technical agricultural knowledge on how to commune with the planet, but also the transmission of knowledge and lessons from seasoned organizers and elders on the radical tradition of Black agrarian organizing for land and power.

Those of us within the Black agrarian dynamic are at an intergenerational crossroads, for we face both the rapid loss of traditional and ancestral knowledge of aging farmers, landowners, and rural peoples—exacerbated by the dispossession and loss of black-owned land—and the massive disconnection between the generations organizing within the Black agrarian community. For Black folk and people of color, this twofold disjuncture is compounded by institutionalized racism, exploitation, violence, and generational trauma from working the land.

Given the proprietary structure of land ownership, the stabilization and transition of black-owned land has always been under threat. This is illustrated acutely in the previous chapters of this section, but the story of Savannah Williams of South of the Ferry Farm in Surry, Virginia provides a point of departure. Savannah is well known within the agricultural community throughout the South. When she arrived on her land, with two other partners, she set out a 60-year plan for the land. One of her first tasks was to establish a way to transfer land and to create homes for the next generation of "land stewards." Savanah shares:

> I think also the interest that I took in the [land] trust, the interest that really sort of presented itself. That is the way of transferring land while you're living, so you can see how people are using it if you want to. It seems that so much of the gift that we give to people, especially if you are poor, are gifts that come at death—especially land. I really felt that one of the best ways I can give to the present and future generation is to have a place while I am living to share with them. And a place where those that become a part of my extended family will recognize that they should not, that they will not, have a worry about a place to call their own, including growing food [and] building a home and community that will be there to give support.

Savannah's paradigm and frame of reference could be viewed as a model and way for other landowners to transition land while living, to provide a "safe place" based on relationships and community, and as an alternative to the market economy, which creates scarcity. This ultimately is something to be examined more closely: the role and ways that the black land-holding class can (re)engage in the current political moment, as they did during the reconstruction and civil rights era in the South (Umoja 2013).

Despite the destruction of rural Black culture, the aggressive dispossession of our lands, and the violent social dismantling of our farms, a base from which to build power still exists. Black folk hold a small but significant land base, and there are still strong (albeit older) pockets of Black and afro-indigenous rural landowners and farmers. Additionally, since the early 2000s, there has been a rise in the regeneration and return of more radicalized forms of Black agrarianism and militancy in rural and urban spaces (USDA 2014b).

The Black Dirt Farm Collective (BDFC), on the eastern shore of Maryland, sprouted from the recognition that the region "lacks a meaningful, critical, and clear form of land-based political and agroecological training for Black folk, and people of color in general" (BDFC 2016). The BDFC operates a two-acre vegetable and seed saving farm. They've situated the farm within organizing efforts to create spaces for healing, building power, and supporting the development of an alternative food system. They are organized by a central coordinating collective. In an interview with members of the BDFC, they shared that, "Afro-ecology came to us through our debates and considerations on an agrarian concept and methodology that spoke to our experience as black folk who do not come from farming backgrounds, yet want to be farmers, connect with the land, and use agriculture via agroecology as a tool for social transformation." The BDFC uses the Afro-ecology methodology to guide their itinerant training process throughout the Chesapeake Bay region.

The methodology is guided by a series of principles and values, as well as internal structures that create space for dialogue and new leadership to emerge, and for older leadership to evolve. They utilize popular education, base groups, intergenerational leadership, and collective work as core pillars:

> We really understand our beginning to have a clear starting point back in 2010, when one of our members had the chance to become part of La Vía Campesina, and began to learn about various forms of collective organization, ecological farming, and political training. Since then, members of our collective have travelled around the country and internationally, learning from farmers and movements like the MST (Landless Workers' Movement), MAB (Movement of Dam Affected Peoples of Brazil), the ANAP (National Association of Small Producers of Cuba), ZIMSOFF (Zimbabwe Small Holder Organic Farmers' Forum), and SAAFON (Southeastern African American Farmers Organic Network) and its members in Georgia, South Carolina, and St. Croix. These learning exchanges have been invaluable (BDFC 2016).

The BDFC believes that through these international and local exchanges, rural peoples, farmers, and organizers can strengthen their mobilizing and farming efforts, while strategically deepening the connections amongst movements. Organized alliances and connections among movements are vitally strategic for our efforts to confront capital, colonialism and all forms of oppression.

Farmers as Activists and Popular Educators

> Without landowning Black farmers, there would have been no Civil Rights Movement.
>
> - Baba Curtis Hayes Muhammad, Civil Rights Movement veteran

The Movement for Black Lives is about the end of state-sanctioned violence against Black and Brown people. Murder by police is just one form of legalized violence. Discrimination in housing and education are others. However, the most deadly form of state sanctioned violence is the intentional policy and practice of flooding our communities with processed foods that make us chronically ill, and the systemic practices driving us off the land that nourishes our bodies and our souls. Black, Latino, and Indigenous people are three times as likely as white people to suffer from food insecurity, and have disproportionately high rates of obesity and other diet related illnesses (Yen Liu 2012; Indian Health Service 2015).

Much like the Black landowners who were also politicians during Reconstruction, returning generation and established farmers are also community activists and popular educators who are working to dismantle this system of food apartheid and restore Black folks' rightful place of agency in the food system.

Dennis Derryck coordinates the Corbin Hill Food Project, a hub that gets fresh produce to over 89,000 New York City residents each year, the vast majority of whom are economically vulnerable. Derryck explains, "The major cause of death for our people is not about AIDS, guns, or crack anymore, and the prison system is doing its own job on us, but still the major cause of death is food. That is what is killing us."

Derryck purchased a 95-acre farm in upstate New York with 72 percent of the equity coming from Black and Latino investors. He combines the harvest from this land and 30 other farms and distributes it to vulnerable people in the city, offering payment plans, third-party subsidized shares, and flexible joining terms. He is also creating micro-hubs where urban farmers can aggregate their harvest and create value-added products. Together with other grassroots activist-farmers, Derryck drafted clear and uncompromising recommendations for the New York State Food Hub Task Force to dismantle structural racism in their programs.

Derryck is still looking for more systemic change. "Even if we reach another 100,000 people and have not provided any changes to the system, then when people say 'you do a great job' it's not true" (2016).

Leah Penniman, a farmer, educator, and activist at Soul Fire Farm in Grafton, NY, situates her work as a farmer firmly in the context of the Movement for Black Lives. She believes, "If we want a society that values Black lives, we cannot ignore the role of land and food." With her kin and chosen family, Penniman operates an 80-family Community Supported Agriculture (CSA) operation that provides weekly doorstep delivery of organic produce to families living in neighborhoods under food apartheid. The farm directly accepts public benefits and charges on a sliding scale based on income.

Soul Fire Farm also provides food justice empowerment training for youth, including those who are court-adjudicated. Through an alternative sentencing agreement with the county, young people who train on the farm can avoid incarceration and other forms of state punishment.

Penniman is committed to reversing the dangerous decline in Black and Brown farmland, and provides culturally relevant, justice-focused farm training for aspiring farmers. She says:

> When we ran our first intensive, I posted the application on Facebook and the spots filled up in 24 hours, so we added another one and the same thing happened. People are telling us they are so discouraged navigating the white farming world and encountering cultural erasure and other forms of racism. Our people want to return to the land.

Soul Fire Farm is also a member of the Freedom Food Alliance, a project catalyzed by Jalal Sabur. Inspired by his friendship with political prisoner Herman Bell and his peers in the Malcolm X Grassroots Movement, Sabur created a farming model that would directly support incarcerated people and their loved ones. He aggregates produce from regional farmers and runs a CSA where members get free trips to visit their family members in upstate correctional facilities.

Chris Newsome is an urban grower, activist, and popular educator in Philadelphia, PA. When Newsome moved from Mississippi to the North, he found himself an immigrant in his own country, surrounded by a Black community with different customs, values, and ideas. Back South, growing food was taken for granted, a part of the landscape. Up North, people could reach the age of 60 or 70 having never planted a seed. "I started growing food kind of out of home sicknesses," Newsome shares.

For Newsome, transmitting African ancestral farming and culinary wisdom to Black youth is a necessary part of liberation. He shows his students how to plant in hills, like his daddy did in the floodplains of Mississippi. He teaches them their traditional foodways, and the spirituals and liberation songs that they did not hear growing up.

> We grow crops that connect us to African heritage and speak to our experience in the diaspora. Black-eyed peas were our common bean and sorghum was our mother grain, fit for our DNA and also appropriate for the changing climate. We grow the black peanut from South Carolina that the Gullah people cultivate and eat.

Newsome has revived and innovated ancestral intercropping strategies, putting together the "three more sisters" of sorghum, sweet potato, and field pea (Bolden-Newsome 2016).

Like Newsome, Fleming uplifts Afrocentric pedagogies and farming techniques on her farm. She uses drumming, call and response, storytelling, and Djare (talking stick). Their bread ovens are made of clay and the learning center is built with a thatched roof, like the indigenous people of Guyana. Fleming is also conducting trials on the impact of electromagnetic energy from Giza-style pyramids on seed germination rates and crop growth. "All of those are African centered ways of farming and being," she says (Fleming 2016).

So much of the traditions of the folk whom are Indigenous to the Americas or Africa are grounded with deep, profound, and animated spirituality surrounding the relations between land, people, and the cosmos. These cosmovisions are systems of reality that carry images and values for ways of relating to people and land in radically different ways than those suggested by the dominant capitalist society. When asked about what Gullah means, Chef Bill Green of the Gullah Grub Restaurant in St. Helena Island, SC shares his cosmovision: "People that live alongside the salt water. People who drink a lot of salt water, that live with the sun. That basically live off the fat of the land. So I always say—when they ask me about Gullah—love and kindness."

Living off the Fat of the Land: Land, Healing, and Being Whole

> Every time an elder dies, a library is burned.
>
> - Matthew and Althea Raiford of Gillard Farms

Many folk speak of being connected to the land (or connected to nature; each person has a different way of relating and describing their connection). Within the current political moment, seeking a greater appreciation and connection to the place from which we come—the land—is important beyond measure. As descendants of enslaved African peoples, we have to come to terms with the generational memory that has been etched by the strokes of violence, pain, and fear. Slavery was and remains an indelibly traumatic event for us.

To move through that terrifying act, and to come to the other side, brings us one step closer to becoming the healers we are. As we study and accept the totality of our contributions to recent human history, we may find the place that the land holds in our process of becoming more whole.

As Chef Green shares from his experience about the importance of land:

> ...the Gullah Geechee people sort of live off of the things they grow on the farm. And the key to that is they learn how to live with the birds, they learn how to live along with the foxes, they learn how to draw a mule cart in the field during harvesting. They have to have that love to be able to deal with all of that. If they want shrimp then look to the season, you go out and see them migrate one place and you go out and cast, and that's where you will find all your shrimp. You're looking for fish, you go out on your boat. . . When you come back to the neighborhood, everybody waitin' on you wit a pan, a pot, or whatever they got to put a meal in. But they used to share, back then. Everybody used to share. Whatever you ain't got, the next one have. That's the true living of Gullah people and how they connect together. When growing on the farm, some of them grow peas, some of them grow corn, some of them grow different type of beans. Whoever grow with whatever yield, help the next one.

So much of our lives and perceptions are controlled by images we saw, see, and had described to us from the moment we came out of the womb. These imparted images shape our reality. Many of us today are not able to recall memories on the farm, nor of our parents on the farm, as Green does. Of the memories we can recall, many may be far from favorable. Savannah Williams shares:

> [They] left because [of] the way in which we had been introduced to the land in this part of the world. It didn't help connect farming to our lives as whole people. And we as a people were used, for economic purposes, but there was not the wholeness of our lives. And out of that, I think, came a continuous need for us to find some other way to be whole. . . and the result, I don't think we stopped to consider that this disconnect has prevented us from being whole, went on to rupture, our future in such a way that we have not taken time to reflect on how we must find a way to return to the land, and to be detoxified from all the, from all of the horror that has built upon it, but on the horror that has been built within ourselves.

She goes on to elaborate: "So we haven't redefined what it is to be whole and people, without us thinking that we have to run away from the land. What we are running to is not evaluated in the same way." Very often, given the capitalist nature of our existence, we approach the land from the narrow frames of economic development and production alone. Expanding through and beyond those two frames is not just transformative; it is a prerequisite to finding *peace* with the land and regenerating radical agrarian ethics and identities. Savannah shares this sentiment:

> I would like for us to give consideration to many alternative uses of land, as reasons why we need to return to it. And the production of our food, and our shelter, as two of the primary reasons why we may want to return. And all of the surplus of our production can be a part of that economic development. I would like for us to consider that. And ask, what would your personal world look like if that would be?"

Advice for the Next Generation of Black Farmers

The water is our bloodline. The land is our family.

- Queen Quet, Chief of the Gullah Geechee Nation

The returning generation farmers who generously shared their stories for this chapter have hundreds of years of combined experience. We get to stand on their shoulders, learn from the experience, and heed their wisdom.

Our farmers tell us that owning land is the basis of our freedom. Corporations are land grabbing all over the planet to claim dominance over this essential natural resource (Bienkowski 2013). When we have our land, we have the wealth and services the land provide, including the soil, water, trees, and clean air. This allows us to provide our own food and shelter and gives us a sovereign space to organize and mobilize our community.

We cannot do this alone. We need to return to cooperatives as the system of economic democracy. Just as African people use the *susu* and *konbit*[1], and as ancestor Booker T. Whatley of the Tuskegee Institute taught us to create clientele membership clubs as tools to organize shared wealth, we now need to create buying cooperatives and producer hubs to increase our

---

[1] Susu is an informal means of collecting and saving money through a savings club or partnership as practiced in Ghana and the Caribbean. Konbit is a traditional form of cooperative communal labor in Haiti, whereby the able-bodied folk of a locality help each other prepare their fields.

power share in the food system. For example, over 40,000 public schools across the nation are committed to serving their students local food (USDA 2012); that's a $3 billion market waiting to be tapped by Black farmers if we can band together and claim our market share.

Our farmers implore us to study and implement our ancestral ways of being on the land, particularly the attunement and patience to let the earth teach us. One of our people's staple crops, the plantain, is from Asia, but our ancestors developed the plant into hundreds of varieties over generations; one is suited for each specific landscape and purpose. To develop a crop that no longer reproduces sexually, our ancestors honed the technology of listening and being in deep communion with the plant. Our current generation is being deluded by the allure of false metrics, such as "we harvested 50,000 pounds of tomatoes," which do not reveal the lived reality behind farming. We need to invest ourselves in the ritual of farming, observing what the earth is saying, and writing prescriptions for future generations. We cannot waste an entire generation writing grants and addressing imaginary concerns designed to take us out of our sovereignty and weaken us as a people. We must not pass on the same level of oppression to our children.

When we reconnect to land, we reconnect to our own power. Returning generation farmers are saying, "I am done with settling. I can't go back to the bullshit. I can't go back to not being my complete self." We need the land to be whole, to resist, to win. And we will win.

References

Bandele, Owusu. 2016. Personal Interview by Blain Snipstal. January 10.

Bienkowski, Brian. 2013. "Corporations Grabbing Land and Water Overseas." *Scientific American,* February 12. Accessed February 1, 2016. http://www.scientificamerican.com/article/corporations-grabbing-land-and-water-overseas/.

Black Dirt Farm Collective. 2016. Personal Interview by Blain Snipstal. March 5.

Bolden-Newsome, Chris. 2016. Personal Interview by Leah Penniman. February 18.

Derryck, Dennis, 2016. Personal Interview by Leah Penniman. February 7.

Fleming, Yonnette. 2016. Personal Interview by Leah Penniman. January 31.

Gilbert, Charlene, and Quinn Eli. 2000. *Homecoming: The Story of African-American Farmers*. Boston: Beacon Press.

Green, Bill. 2015. Personal Interview by Blain Snipstal. August 28.

Indian Health Service. 2015. "Disparities." Accessed March 8, 2016. https://www.ihs.gov/newsroom/factsheets/disparities/.

Muhamin, Yasin. 2016. Personal Interview by Blain Snipstal. January 10.

Newsome, Demalda. 2016. Personal Interview by Leah Penniman. February 7.

Newsome, Rufus. 2016. Personal Interview by Leah Penniman. February 7.

Raiford, Matthew. 2016. Personal Interview by Blain Snipstal. January 28.

Rosenburg, Nathan. 2015. "The Whitest Profession: Jim Crow and the Development of Modern American Agriculture." Proceedings of *Just Food: Forum on Justice in the Food System*. Harvard Law School, Cambridge, MA.

Sabur, Jalal. 2016. Personal Interview by Leah Penniman. January 31.

Snipstal, Blain. 2015. "Repeasantization, agroecology and the tactics of food sovereignty." Canadian Food Studies / La Revue canadienne des études sur l'alimentation, [S.l.], v. 2, n. 2, p. 164-173. Accessed February 19, 2016. http://dx.doi.org/10.15353/cfs-rcea.v2i2.132.

Umoja, Akinyele Omowale. 2013. *We Will Shoot Back: Armed Resistance in the Mississippi Freedom Movement*. New York: NYU Press.

USDA. 2012. "Community Food Systems." Farm to School Census. Accessed March 06, 2016. http://www.fns.usda.gov/farmtoschool/farm-school.

USDA. 2014a. "2012 Census of Agriculture: Race, Ethnicity, Gender Profile." USDA Census of Agriculture. Accessed February 1, 2016 http://www.agcensus.usda.gov/Publications/2012/Online_Resources/Race,_Ethnicity_and_Gender_Profiles/cpd99000.pdf.

USDA. 2014b. "News Release: 2012 Census of Agriculture Reveals New Trends in Farming." USDA Census of Agriculture. Accessed March 8, 2016. https://www.agcensus.usda.gov/Newsroom/2014/05_02_2014.php.

Wellington, Frederick. 2016. Personal Interview by Leah Penniman. January 30.

Williams, Savannah. 2016. Personal Interview by Blain Snipstal. February 10.

Yen Liu, Yvonne. 2012. "Good Food and Good Jobs for All: Challenges and Opportunities to Advance Racial and Economic Equity in the Food System." Race Forward. Accessed February 1, 2016. arc.org/foodjustice.

SECTION 2:
Gender and Land

CHAPTER 4

Changes on the Land: Gender and the Power of Alternative Social Networks

Angie Carter

I have to be kind of careful because my attitude is we don't need to feed the world. We don't need to feed the world! I understand it's an agroeconomy. I understand that. We have to have jobs in this state—I totally get it. But it is not our inherited responsibility to feed the world, not at the cost of depleting our natural resources. I don't believe in that.

- Rachel[1]

Rachel and I sat at her dining room table in an Iowa city, halfway across the state from her farm. Between us sat an album of pictures documenting the changes she had made during her time as its owner: tree plantings, prairie buffers, a wetland. As we flipped through the album's pages, she shared with me the great responsibility she felt for these acres of farmland and the many things she had learned—about federal programs, agricultural service providers, conservation practices—in order to take care of the farm.

She did not grow up on the farm, and neither had her parents—they purchased the farm as an investment property. She had never been expected to do more than leave all the decisions to the farm management company, who handled all of the business with the tenant who cash-rented the land in order to farm conventional row crops. However, her interest in and growing

---

[1] Quotations are verbatim transcriptions from recorded conversations from group meetings or in-depth interviews. All names have been changed to protect the identities of the women farmland owners who shared their stories with me.

knowledge about the importance of soil conservation inspired her to spend many weekends out at her farm, working on increasing biodiversity through conservation. She was proud of her status as a landowner in Iowa, and was eager to share the story of her land in the hope that it might inspire others.

Rachel's comment that she felt she had to be careful in talking about her land because she did not feel a responsibility to "feed the world" was in reaction to the expectations she felt from her neighbors and others in the community. A dominant paradigm in Iowa, as well as the larger United States, is that input intensive, industrialized agriculture is necessary to mass produce agricultural commodities and feed the growing world population. However, scientists are increasingly documenting how the industrial agricultural system is *not* actually contributing to greater food security. Instead, this system mines our soil and pollutes our water, jeopardizing the farmland's future fertility while sending pollution downstream (Cox, Hug, and Bruzelius 2011; Naidenko, Cox, and Bruzelius 2012). Recognizing this, Rachel was focused on healing the land rather than maximizing its profit. She explained, "So I am not defined as a 'tree hugger' per se. . . . I believe in business. I believe in the fairness between what has to happen with the land, the economy, supporting of families." However, she also rejected the conventional approach to agriculture, criticizing that too often in agriculture today, "everyone always looks at the bottom line—Monsanto, Pioneer, their investors, their stockholders—and basically the one word that seems to permeate everyone's lives, no matter at what cost, is greed."

On a different afternoon, I sat on a couch in a living room drinking a glass of lemonade and talking with Mary—another woman farmland owner—about her land. Mary shared with me that her time off the farm gave her a newfound appreciation for the importance of being a landowner:

> The life I had off of the farm gave me a different perspective. And now, it's just very, very important to be able to be here at this point in my life. I'm 59 years old. I'm getting really old, but it's like this is where I should be, and this is the kind of thing that I should be focused on, not just for myself. . . I want to be able to tell other people this is what's happening, this is what's important to future generations.

Mary continued to share more with me about her plans for the land she farms with her partner and about the land she co-owns with her sister. Like Rachel, she recognized the dominance of the "feed the world" narrative and its problematic nature, but on a more hopeful note she emphasized,

"There's some positive things going on, but I don't know what's going to happen; I think we have to be very vigilant and draw on each other's strengths as much as we can. There are some very strong, powerful women here in Iowa. That's good."

Statistically, as women farm owners, Rachel and Mary are in good company—women own or co-own about half of the farmland in the United States (Duffy, Smith, and Reutzel 2008). Like many women farmland owners, Rachel and Mary do not farm their land, but instead lease out their farms to tenant-operators. In the Midwest, research has found that women farmland owners often cede their power to men—their tenants, family, or co-owners—rather than actively managing the land themselves (Wells and Eells 2011). Yet, as Mary suggests, some women are challenging these norms through active management of their farmland. In many ways, Rachel and Mary are not the norm when it comes to farmland ownership in the United States.

What makes Rachel and Mary unique is that, despite leasing their land to tenant-operators, both have taken action to change and engage directly in the management of their farmland. Both are concerned with the expectations and path of our current agricultural system and are suspect of its claims to "feed the world." Both are redefining what it means to be a landowner in a landscape where more yield and more profit are generally thought to be better. Most importantly, both had connections with alternative agricultural networks—not institutionalized agricultural service offices such as land grant university extension services or United States Department of Agriculture (USDA), but nonprofits and local, informal networks. My research found that these alternative social networks are a key resource providing women like Rachel and Mary with paths forward to act on their beliefs about their farmland in ways that may not fit with expectations in their communities.

Farmland ownership is changing in Iowa and across the country, and the social relationships involved in managing farmland are changing, too. Increasingly, Iowa's farmland owners do not actively farm their land, but instead rent it out to a tenant-operator (Duffy, Smith, and Reutzel 2008). In Iowa, women own or co-own 47 percent of Iowa's farmland and 52 percent of its leased farmland (Duffy, Smith, and Reutzel 2008). The concentration of farmland means there is increasing competition for it. Farmland ownership has long been a complicated arrangement—often combinations of family members may inherit or co-own a farm—but these new trends mean that a landowner's relationship with the tenant-operator is of increasing importance to understand for those interested in landscape level changes, especially conservation and diversification.

From 2012 to 2015, I traveled my home state of Iowa meeting with women landowners to learn more about these changes on the land and what lessons might be useful for others engaged in landscape-level change. I attended ten meetings across the state, and also conducted in-depth interviews with 28 women farmland owners. I recruited interviewees through a variety of agricultural and community organizations and lists, some associated with extension programs at Iowa State University, our state's land grant institution, as well as nonprofit groups such as Practical Farmers of Iowa and Women, Food and Agriculture Network (WFAN).[2] Our conversations were as short as a few minutes, and sometimes extended over days. Some have still not ended.

As sociologist Dorothy Smith (1987) reminds us, studying the points of view of women "does not imply a common viewpoint among women" (p. 78). Collecting data from multiple events and using multiple methods allowed me to identify both differences and commonalities among different types of land ownership and landowners. The findings I share in this chapter should not be interpreted as being "the experience of all women farmland owners," or even "the experience of all women farmland owners in Iowa." Rather, this research reflects the experiences of those women farmland owners in Iowa who responded to my query shared across numerous organizations, listservs, and through word-of-mouth. Their experiences as landowners in the heart of the Corn Belt, where commodity agriculture is king, help us to understand how land remains a site of patriarchal power and the ways in which gendered social processes continue to influence decision-making about farmland transition and change.

My conversations with these women were anything but similar—each conversation, each woman's life, and the various tracts of land in question were very different. These conversations took place as we walked through timbers and past century oaks, through fledgling orchards, and along riparian buffers bordering creeks. I met with women in late winter snowstorms and on early spring mornings. We climbed over fences, up hills, and walked down gravel roads. We talked in library meeting rooms, coffee shops, living rooms, at kitchen and dining room tables, quiet corners at conferences, and in church basements. Usually in person, but sometimes by email or over the phone, I listened to stories about families, love, loss, heartache, and hope—but always land.

---

[2] Practical Farmers of Iowa is an organization for farmers with a mission to strengthen farms and communities through farmer-led investigation and information sharing. Women, Food and Agriculture Network (WFAN) is a national non-profit based in Iowa serving women in sustainable agriculture. Its mission is to engage women in building an ecological and just food and agricultural system through individual and community power.

They owned Iowa farmland with spouses, cousins, siblings, parents, children... They owned land alone. They had inherited land or bought it, sometimes both. Land was an investment, a burden, a joy, and a future. They lived near their land, on their land, and across the state or country from their land. They drove past their land on the way to church each Sunday, walked its woods every evening, or visited it only upon the occasion of a family event. They were widowed, married, divorced, partnered, and single. They ranged in age from their 30s through their 80s. Their land was both wild and cultivated, growing soybeans, corn, trees, prairie, livestock, monarch habitat, and hay.

We laughed and cried. Throughout, I took detailed field notes, recorded and transcribed conversations, and then coded and categorized data. Across the myriad of ownership situations, life statuses, and histories, I identified commonalities and exceptions. "Do you find that some of these interviews are kind of emotional?" Mary asked me when we met for our interview at her house. "It's hard to talk about land," she said. "You're also talking about family and life transitions, and it's hard." I nodded and listened.

Was I surprised that talking about land was so hard? No. My own background in Iowa and experience growing up in a rural space during the 1980s Farm Crisis had taught me a lot already about how emotional and central land is to the identity of a person, a family, or a community.

Was I surprised to learn that despite their near parity as landowners, women are still often expected—by their co-owners, tenants, neighbors, and agricultural and conservation service providers—to be placeholders on the landscape rather than active managers of their farmland? No. Previous research in the Midwest has found that despite their status as farmland owners, women continue to experience gender-based challenges in land management (Petrzelka and Marquart-Pyatt 2011; Wells and Eells 2011; Carolan 2005).

What *was* surprising to me—and is hopeful for those engaged in agricultural change—was the importance of alternative social networks for those who are changing the management and use of their farmland. Some of these networks were agricultural non-profit organizations serving women explicitly (such as WFAN) or were agricultural organizations of farmers who had self-organized to try new agricultural practices (such as Practical Farmers of Iowa); others were groups of people interested in conservation, prairies, or wildlife. Of those women I met with who were successful in creating change on their farmland, many were involved in more than one of these organizations. Through these networks, women found mentorship, access to agricultural information and services, and validation of their land management approaches.

Land as Power

The women I met with were all privileged in that they own farmland, a limited resource and one that, in the settler-society of the United States, has been used historically to centralize power among white men (Donahue 2007; Edelson 2011; Faragher 1988). Many of the women I met with acknowledged their responsibility as landowners, and some of them specifically acknowledged the colonial legacy of their inheritance. For example, Mary acknowledged her family's ties to settler society:

> And there is a connection, of course, yes, and what's cruel about it is that, yeah, it is a piece of land in Iowa. And on the one hand it's nothing unique, it's nothing special; but on the other hand, it really is, because it is something that once was prairie and now has been sustaining Iowans and their families and the people here for many generations. I did some family research a few years ago and looked at how the farmland in Iowa was, what's the word, bought and given away, how it was first acquired from. . . well, not from the Indians, 'cause they [the government] just took it. But I mean how Civil War veterans were given land as a payment and that's how a lot of the land here in Iowa was first owned. So my family farm where I grew up had some ownership like that, too, and then some of it was just bought outright from the government, I think, if I remember correctly. So, yeah, I mean there's a history there.

The imperialism of land's symbolic power continues. The lack of research about women farmland owners, even as their numbers are in near parity with men, is an example of the "conceptual imperialism" (Smith 1974) in which the standpoint of men assumes the knowledge of women.

Historically, US women were excluded from land ownership, as land was passed on between generations of male family members. *The Invisible Farmers: Women in Agricultural Production,* by rural sociologist Carolyn Sachs (1983), chronicles the long history of women's marginalization in US agriculture. Fathers controlled the transfer of farmland and determined its future distribution among their sons. A daughter could inherit land only in the case that a father had no living sons and, once the daughter married, she lost the title again to her husband. Widows did not have legal control over their deceased husband's land until the 19th century, and, even then, they were expected to manage it only until their children reached adulthood. Though the United States Department of Agriculture (USDA) began collecting demographic information about race as early as 1900, it did not begin collecting information about gender until 1978 (Druschke and Secchi 2014), and it was not until the 1981 changes in US inheritance taxes that women were recognized as legal co-owners of farm operations upon the death of their husbands (Jensen 1991).

Today, the mediation of farmland access and management continues to be centralized in the power of white men. The marginalization of women and people of color in agricultural policy is not yet even recent history, as the claims process of the *Love v. Vilsack* lawsuit and *Pigford, Garcia,* and *Keepseagle* cases illustrate.[3] An ethnographic study of an Iowan agricultural community found that the women who did own land had primarily inherited it or acquired it through marriage (Fink 1986). Studies by Wells and Eells (2011) and Carolan (2005) in Iowa found that women defer decision making about their farmland to men—spouses, family members, tenants, and influential others. Other studies have found that the legal power inherent in land ownership does not translate into social power for many women farmland owners in the US, who continue to face barriers within their communities and families when it comes to making changes on their land (Petrzelka and Marquart-Pyatt 2011; Salamon and Keim 1979).

In my conversations with women—Rachel, Mary, and many others— I learned the importance of alternative networks in providing space, resources, and community for those engaged in changes on their land as they navigated gendered constraints in land management. Through the sharing of resources and experiences, some landowners were able to circumvent the status quo—the expectation that "feeding the world" necessitates maximizing commodity production rather conservation of soil and water—and instead act on their values of responsibility, stewardship, and care for the land.

Changes On The Farm

Conserving a prairie, restoring a wetland, installing a stream buffer—these are radical acts for farmland owners in the middle of the Corn Belt, where state fairs and state leaders regularly celebrate the monoculture of corn and soy. This material monoculture is rooted in a "monoculture of the mind," created by research and practices that devalue alternative systems and limit the possibilities for inclusivity and diversity on the ground (Shiva 1993).

---

[3] The *Love v. Vilsack* lawsuit filed in 2000 by women farmers against the United States Department of Agriculture (USDA) alleged gender discrimination in the administration of the USDA's farm loan programs. As a result, women farmers were allowed to file claims from September 24, 2012 through June 8, 2015 (Women Farmers n.d.). See also the *Pigford, Garcia,* and *Keepseagle* cases in which the USDA paid settlements to African Americans, Latino/as, and Native Americans as compensation for discrimination in farm service programs and loans (NRCS n.d.).

The tendency to devalue alternatives and limit possibilities is also reflected in the social norms of agricultural communities, where important agricultural information is discussed and exchanged most often at the coffee shop or local seed or fuel co-operative. "Men at the co-op don't talk. Some men try to help you. Some men don't want you to farm at all; they want to buy the land, and they basically want you to give it to them," a woman at a northeastern Iowa meeting explained to me. Excluding women may not be the explicit agenda, but it persists through unquestioned conventions. Through these social interactions and expectations, historic patterns of land tenure continue to influence both how land is used and who makes decisions about land use today.

Iowa is an ideal site in which to study these gendered dynamics of farmland ownership. As a state with over 90 percent of its land used for agricultural production (IDALS 2014), farming is both an important business and a cultural identity here. Iowa ranks first in the US for production of corn and soybeans, as well as hog and egg production. It also produces nearly 30 percent of the nation's ethanol (IDALS 2014). In 2012, Iowa exported over $11.3 billion in agricultural products (IDALS 2014). The type of agriculture practiced by the majority of Iowa's farmers can be characterized as productivist agriculture, described as promoting the intensification of technology, concentration of farmland, and specialization of production rather than diversification (Trauger 2001, 154). The "feed the world" narrative of dominant agrofood systems is alive and well here, and those who choose to farm something different are subject to scrutiny, even as Iowa's rich topsoil washes downstream and our water is increasingly polluted (Cox et al. 2011, Naidenko et. al. 2012), compromising future fertility of our farmland. Thus, tensions between different agricultural approaches, in which gendered dynamics often manifest, can be acute and emotional.

Emily, a farmer running a vegetable farm that frequently hosts field days, shared an example of this tension in her relationship with her neighbor:

> The number one reason why we have trouble with [our neighbor] is because of our concerns about [pesticide] spray. That is his number one reason why he doesn't want us here: because we don't want to get sprayed. For some reason he feels like that's outrageous of us, and that we're totally irrational about spray. It is illegal to spray us. It's not like it is our personal feeling whether or not he thinks his spray is good for us. We have public events. When we have 30 people on the farm and all of a sudden there's airplanes spraying a quarter mile away, or even

hundreds of feet away. . . [They tell us] if they're spraying to go indoors and close your windows. There are weeks where they're spraying every day. [...] I know that people want to spray, and I know that's how their agriculture works. I don't want to be sprayed, and I would like to be able to know when they're going to spray. I hate when we're sprayed during a public event— that's just, just extremely difficult.

Landowners prioritizing community, soil, and water health over short-term yield bumps and profit can face challenges within their families, communities, and even from agricultural service providers because these practices do not fit with socially accepted uses of farmland or how that farmland has historically been managed. When these actions are made by women, and especially when these actions involve ignoring the advice of an uncle who has managed the farm, or firing the neighbor who has rented the acres since he was a young man, these changes also challenge who has historically made decisions about farmland management and transgress who is accepted as a legitimate decision maker on the land.

Elizabeth's story of land transition illustrates how skillfully some landowners learn to navigate gendered challenges in land management. She is now the manager of her inherited farmland, but the transition was not easy for her or her family. She explained that when she first planned to approach her father about taking over active management of her farmland, she weighed the best methods of approach and first gained approval from her brother. She knew that she would not be effective in her meeting with her father if she discussed how her brothers had been favored in the family when it came to business and land decisions. Instead, she emphasized her interest in the farm in the context of her grandmother's and great-grandmother's interest in land stewardship. She said that these women would have been good farm managers. Her father's response surprised her:

He said, 'Well, yes, you're right. Your [great grandmother] would have been.' And then he said, 'And you know [your grandmother] would have been, too.' And he said, 'Well, you know, and your sister would.' And so it sort of shifted the tone of the conversation. It could have been a really uncomfortable. . .

While the transition worked out within her family, Elizabeth faced negative repercussions from the farmland's previous tenant, who publicly rebuked her in town for having hired a new tenant who would farm in accordance with her land management plan.

Creating changes on their farmland was not without consequence for many of the women who shared stories with me. Bev crop-shared with a tenant, splitting the investment and decision-making regarding the farming of her land, and had done extensive conservation work on her farm to improve soil conservation and water quality. She shared that these acts were viewed as "crazy" in her community:

> I have taken cropland out of production, which makes me look crazy. [. . .] You know, some people think that you should grow corn on every acre or soybeans on every acre, and here's this crazy woman taking cropland out of production when they're tearing up things and putting it into production. And what is she doing? And why? And why is she putting cover crops on and all those things over the years?

As is common in many land transfer situations, Bev had inherited her farm's operator-tenant when she inherited the family farm. After many years of working together, she learned that this tenant was not respecting her plans. When she confronted him, he admonished her decision, telling her "[Your dad] would never do that," to which Bev replied, "You're not dealing with [my dad]." She explained to me, "It was *my* farm. And he hadn't got that through his head yet, and that was the last year that he farmed for me." In addition to illustrating the assumption that men know best about farmland management, Bev's story also illustrates the dominance of the "feed the world" narrative: growing corn on every acre is seen as good, whereas doing some conservation work is seen as "crazy."

Despite these challenges, women are making changes on their farms. The alternative networks agricultural women have formed as a response to their historical exclusion provide women a unique opportunity when it comes to landscape level changes in our agricultural system. These alternative networks are places where community, landownership, and stewardship can be redefined on women's own terms. Having these networks inspired Kristin with the notion that change was possible:

> I cannot do it alone, and that's why these meetings [for women] are so important to me, because I know that there are programs out there to help us, but I need to know what they are. And I need to know how to get the help that I need. And this is grassroots stuff—we can do this.

Cultivating these networks where they are growing may help us translate landscape-level shifts in power to institutional shifts, not just for women, but for all who are challenging dominant paradigms of land use and land power.

Alternative Social Networks and Social Change on the Farm

The women I spoke with identified two challenges to actively managing their farmland—exclusion and isolation. Those who were successful in changing or putting in motion eventual changes on their farms were all a part of alternative networks. Through these alternative networks, women found information and support to change the default social relationships involved in their farmland management. An ethic of care was also common across the stories of those engaged in changes on their farms—care for the water, the soil, those downstream, wildlife, and the planet.

Alternative social networks were essential to landowners who were doing something different than the status quo, and who instead were focused on conserving soil and water while ensuring farmland for future generations. These alternative social networks provided validation; they proved that even if they, as women, did not fit expectations about who makes decisions about farmland, they were not alone. As Karen, who co-owned inherited farmland with her siblings, shared:

> I mean, obviously, I think Women, Food and Agriculture Network definitely helps with that [learning about conservation]. You feel sane because there's a whole network for it. When I came here, it just was a godsend just to know I had a safe place where somebody understood me and I could learn, really. Other people's stories are important.

Connie explained that it was thanks to her involvement with the Iowa Prairie Network that she learned the language of conservation and developed the confidence she needed to make changes on her family's century farm. Her mother had been eager to "do prairie" but had been "ahead of her time" and never got to it, she imagined, "because she didn't know where to go." When Connie inherited the farm, she began to work closely with her tenant—a cousin—to integrate prairie as a conservation measure on the farm even though she recognized it challenged beliefs about how farmland would be used. "People say you have to farm every inch," she said. "I say no, you can put some aside for wildlife." She shared that her tenant/cousin is supportive of the prairie conservation, though he "gets harassed" by "the coffee shop crowd" in the community because they did not think taking 40 acres out of production and putting it into prairie was an appropriate use of farmland. Her tenant/cousin replied to them, "Would you like the government to come in and tell you what to do with your land? Why do you think you should tell Connie? She owns it." In this way, having a network to validate her decisions not only inspired her own efforts, but also influenced her tenant to stand up to dominant narratives of gendered decision-making and farmland use.

These networks also provided landowners with much-needed information for farmland management. Cathy, upon being widowed, took a more active role in learning about farmland management through information she learned at Practical Farmers of Iowa meetings. This information helped her to renegotiate her lease with her tenants, and shifted power in their relationship:

> I think they [the tenants] perceived me as the clueless widow from [the city] who didn't know what rents were, and they kind of got one over on me. And then we had kind of a talk a year ago, and I pointed out to them that I knew what I was doing and that I was very intentional about giving them the rental rate and the five-year lease because I wanted to help them. And I think that might have changed their perception a little bit, not so sure but it was a real eye-opener for me, because now I understand the importance of putting in the lease conservation practices, tilling practices, requirements for cover crops, all of those kinds of things that I thought weren't necessary.

Bev, the farmland owner who fired the tenant she inherited with her family's farmland, expressed similar appreciation for WFAN's validation of her actions:

> That's why that person doesn't farm for me anymore, because his standpoint was: anything I was trying to do was costing him money. My standpoint was: anything he was trying to do was costing me my farm and my way of life. So it was a philosophy thing more than he's a bad farmer or more than I was a bad landlord. It was a philosophy. It was never more apparent. And Women Food and Agriculture is the reason this man is not farming for me anymore. [. . .] His idea was: it has to make money. And mine was: you have to save the water.

Whereas some landowners shared how dependent they were upon their tenants or that they did not feel change was possible, those connected with alternative agricultural networks found examples in other women's stories through opportunities to learn from one another's successes and failures as they engaged in active management of their farmland fitting with their vision.

For landowners living out of state, connecting to local networks of like-minded women was difficult. Brenda was a landowner living out-of-state who expressed her desire to change the current land use on her farm "to do the right thing for the land." However, she explained that it was hard because "there's just not a lot of support out there." She also commented, "We don't know the questions to ask." Rose, another out-of-state landowner, shared that she had hired an attorney to set up a trust for her farmland and had not shared these plans with her current tenant, who was a family member. "I don't feel like I need to deal with their reaction," she said. When I asked her to clarify, she explained, "I think for some farmers, it's kind of an arrogance or sense of entitlement. I think it's more than that... it's not all farmers, but I would say for some there is a sense of entitlement about farmland, and I don't think that some farmers respect women as much as they should."

Laura, an out-of-state landowner who did not grow up on a farm and had no farm background, shared that it was thanks to WFAN that she had been able to implement changes on her land: firing her former management company, hiring new tenants fitting with her vision, learning more about soil health, and, ultimately deciding to move to Iowa to be closer to her farmland:

> I didn't have any mentors that could help me through what this was. I felt very isolated and alone a lot of the time. I mean, WFAN was amazing . . . But I just feel like for women in a men's farming world, it can be very intimidating, extremely. And I think that a lot of the men that I've worked with just never knew how serious I was about stuff until they finally got it now that I was checking everything out.

Even without distance as a factor, women landowners experienced gendered constraints to creating change on their farmland. Cathy, who co-owned some of her family's multi-generational farmland with her sisters, shared with me her plan to place her family's farmland into a land trust upon the death of an extended family member. The extended family member had been the farm manager for decades but had no legal authority over the land now. Cathy shared that she and her sisters had initially approached the family member in effort to share the idea as one possible option for the land's future, but the family member's reaction was one of anger:

> So, anyway, we all agreed that it would be a wonderful thing to sell this land to the DNR. And then when I told my uncle, he just freaked out. He's in his seventies; he grew up on that farm, and to him it was just the worst possible thing you could do. I mean, if I had gone out there and sprayed Roundup over the whole farm, he'd think that was wonderful, but to sell it as conservation ground is 'destroying that land, absolutely destroying that land and destroying everything' that his father had worked for.

The family member expected that Cathy and her sisters would defer decision-making about the land to him, even though he no longer was employed as the farmland manager. He told them that their plan was inappropriate for the farm because it would not "feed the world:"

> And there was no middle ground on this thing. It was a very hard, difficult situation to. . . Well, there was no negotiating. [T]here were two issues here [from his point of view]: one was it was destroying the land [by taking it out of production], and then we would be starving children across the globe—"How are you going to feed the people?" are the words that I so have burned into my brain. "You can't feed the people." And there's no use pointing out that the crop goes to the ethanol plant and that it goes to industrial uses that have been created to use the surplus of corn and beans. [N]o matter who you're talking to—it's the same words: "You have to feed the world." And the only way you can feed the world is to grow corn and beans that not a single human being on the planet eats.

Cathy's extended family member's influence, and the potential for conflict within the family and extended community, was too great a risk for Cathy and her sisters to continue on with their plans in that moment:

> It was a very emotional time. And so my sisters and I did not, at that time, have the stomach to go ahead; we just felt like it would be too destructive to the family relationships. My feeling was, well, quite frankly, he's going to die before I do. I intend to live a long time, and when he's gone and not managing the farm, then we'll do whatever we want.

Cathy shared with me that even though they have abandoned their plans to sell the land to the land trust, she still wanted to make a change: "I want to take a stand here somehow. And so I told him that we wouldn't sell the farm at that time, but I would like to manage the farm, because I want the farm organic. And that also engendered conflict, because 'you can't feed the world' with an organic farm."

The roots of systemic change are taking hold in these alternative networks. Maintaining these networks will be a challenge, and one that researchers studying women's agricultural organizations in the Eastern United States have already found to be threatened by co-optation and economic pressure (Sachs et al. 2016). A first step to cultivating the future of these networks is to understand their importance and share their stories. In Iowa, for women farmland owners, alternative networks provided a sense of the possible, mentorship, needed information, and inspiration.

Iowa land owners at a field day. Courtesy of the author.

Sustaining Landscape Change

Centering justice—for our soil, water, wildlife, and the next generation of farmers and landowners—requires changes, urban and rural, local and global. I find hope in the understanding that our agrifood system is one that we—as individuals and as a society—have made; this means that it can be remade to better fit our shared values. Alternative networks offer sites for these changes to begin.

It should not be a surprise that landscape changes challenging land use and gender norms are supported by alternative agricultural networks. The historic site of information exchange and education for agriculture—our land grant university system—is increasingly co-opted by corporate interests manufacturing the "feed the world" narrative (Food & Water Watch 2012). As Patricia Allen (2004) has written, universities are increasingly "'hegemonic" institutions in the sense that they develop and transmit ideas, discourses, and practices that constitute the "common sense" of the agri-food system" (p. 55). The work these women farmland owners are doing on their farms and within these alternative social networks offer alternatives to the hegemony of the dominant agricultural system. Identifying how these women have worked to overcome barriers of exclusion and intimidation through these networks can help us identify possible points of intervention, or "leverage points," (Meadows 2008) within systems of power and monopolies of knowledge.

Through peer-to-peer networking, these women farmland owners in Iowa are redefining what it means to be a landowner—shifting from someone who cedes power for profit to someone who uses their authority for more collectivist ends. Their stories share some of the first steps toward landscape-level change. As Kristin reminds us, the knowledge shared through these alternative social networks, the community they create, and the passion they tend offer hope for change:

> When I was growing up, I never saw an eagle, but just in the last 15, 20 years we have that resurgence because of what Rachel Carson did. And she said, when teaching children about nature, it's not half so important to know as it is to feel. So we love this land, and we want to take care of this land, so we need to do whatever we can to do that. And that's something that I truly believe in.

References

Allen, Patricia. 2004. *Together at the Table: Sustainability and Sustenance in the American Agrifood System.* University Park, PA: The Pennsylvania State University Press.

Carolan, Michael S. 2005. "Barriers to the Adoption of Sustainable Agriculture on Rented Land: An Examination of Contesting Social Fields." *Rural Sociology* 70(3): 387-413.

Cox, Craig, Andrew Hug, and Nils Bruzelius. 2011. "Losing Ground." Environmental Working Group. Accessed April 20, 2012. http://static.ewg.org/reports/2010/losingground/pdf/losingground_report.pdf.

Donahue, Brian. 2007. *The Great Meadow: Farmers and the Land in Colonial Concord.* New Haven: Yale University Press.

Druschke, C.G. and S. Secchi. 2014. "The impact of gender on agricultural conservation knowledge and attitudes in an Iowa watershed." *Journal of Soil and Water Conservation* 69(2): 95-106.

Duffy, Michael, Darnell Smith, and Jennifer Reutzel. 2008. *Farmland Ownership and Tenure in Iowa 2007. Extension Outreach and Publications.* Book 68. Accessed September 1, 2016. http://lib.dr.iastate.edu/extension_pubs/68.

Edelson, S. Max. 2011. *Plantation Enterprise in Colonial South Carolina.* Cambridge: Harvard University Press.

Faragher, John Mack. 1988. *Sugar Creek: Life on the Illinois Prairie.* New Haven: Yale University Press.

Fink, Deborah. 1986. *Open Country, Iowa: Rural Women, Tradition, and Change.* Albany: State University of New York Press.

Food & Water Watch. 2012. "Public Research, Private Gain: Corporate Influence Over Agricultural Research." Accessed September 24, 2016. http://www.foodandwaterwatch.org/sites/default/files/Public%20Research%20Private%20Gain%20Report%20April%202012.pdf.

Iowa Department of Agriculture and Land Stewardship (IDALS). 2014. "Iowa Agriculture Quick Facts: Quick Stats." Accessed June 10, 2015 http://www.iowaagriculture.gov/quickfacts.asp.

Jensen, Joan M. 1991. *Promise to the land: Essays on rural women.* Albuquerque: University of New Mexico Press.

Meadows, Donella. 2008. *Thinking in Systems: A Primer.* White River Junction, Vermont: Chelsea Green Publishing.

Natural Resources Conservation Service (NRCS). Discrimination Lawsuits. Retrieved September 24, http://www.nrcs.usda.gov/Internet/FSE_DOCUMENTS/nrcs141p2_015583.pdf.

Naidenko, Olga V., Craig Cox, and Niles Bruzelius. 2012. "Troubled Waters: Farm Pollution Threatens Drinking Water." Environmental Working Group. Retrieved April 20, 2012, http://static.ewg.org/reports/2012/troubled_waters/troubled_waters.pdf.

Petrzelka, Peggy and Sandra Marquart-Pyatt. 2011. "Land tenure in the U.S.: power, gender, and consequences for conservation decision making." *Agriculture and Human Values* 28(4): 549-560.

Sachs, Carolyn. 1983. *The Invisible Farmers: Women in Agricultural Production.* Totowa, New Jersey: Rowman & Allanheld.

Sachs, Carolyn E., Mary E. Barbercheck, Kathryn J. Brasier, Nancy Ellen Kiernan and Anna Rachel Terman. 2016. *The Rise of Women Farmers and Sustainable Agriculture*. Iowa City: University of Iowa Press.

Salamon, Sonya and Ann Mackey Keim. 1979. "Land Ownership and Women's Power in a Midwestern Farming Community." *Journal of Marriage and Family*. 41(1): 109-119.

Shiva, Vandana. 1993. *Monocultures of the Mind: Perspectives on Biodiversity and Biotechnology*. London: Zed Books.

Smith, Dorothy E. 1974. "Women's Perspective as a Radical Critique of Sociology." *Sociological Inquiry*. 44(1):7-13.

Smith, Dorothy. 1987. *The Everyday World As Problematic: A Feminist Sociology*. Boston: Northeastern University Press.

Trauger, Amy. 2001. "Women farmers in Minnesota and the post-productivist tradition." *The Great Lakes Geographer* 8(2):53-66.

Wells, Betty, and Jean Eells. 2011. "One size does not fit all: Customizing conservation to a changing demographic." *Journal of Soil and Water Conservation* 66(5):136A-139A.

Arent Fox LLP. 2007-2015. "Women Farmers Litigation: Love v. Vilsack." Retrieved May 19, 2014, www.womenfarmers.com.

CHAPTER 5

Womanism as Agrarianism: Black Women Healing Through Innate Agrarian Artistry

Kirtrina Baxter, Dara Cooper, Aleya Fraser, Shakara Tyler (Equal Authorship)

> We are spiritually connected to that land and must return. Our mitochondrial pull back to our original land is so deep that it is now all the plants speak to us about. Sorghum speaks the loudest. She says that we must take her there to repair the soils and feed us and our animals until we begin growing her brothers and sisters.
>
> - Aleya Fraser (2016)

Womanism, as conceived by Alice Walker (1983), is a praxis rooted in the audacious reclaiming of Black women's intersectional power that inevitably corresponds to our race, gender, class, and sexual oppression. Intersectionality honors many branches of oppression that work together to produce injustices (Collins 2009). Isolating these branches that have become influential identity markers—race, gender, etc.—homogenizes and forces a cherry picking of the dominant forms of oppression, while erasing the others (Crenshaw 1995). Womanism counters this erasure. Through our experiences, we are conscious of how our intersectional power and oppression is rooted beyond the routinely conceptualized race, class, and gender trilogy. Land is also a significant factor in the intersectional realities of Black women (Tyler and Fraser 2016) because, as Psyche Williams-Forson (2006) argued—specifically in terms of food and power for Black women—producing one's own knowledge of self and community happens not only through race, class, and gender, but land as well. This is where we believe womanism meets agrarianism.

Agrarianism, as a philosophy of land as a way of life and/or livelihood, is the crux of our womanist ethic. As farmers, gardeners, seed-/cultural-keepers, healers, and spiritual matrons, we fully realize our womanist praxis of land-based resistance, and are able to contribute to the collective cultural healing of our communities. Situating our identity as Black women resisting in, on, and through the land, womanism as agrarianism honors Black women's leading contributions to land-based resistance. It deciphers the land as the womb through which all self-determining resistance efforts are birthed and sustained. Further, it emphasizes Black women's pasts and ongoing roles as vanguards in communal struggles for self-determination and liberation (Davis 1990; Davis 1971; James 1999).

In *Black Women: Shaping Feminist Theory*, hooks (1984) proclaimed, "any movement to resist the co-optation of feminist struggle must begin by introducing a different feminist perspective—a new theory—one that is not informed by the ideology of liberal individualism" (p. 8). In an attempt to reappropriate feminism, womanism theorizes that to be "feminist" in any authentic sense of the term is to insist on the liberation of all people from sexist role patterns, domination, and oppression (hooks 1981). It articulates Black women's liberation as the seed to the collective liberation of humanity. When Black women, often thought to be the "mule of the world"[1] (hooks 1993, Walker 1983) are liberated, those depending on the physical, mental, and psychological toilage of supposedly mule-like Black women are also liberated; oppressors are liberated from their oppression when the liberation struggle at hand is led by those in the oppressed societal positions (King 1988). In this light, we create a counter-movement to this dominant oppression through the formation of a liberationist feminist theory and praxis (hooks 1984), and by sharing how we situate agrarianism within our womanist ethic.

Innate Agrarian Artistry

This chapter illuminates how Black women have influenced and continue the tradition of seed keeping within Black agrarian organizing, particularly in the US. We reflect the light of truth that emerges when the agrarian artistry of Black women is manifested through feminine creative energy. According to Alice Walker, "the work of an artist is to also create and to preserve what was created before him" (Walker 1983, 135). Black

---

[1] Honoring the non-exclusivity of our oppression, we acknowledge our shared position with other women of color who also reside in the basal depths of the "white supremacist capitalist patriarchy" (hooks 2013, 4).

women's acts of creating are often relegated to carrying the seeds of the human population, as giving birth is sometimes treated as the only type of creation we are capable of. In reality, Black peoples' artistry is predicated on the endowed feminine creativity of Black women. Thus, we lift up Black women's creative use of the land as a healing mechanism of innate agrarian artistry. Through historical and contemporary narratives of Black women agrarians, activists, and organizers, we describe innate agrarian artistry as the creative, feminine use of land-based resistance to simultaneously preserve the people and soil.

In an interview with Eugene and JoVonna Cooke, of Atlanta, Georgia, proprietors of Grow Where You Are and Maitu Foods, they shared: "While some people are searching outside of themselves to find solutions, some people just revert that internally. So, by being an artist, I'm constantly going inside to find the world that I want as opposed to searching externally" (E. Cooke 2016). As we search our mother's gardens or search for the truths that can set us free, Alice Walker reminds us that in "the far-reaching world of the creative black woman, often the truest answer to a question that really matters can be found very close" (Walker 1983). Both of these quotes resonate with our understanding of innate agrarian artistry. Eugene's internal searching reflects how the search for the soil and the search for the soul become the same journey, and it is through this unified search that we begin to understand the key element of agrarian artistry. As JoVonna describes: ". . . it's already innate. If it's not our grandmothers, it was our great grandmothers (who) were growing stuff in their front yards to keep themselves connected to what they grew up with. It's already there" (J. Cooke 2016).

In this light, innate agrarian artistry is the lens through which we view Alice Walker's nuanced conceptualization of womanism as black women's resistance to various faces of oppression, and as acts of loving nature and nurturing the gardens from which Black people's resilience grow. Our continuous connection to the land, despite the white power structure's diligent attempts to excise it from our innate knowing, is a "womanish"[2] act that challenges the subservient role Black women are expected to play. In the words of Alice Walker (1983), "To be an artist and a black woman, even today, lowers our status in many respects, rather than arises it: and yet, artists we will be."

During the enslavement era, Black female slaves showed they were capable of performing the so-called "manly" labor of field work in gruesome

---

[2] The womanist theorization refers to wanting to know more and in greater depth than is considered "good" for one or being "womanish".

conditions, but also that they could also perform those so-called "womanly" tasks of housekeeping, cooking, and child rearing (hooks 1981). Throughout their varied realities—chattel enslavement, Jim Crow, northern migrations, and Civil Rights struggles—Black women have always had to combine the labor of the land, labor of birthing, and labor of kin. As agrarian artists who continuously served their communities through land, Black women often "left their mark in the only materials" afforded to them and through "the only medium [their] position in society allowed [them] to use" (Walker 1983, 239). Whether through their ability to create subversive methods to protect and provide for communities or through finding creative ways to utilize the tools at their disposal, Black women possess knowledge that comes from a deep place of knowing and nurturing. For example, relating womanism to agroeoclogy as an ecological praxis of food and power, Tyler and Fraser (2016) argue that seed keeping, as an act of political warfare, is the womanist love song that militantly and creatively transforms earthly destruction back to its rightful place of peace and wholeness. Being so, seed keeping is a method of innate agrarian artistry.

Innate agrarian artistry—as a praxis—provides us with language to celebrate the historical resistance of which Black women have woven quilts, sang spirituals, and foraged from the land for survival. In a world that erases, silences, ignores, misappropriates, murders, and dehumanizes us, the paths blazed by our ancestors show us that survival is resistance. There are many uncaptured stories of women resisting through land within our history, and for this chapter we have chosen to highlight women who we feel a personal connection to "the creative spark, the seed of the flower they themselves never hoped to see" (Walker 1983, 240). These are the shoulders upon which we stand, and they remind us "we cannot be ourselves without our land" (Walker n.d.). Historically, who are these women who have been armed with audacious visions, experiential wisdom, and gifts from the land?

A *Herstory* of Innate Agrarian Artistry

There is a long history of examples from Black women regarding innate agrarian artistry that goes back to the times of enslavement. An important example of this is the work of Araminta Ross, also known as Harriet Tubman, whose exploits regarding Black women's resistance to enslavement are well known. Lesser known are the kinds of agrarian knowledge she mobilized that assisted in her superior organizing around the passage from South to North through US terrains. Likewise, the celebrated quilts of the women of Gee's Bend are not always recognized as being an economic strategy employed to save community land. These herstorical accounts, along with those of Fannie Lou Hamer and her fiercely intuitive understanding of how to meet community needs, are honored ancestral legacies that exemplify innate agrarian artistry.

Araminta Ross

Araminta Ross (Harriet Tubman) epitomized innate agrarian artistry through her inconspicuous, organized means of escape from enslavement through the Underground Railroad. As the product of a timber farming family, she knew all about the forest, which vines were good for water, what leaves were good for poultices, and more. Her father taught her many things about the treasures the forest held (Lewis 2016). Along her escapement journeys from South to North, she employed her knowledge of the forest and land as a survival tactic: knowing what could protect, feed, and heal on the journey to freedom. Even still, there had to be fear and anxiety around the land as well. Traps were laid out in the woods, shielding her would-be captors; there was certain death all around her as she made her way across the land. However, she kept working through that internal struggle. Eastern Shore historian Pat Lewis explains, "All the things that she knew helped to nurture her and give her faith through the journey" (Lewis 2016).

The Quilters of Gee's Bend

Another historical account that illustrates how women used innate agrarian artistry to resurrect their community lies between the threads of the Quilters of Gee's Bend. Quilting was a common practice of Black women in the south, likely beginning in the 1800's (Wallach 2006). The ritual of quilting was a means to keep families warm and to spend quality time with the women of the community: sisters, daughters, grandmothers, weaving stories while binding protection. A cloth of familiarity in times of cold, violence, and oppression, the women of Gee's Bend spun threads of resistance.

Established in 1937 by the Farm Security Administration (FSA), Gee's Bend Farm, Inc. is a river community on the bend of the Alabama River. The FSA sold small tracts of land to the Black tenant farming families who had resided there since before emancipation, making them primary landholders. When the combined threats of cotton mechanization and farm flooding caused by dam development threatened their livelihoods, these resilient women created salvation in the form of quilting. Selling their craftwork gave women in Gee's Bend the financial means needed to save their community's farmland from the encroaching progression of capitalist dispossession.

Fannie Lou Hamer

Similar to this artistic institution building, Fannie Lou Hamer's Freedom Cooperative also exemplified innate agrarian artistry in the 1960s Mississippi Delta. The daughter of sharecroppers, Fannie Lou Hamer possessed experiential knowledge of how the white racist establishment used starvation and land dispossession of Black tenant farmers as a political weapon. This allowed her to identify these structural obstacles to collective Black progress and develop Freedom Farms as a locale of resistance against the oppressive white establishment (White 2015). The Freedom Farm Cooperative was a political institution of communal wellbeing that grew out of her innate understanding of how to respond to communal struggles through physical, emotional, and psychological nurturance. Whether it was singing Negro spirituals as a calming mechanism during contentious moments like protests and sit-ins (White 2015), or using land-based resistance to ensure that housing, healthcare, employment, education, and access to healthy food were available at times when the white power structure of rural Mississippi purposefully withheld them, Hamer used the art of cultural song and political institution building to remedy the ailments of Black agrarian communities.

Speaking Our Truth

The historical narratives above are only a few examples of the precedents of Black women trailblazing the Black agrarian legacy by creating self-reliant institutions, cultural and material artifacts, and liberating processes that carry over to our contemporary organizing spaces, building community self-determination. In *Sister/Outsider*, Audre Lorde (1984) affirmed, "it is necessary for us to teach by living and speaking those truths with what we believe and know beyond understanding. Because in this way alone can we survive. . ." To this point, food justice activist and co-creator of the Black Urban Growers Conference (BUGS), Karen Washington, reminded us: "Women need to be more vocal and claim their work. Complacency and silence is most damaging. . . There's no shame in staying home and raising kids, growing food to feed your families. . . Women are powerful. Embrace that innate power!" (Washington 2016). It is this sentiment that is seeded throughout Black women's ancestral agrarian legacy.

Answering this plea, we center Black women's knowledge in the reaffirmation of Black communities and how land is deeply intertwined with how Black women position themselves as agrarians, creatively using their erotic senses (Lorde 1984) to nurture us all B(l)ack to Earth. The complicated, though beautiful, relationships Black women have with the land have not been written about sufficiently. This narrative contains the healing strength of who we know ourselves to be to in our communities and radically lifts up the work of women around us. Three thematic threads emerged from interviews, portraying how Black women relive and reinscribe our relationships to the land: healing creatively with the land; ancestral honoring/remembering; and community self-determination and liberation.

Creatively Healing Our Connection to Land

We need to understand the complexities of Black women's experience with land in this country. It is difficult to separate our experiences of violence on the land from our reverence towards the land, since this reverence creatively emerged out of situations of violence and oppression on that land. Throughout history, women have served as the primary keepers of cultural traditions (Shiva 2015). In this respect, Black women have historically served to preserve and empower communities, while resisting the dominant paradigm and violent structures.

In her book, *Sisters of the Yam: Black Women and Self-recovery*, bell hooks speaks about the adverse effects on the psychological health of Black people due to the inaccessibility of land. She writes, "Without the space to grow food, to commune with nature, or to mediate the starkness of poverty with the splendor of nature, black people experienced profound depression" (hooks 1993, 179). Allison Guess, a Ph.D. student in geography, comes from a long lineage of women growers with reverence for the Earth and speaks of this desolation. Aware of the healing power of the earth, she said, "Just being in the presence of nature and the land really helps to shape and inform our personal health and wellbeing. . . we are being stripped from the earth. . . we are in these boxes, in these capitalist offices . . . for some of us, we are in these cages. . . jail cells and prisons. A lot of that healing that we once achieved has become inaccessible to us" (Guess 2016). In a similar vein, hooks asserts, "Recalling the legacy of our ancestors who knew that the way we regard land and nature will determine the level of our self-regard, black people must reclaim a spiritual legacy where we connect our well-being to the well-being of the earth" (1993, 181). Jenga Mwendo, of New Orleans, speaks about how her work with the land has led her to experience the many healing attributes inherent in the land. After being introduced to gardening from an elder woman who activated the community around revitalizing an old garden, Jenga now does the work of creating backyard gardens in the Ninth Ward, where they grow on the land to help heal people. She said, "We have a 'food as medicine' series... that teaches food as a primary source of healing, and looking at a very base level that's what the earth is for" (Mwendo 2016). There is an artistry to how Black women intuitively feed the needs of the community through the bounty of the land and recognize that healing comes in many ways.

Along similar lines, Maya Blow also uses the land as a healing mechanism. She, her husband, and two children have an urban homestead named Soul Flower Farms, in the East San Francisco Bay Area in California. Soul Flower Farm is a magical mecca of plant, animal, herbal, and human life. Maya's experiences on the land reflect the cyclical relationship between women's wholeness, land, and community action. The formation of her activities enacts innate agrarian artistry in motion. She eloquently describes her healing process on the land:

> Coming to this space I came with a lot of trauma from other experiences in life. I would call it PTSD [post-traumatic stress disorder]. So to have this amazing piece of land to heal to get a deeper understanding of myself has been a profound healing experience for me... over the course of three years I realized I felt better, but now what? Realizing that I had already done my personal healing work... the obvious question was, how do I give back? So that has manifested in many different ways (Blow 2016).

Healing is an essential aspect of innate agrarian artistry. Healing the psyche, as bell hooks points out, helps restore our connection to the natural world (hooks 1993). Dorathy Barker farms with her husband in North Carolina. As the daughter of a sharecropper and shop owner, she has always been close to the land. She explained, "I think as women we have always been empowered especially when it comes to the land because we know we are connected to the land. Even though the man [typically] works the land, women have a spiritual connection with the land" (Barker 2016). This association between women, health, and the land is a salient theme for Black women. Dorathy continues: "Just like in Africa, when you put your feet down in the earth, it comes up all through your body. It's just healing to me. I know the powers that have gone into that land and I just have to step out on that land to feel like I will be rejuvenated" (Barker 2016).

Karen Washington, co-creator of the Black Urban Growers Conference (BUGS), reiterates this physical feeling of healing recognition from an experience in Santa Cruz. She said, "I put my hands in that soil. It was like 'you belong here.' It was such a connection. Something that pulled me and said this is mine—my connection" (Washington 2016). Although Karen lives in New York, she had this experience on the other side of the continent.

This story illustrates the innate connection of Black women with the land, grounding us in places even outside our places of origin.

It is also important that we cultivate these connections between our children and the land. Affording our children time and space on the land will garner a love and respect for the earth. One of the authors of this chapter, Kirtrina, made sure that as a child her daughter, Enlylh, spent a lot of time in nature. She was allowed to play uninhibited, to experience the freedom that comes from running wild without limitations. As a result, Enlylh not only seeks the land when in need of balance and peace, but is studying environmental engineering in college. Enlylh shared:

> During early childhood my mother managed to teach me the beauty of every lifecycle on this planet. . . It was during those many moons of my adolescence that I came to love nurturing the earth the same way it nurtured me. It became clear that my purpose would be to hold hands with nature, serving it in every way I could. Nothing could ever sever the relationship that I have created with the elements around me and because of this environmental science became my focus (Baxter 2016).

Allison also spoke of how the reverence her family showed in the garden taught her as a child and such memories are healing in traumatic times:

> My family placed me in our family garden right as I was learning to walk. I like to think that the tomato plants helped me to learn to walk. I learned very early on to watch my steps when I was in the garden because I did not want to 'hurt' one of the plants by stepping on them, so I was determined not to fall. That is how I learned how to walk, out of concern and care for the plants (Guess 2016).

As we see in the expressed sentiments above, "reclaiming Earth is not an abstract state of affairs but rather is inextricably tied to the survival of our peoples" (Riley 2004). As Africans were separated from the motherland (the continent of Africa) in the onset of the colonial settler "New World," their enslavement resulted in the deep assault on their spiritualties, health, identities, and more. Their recovery is possible—as it always has been—through creative healing with the land. If spirituality is the basis of art, as postulated by Alice Walker (1983), the reclamation of their agrarian principles is an artistic responsibility to their ancestors and future generations to transcend beyond the myths that the oppressive system has imposed upon our communities.

Ancestral Honoring and Remembrance

Honoring ancestors is a foundational aspect of African life. Luisa Teish points out that it is "through reverence of them [that] we recognize our origins and ensure the spiritual and physical continuity of the human race" (Teish 1985). Speaking of our ancestors and honoring their presence ushers their power back into our lives and reconnects us with a long tradition of agrarian knowledge and practices. This practice is making its way back into the hearts of many women working the land today. As one woman asserts, "When I look back I see the women because women, we struggle. It's hard sometimes but just to know I have all the mamas and grandmamas and aunties and sisters that came before. . . . This is a really strong source of strength for me" (Blow 2016).

Sophia Buggs of Lady Buggs Farm in Youngstown, Ohio, also speaks of both her reverence for the women in her family and also to those ancestors long past. She is a single mother and urban homesteader who lives in the home she inherited from her grandmother and farms on the seven lots that surround it. She said, "So I honor the space, grateful for what I've got. I honor it by doing what I'm supposed to do. I remind others that there were people prior to me whose shoulders I'm standing on" (Buggs 2016). Sophia also spoke of all the old houses in her community that have been lost and torn down, previously Black-owned properties. In her quest to rehabilitate her ancestral land and growing practices, she is also revitalizing her community through farming, natural healing practices, and healthy living education. Related to the ancestral reverence and remembrance of Black women working with the land, it is also the connection of spiritual practice, which has ancestrally been Earth-based. Some religious vestiges of the past have been maintained through resistance and reclaimed in the form of various African religions, such as Yoruba, Candomble, and Santeria. "There is an abundant feminine energetic connection to land . . . displayed in our Afro-diasporic and Afro-indigenous religions . . . that brings forth Yemaya, Oshun, Oya [Black female deities] . . . " (Guess 2016). The ability to practice these cultural forms of worship and sacredness in an authentic way is also tied to the land. Dorothy Barker, who is a priestess of indigenous Yoruba culture, mentioned:

> I feel that we need this land because there [are] so many places that we cannot worship. We need the land just to know that when some people come here they see the ancestors coming from the back where the graveyard is . . . I just feel like everything I need can be grown here . . . It's just having that freedom . . . Just having the things on my farm I need for my religion (Barker 2016).

Still, there are more ways Black women honor the ancestors. Paulette Green and Donna Dear are rural farmers on the Eastern Shore of Maryland who moved back South to purchase Paulette's family land. They ended up purchasing 120 acres of Araminta Ross's (Harriet Tubman) ancestral lands. Paulette and Donna consistently find ways to honor Harriet Tubman's memories. One of the most profound ways they do this is by introducing visitors and neighbors to the "witness tree," an old growth tree that is rumored to have been a meeting place for the Underground Railroad. In their community, "the Aunties" are highly respected elders who keep the culture through their relationships to each other, the land, and their community. This, too, is the work of honoring our ancestors. Donna told us:

> The people in the community, they seem to be very happy that we bought this property because it reflects them and the whole community. And we are them. . . I know they see us as Donna and Paulette, but they don't necessarily see us as gay. They see us as two women who are movers and shakers, and I say that because every time somebody needs something or needs to know about something they call us. . . And that is a good thing to know that you are able to help your community (Dear 2016).

Just like the Aunties, Mrs. Barker, and so many others, we must create what bell hooks calls "communities of resistance," spaces that "can emerge around our struggles for personal self-recovery as well as our efforts to organize collectively" (hooks 1993, 161).

Community Self-determination and Liberation

For Black people here in the US, agrarianism must be an ecology of resistance that reclaims self-determined paths for sovereign communities. In communities of resistance such as Hamer's Freedom Farm Cooperative, land is used towards community autonomy over the process of community development. By possessing cultural control, the ecology of the people and the ecology of the land give birth to an ecology of resistance. We see this reflected in New Orleans, where Jenga Mwendo suggested, "Land can be a foundation for organizing. When we think about the spaces in our community where we can bring people together like the churches in our neighborhoods where we have meetings or even our garden space now can be a place for people to come together and organize around issues that affect all of us" (Mwendo 2016).

Concepts of community self-determination and liberation as it relates to land-based resistance extend far beyond community gardening and the farm and are, in fact, at the heart of the recent uprisings under Black Lives Matter (BLM) and the larger Movement for Black Lives (MBL) banner. This contemporary social movement continues a long lineage of freedom fighting rooted in self-determination, yet advances the movement to an entirely new level by intentionally centering the voices and leadership of Black women particularly.

One of the authors of this chapter, Dara Cooper, has been organizing within various intersections of this movement. A Black feminist activist, co-lead on the National Black Food and Justice Alliance, and a member of the leadership team of the MBL policy table, Cooper left her job after launching various projects supporting local Black agriculture in New York to work deeper in the national movement escalating under the banner of Black Lives Matter. As a national organizer with the National Black Food and Justice Alliance, a member of the Malcolm X Grassroots Movement, and an activist committed to sustainable, community-based Black self-determination most of her life, the time she spent supporting protesters on the streets of Ferguson, Cleveland, Chicago, and New York indicated the time was ripe to escalate the call for revolutionary transformation in the broadest and most radical sense.

Although largely framed as a response to police violence, Cooper and many of the contributing organizers under the Movement for Black Lives have helped shape much broader communities of resistance around the political, economic, social, and psychic stakes for Black communities today, particularly relative to Black land and all of the myriad ways in which state violence is perpetuated.

Black land justice has always been an essential component of so much of our organizing historically and continues in today's work. In a conversation about the movement today, Fresco Steez of the youth organizing group BYP 100 (Black Youth Project) shared, "I don't see Black self-determination without Black land. I just don't see it because as advanced as we get, I don't see any technical solution for the need to be in control of land if we want to be in control of our destiny politically." BYP 100 released an Agenda for Black Futures and later, the Movement for Black Lives (which includes BPY 100) released a broad policy platform document called "A Vision for Black Lives," which details a comprehensive range of demands, from community control to reparations to land justice to a call for investments in cooperatives and community land trusts. Steez went on:

> So when we talk about land trusts, the reclamation of land and the demand for land—that we are entitled to land—that is reclaiming our identity and saying 'you have stripped land from

us in a history of anti-blackness . . . so in order to repair that harm, you have to allow us our own land . . . so we can sustain our communities. So us needing land trusts—it's a sustainable anchor for control over our own homes our own food and that being an effort of sustainability that is included in economic justice. Because when we can make our own food, we can make our own models (Steez, BYP100 2016).

Valuing land access and unapologetically calling for reparations is yet another embodiment of innate agrarian artistry. It underscores MBL organizers' focus on history as they work toward Black liberation. Savi Horne of the Land Loss Prevention Project, a longtime activist, lawyer, and freedom fighter, cautions, "If we don't do anything about land, the very thing that connects us with freedom, connects us with our civil rights, our food ways, our family life . . . If we lose all of that, then what is there? Why struggle? Land MUST be re-centered in our struggle because it connects us to everything." Black farmers and food activists have always been a part of the Black Freedom Struggle and continue today.

Conclusion

Innate agrarian artistry is the womanist praxis of using deep-rooted knowledge as a creatively healing, ancestrally honoring, and community self-determining act of land-based resistance. These narratives reflect how we—as Black women/people—continue to hold tight to the faint but formidable ancestral whispers that assure us that land is a loving lifeline, holding us close, the way a mother holds her child. It is the way Araminta Ross used knowledge of the land as a survival tool to feed and cure the body during the escape from enslavement. It is also how Jenga Mwendo of New Orleans and Maya Blow of the East Bay (California) use the land as a medicinal healing tool in their communities. We see it come full circle in the way "the Aunties" on the Eastern Shore of Maryland continue to use Ross's land as a resource for community healing by sharing the cultural stories of the "witness tree" and the Underground Railroad. We also see how Gee's Bend used the art of quilting to "save the farm" and for women's economic development in similar ways Sophia Buggs uses the art of natural healing practices on the land to revitalize her urban community. The community-self determined visions of Fannie Lou Hamer and her Freedom Farm Cooperative and the Movement for Black Lives (MBL) both exemplify how land-based healing and resistance efforts are critical elements to all Black liberation models.

If, as hooks notes, "choosing 'wellness' is an act of political resistance" (1993, 14), then the trajectory outlined above demonstrates how the ability of Black people to heal and thrive is directly related to the land-based resistance efforts that Black women continue to lead as the vanguards of the innate agrarian artistry. That is, "to know the work we are called to do in this world, we must know ourselves" (hooks 1993, 52). The land has always held the key to wellbeing, and in many ways serves as the cipher to unlocking our nuanced understandings of self. As Black women who have found each other on this very journey, our whole being is reaffirmed through the act of working the land and organizing around land-based resistance. Womanism as agrarianism is honoring the creative labor and utility of the land as the "work that makes life sweet" (hooks, 1993); it is the only work that will birth the authentic, community-based, self-determined liberation sought by all of humanity.

References

Barker, Dorathy. 2016. In person interview by Dara Cooper. February 11.

Baxter, Enlylh. 2016. In person interview by Kirtrina Baxter. August 25.

Blow, Maya. 2016. Personal Interview by Kirtrina Baxter. Feb 2.

Buggs, Sophia. 2016. Personal Interview by Kirtrina Baxter. Feb 1.

BYP100. 2016. "Solutions." Agenda to Build Black Futures. Accessed March 1, 2016. http://agendatobuildblackfutures.org/our-agenda/solutions/.

Callahan, Nancy. 2005. *The Freedom Quilting Bee.* 1987 Reprint. Tuscaloosa: University of Alabama Press, 2005. Accessed September 17, 2016. http://www.encyclopediaofalabama.org/article/h-1628.

Collins, Patricia Hill. 2009. *Black Feminist Thought.* New York: Routledge.

Cooke, Eugene. 2016. Personal interview by Dara Cooper. January 15.

Cooke, JoVanna. 2016. Personal interview by Dara Cooper. January 15.

Crenshaw, Kimberlé. 1995. "Mapping the Margins: Intersectionality, Identity Politics, and Violence Against Women of Color." *Critical Race Theory: The Key Writings That Formed the Movement,* edited by Kimberlé Crenshaw, Neil Gotanda, Gary Peller, and Kendall Thomas, 357-383. New York: The New Press.

Davies, Ken. 2014. "Unlocking the power of women farmers." The Guardian. Accessed June 12, 2016. http://www.theguardian.com/global-development-professionals-network/2014/jun/12/women-farmers-world-food-programme.

Davis, Angela Yvonne. 1990. *Women, culture & politics*. New York: Vintage Books.

Davis, Angela. 1971. "Reflections on the Black Woman's Role in the Community of Slaves." *The Black Scholar* 3(4): 2-15.

Dear, Donna. 2016. Personal interview by Aleya Fraser. February 7.

Fraser, Aleya. 2016. Good Sense Farm Blog Post. Accessed October 4. http://goodsensefarm.tumblr.com/post/133759485620/i-met-aleya-fasier-hunched-over-sweet-potatoes.

Guess, Allison. 2016. Personal Interview by Kirtrina Baxter. Feb 3.

hooks, bell. 2013. "Racism: Naming What Hurts." In *Writing Beyond Race: Living Theory and Practice*. New York: Routledge. 10-25.

hooks, bell. 1993. Classic Series. *Sisters of the Yam: Black Women and Self-recovery*. Boston: South End Press.

hooks, bell. 1981. *Ain't I A Woman: Black Women and Feminism*. Boston: South End Press.

hooks, bell. 1984. "Black Women: Shaping Feminist Theory." In *Feminist Theory: From Margin to Center*. Boston: South End Press. p. 1-15.

James, Joy. 1999. "Resting in gardens, battling in deserts: Black women's activism." *The Black Scholar* 29(4): 2-7.

King, Deborah K. 1988. "Multiple jeopardy, multiple consciousness: The context of a Black feminist ideology." *Signs* 14(1): 42-72.

Lewis, Pat. 2016. Personal Interview by Kirtrina Baxter. Aug 31.

Lorde, Audre. 1984. "The transformation of silence into language and action." In *Sister Outsider: Essays and Speeches,* 40-44, California: The Crossing Press.

Lorde, Audre. 1984. "Uses of the Erotic: The Erotic as Power." In *Sister Outsider: Essays and Speeches*, 53-59, California: The Crossing Press.

Lugones, M. 2007. "Heterosexualism and the colonial/modern gender system." *Hypatia*, 22(1): 186-209.

Mwendo, Jenga. 2016. Personal Interview by Dara Cooper. Jan 29.

Nembhard, Jessica Gordon. 2014. *Collective courage: A history of African American cooperative economic thought and practice*. Pennsylvania: Pennsylvania State University Press.

Riley, Shamara Shantu. 2004. "Ecology is a Sistah's Issue Too: Politics of Emergent Afrocentric Ecowomanism." In Gottlieb, R.S. (ed). 2004. *This Sacred Earth: Religion, Nature, Environment,* 412-427. New York: Routledge.

Shiva, Vandana ed. 2015. *Seed Sovereignty, Food Security: women in the vanguard.* New Delhi: Women Unlimited.

Steez, Fresco. 2016. Interview by Dara Cooper. February 24.

Teish, Luisah. 1985. *Jambalaya: The Natural Woman's Book of Personal Charms and Practical Rituals.* New York: Harper Collins.

Tyler, Shakara, and Aleya Fraser. 2016. "Womanism and agroecology: An intersectional praxis seed keeping as acts of political warfare." In *Emergent Possibilities for Global Sustainability: Intersections of race, class and gender,* edited by Phoebe Godfrey and Denise Torres, 19-30. New York: Routledge.

Walker, Alice. n.d. "We Cannot Be Ourselves Without Our Land." *Grassroots Economic Organizing.* Accessed May 2, 2014. http://www.geo.coop/node/522.

Walker, Alice. 1983. *In Search of Our Mothers' Garden: Womanist Prose.* San Diego: Harcourt.

Wallach, Amei. 2006. "Fabric of Their Lives." *Smithsonian,* October.

Washington, Karen. 2016. Personal Interview by Kirtrina Baxter. Feb 1.

White, Monica. 2015. "'A Pig and a Garden': Fannie Lou Hamer as organic intellectual and the freedom farms cooperative." In *Freedom Farmers: Agricultural Resistance and the Black Freedom Movement,* 1880-2010. Unpublished manuscript.

Williams-Forson, Psyche A. 2006. *Building houses out of chicken legs: Black women, food, and power.* Chapel Hill: University of North Carolina Press.

Land Access, Social Privilege, and the Rise of Indigenous Leadership

CHAPTER 6

Notes from a New Farmer: Rent-Culture, Insecurity, and the Need for Change

Caitlin Hachmyer

I t is early. The fog won't lift for a few more hours. The light is calm and new. I look out over my crops and beyond to the fields dappled with oak trees and eucalyptus. I have done this many times now: looked over and across many stretches of land, rolling landscapes that I can touch but which are just out of grasp. I don't own this land. I won't. Ever. It feels quite certain. I farm the land, I steward the soil—and have for over six years now. Moving from plot to plot, working with landowner after landowner in search of a connection I have not been able to find on rented land. My care for the land—my desire to not only sustain, but also to regenerate it—is in constant conflict with the knowledge that I put money and more money into something that I do not own. I work to build something that could slip through my fingers at any moment. An investment whose return I might never know.

I am a new farmer. Born and raised on an acre of land in rural Sonoma County, California, I do not come from a farming family. I studied the food system in college, spent a year and a half working on farmer advocacy in the non-profit sector, and then decided some on-the-ground experience was critical to doing the work in a genuine way. While I was apprenticing on a farm in rural Minnesota, the economy collapsed. Equipped with a new skill set, facing a hostile job market, and having direct access to the land on which I grew up, I stumbled into a career in farming. It started small, slow, and somewhat without specific intention. I had access to my parents' land, so why not try it out? Red H Farm was born.

Nuances of Access

Taking a moment to understand the complexities of the concept of access, its relation to the notion of property, and the implications of these nuances for the food system and new farmers is important in this conversation about land justice and food systems change. Ribot and Peluso (2003) distinguish access from property, explaining that property provides one form of access, but that access is, in fact, grounded in the ability (not necessarily the right, as recognized by law, custom, or convention) to benefit from something. This means, one can have access without having property. The ability to benefit from something (like land) is primarily determined by a "bundle of powers," situated firmly in specific social and political-economic contexts, and affected by a variety of mechanisms, including access to technology, capital, markets, labor, knowledge, authority, identity, and social relations (Ribot and Peluso 2003, 173).

These mechanisms become important in the context of young or new farmers' access to land, primarily because, in most cases, this new farmer demographic is unable to access land through property rights, and thus relies on more nuanced forms in order to farm. Beyond land ownership, and because the United States is very firmly grounded in the principle of private property, the primary mode of access in the American context is through renting, either through short-term or long-term leases. Less common modes include the use of public land, non-profit land, and land-trusted land, but in most cases these forms of access still engage with renting culture.

The challenge small-scale producers face in owning land is not divorced from the fact that the local food system falls victim to gentrification. These farmers, working within the local food system paradigm, necessarily farm in landscapes where there is a direct market for their products. Development pressure, and highest and best use as defined by the market, make urban and peri-urban land inherently expensive when compared to the value of crops that can be produced on that land. When these farms are located in rural areas, they are typically either in close proximity to an urban center or are situated in a community in which local food is a cultural cornerstone. Sonoma County, California fits both rural models. It is a mere hour from the San Francisco Bay Area and is also a hub for local food and wine. Communities like Sonoma County, with rural charm and access to "nature," coupled with urban amenities (ie. great local food, music, bars), suffer from forms of gentrification that are similar to what is seen in urban neighborhoods.

And so to gain access, new and young farmers typically rent. This system relies heavily on Ribot and Peluso's mechanisms of access; things like knowledge of formal networks through which land may be accessible (particularly public and non-profit), social identity, and social networks by which land can be made available. Success in this system also relies on developing a market niche through which a new farmer can move her or his products after securing land. These mechanisms are restrictive and often favor educated, networked individuals who matriculate in particular socio-economic circles or who have a history in the region that may provide them access to land acquired before the forces of gentrification took hold. It is important to note here that in Sonoma County, the prohibitive nature of purchasing and the nuanced mechanisms facilitating renting disadvantage a large segment of the agricultural workforce. The vast network of farmworkers hailing from Mexico, for instance, that work in the vineyards and often have stronger agricultural backgrounds and knowledge sets than most young, aspiring farmers, lack the social and financial capital necessary for access. In short, race and class create barriers to entry.

In addition to being socially restrictive, the culture of renting also makes it difficult for small-scale farmers to simultaneously achieve ecological and financial sustainability. If our goal as farmers and activists is to transform the food system in the US—socially, economically, and ecologically—it is unclear if access attained through Ribot and Peluso's "bundles of powers" will allow for success.

This chapter explores the struggles new farmers face in accessing and properly managing land through the narrative of Red H Farm and the community of Sonoma County. It will explore the question of whether or not the national focus on developing strong lease structures for new farmers is in fact where energy should be focused in the effort to build a new and changed food system. It will look at possible solutions whereby US farmers can access land by *right*.

The Building of a Farm: Renting in the Food System

In my first year running Red H Farm I understood the land I had known for 24 years in a new way. I felt its contours and I marveled at its bank of weed seeds. I realized there was some kind of underground water feature at the very far end, and I appreciated that it wasn't until July or August that I needed to worry about irrigation. The land was low, with the gradually sloping hills leading to a point where collected rainwater and groundwater runoff essentially formed a marsh in the winter. This meant there was enough moisture to provide natural irrigation very late into the season. It also meant that every June a tractor would get neatly stuck to the point that only a well-positioned truck outfitted with a winch could pull it out.

I realized that to not only scale up, but to farm at all in California, where year round production is the expectation, I would need to add more land to my system—land that sat high or was sloped—so that I could produce winter and early spring crops. Surprisingly, such land was easy to come by. In the last decade, more and more people have become interested in engaging with a localized food system, and for some landowners this includes making their land available to aspiring, landless farmers. Currently, this plays a critical role in building local food systems, particularly in places where the price of land is prohibitive to purchasing it. I quickly found a generous and excited neighbor who wanted his land put to use. Over the next five years, I moved through three secondary properties.

* * *

According to the USDA 2012 Census of Agriculture, 40 percent of US land in production is farmed under lease agreements. The trend toward renting land is common across all scales of agriculture, from micro specialty crop productions to the industrial farms blanketing the Midwest. As the number of industrial farms shrinks—a result of farmers aging out, passing away, or being unable to compete in an economy of scale system—their size grows (USDA 2014). Enveloping neighboring land into existing operations through leases is a widespread phenomenon in the industrial system.

Among new, small-scale producers, the trend toward renting is a matter of necessity. In Sonoma County, gentrification means that the price of land has been steadily increasing over the years, with prices ranging from $35,000-$85,000/acre for open, arable land (Forcey et al. 2015, 28-29). Land pressure from the wine industry (which occupies over 62,000 acres of cropland in Sonoma County), the geographic proximity to the Bay Area, proliferation of vacation and "lifestyle" properties among the elite, and wealth from the marijuana industry, have all contributed to prices that are seven to seventeen times higher than the Pacific cropland averages of $5,000/acre (Sonoma County Department of Agriculture 2015, 5; Nickerson et al. 2012, 3).

Ironically, it is this proximity to the Bay Area and the local food and wine culture that create strong regional markets for small-scale agriculture in Sonoma County. This is not uncommon; an urban population is a key factor when doing market analysis for small-scale specialty crop production all over the country. And yet, the negative impacts of gentrification and development pressure typically seen in urban and peri-urban settings are constantly at work in rural Sonoma County.

According to Agrarian Trust, one acre of American farmland is lost to development every minute, and the value that could be earned from production on that land is far below the value it sells for on the market (Agrarian Trust, accessed 2016). This leaves new, young agricultural entrepreneurs in a conundrum. Our products are fresh and perishable and our market niche is local. Combined, these factors mean that we must be in close proximity to our markets, which are typically urban and peri-urban, or are rural communities where the local food system and agricultural heritage forms a cultural cornerstone. In other words, we need to farm in precisely the places where land prices are at a premium. This financial hurdle is often compounded by additional pressure from burdens like student loan debt. Combined, these factors make purchasing land an unlikely feat. Furthermore, because many new farmers are not from farming families or even rural communities, most are not in the position to inherit farmland. Or, like me, if they do inherit land, it may not be enough land or in the right location for a farming operation to make sense.

And so we rent.

Small farmers face many challenges when they rent. These include conflicts resulting from land-owners misunderstanding the realities of farming (the aesthetics, the sights, the smells); handshake agreements that fall apart because of differing expectations; short term leases that undermine the motivation to invest in the land and soil; sale of the land or death of the landowner; loss of land to "highest and best use" development;[1] inability to invest in perennial crops; personality conflict; and so on. Even when these challenges are not starkly present, the inherent instability of working land you do not have ultimate control over persists. In my case, the landowners that rent to me have generally been supportive and flexible. Nonetheless, lengthy dialogue, constant points of negotiation, and boundary setting have often been necessary. Beyond that, many farmers experience an inherent difference—whether emotional, spiritual or practical—between the land they tend temporarily and the land they are grounded-in for the long run. While you can love the land you rent, there is something deeper—at least for me—about knowing that I am tending a piece of land that I am permanently connected to. I have found that I have never really sunk into a piece of rented land the way I do at my home farm.

These less tangible factors have been my reason for rotating my secondary farm plot over the years in constant search of something that makes

---

[1] "Highest and best use" development refers to the development of land based on the use that commands the highest financial value in the market. In high-value land markets, the potential agricultural output a parcel of land can produce rarely out competes the market value that land can command for housing, commercial, or retail development. This makes land out of reach for farmers whose income is based on agricultural output.

more sense, requires less negotiation, and necessitates less justification for what is happening at any given time. These things are not necessarily unexpected. Farming in more urban or developed areas, on smaller scales, means that your agricultural work is in the public or landowners' view. This is a large part of why small-scale renting differs from large-scale, commodity crop systems. Your work impacts your landowner in unexpected ways, and this learning curve and education is part of the process. Continual dialogue often spurs out of genuine interest and relationship building. However, for an entrepreneur working 70 hours a week, it can also provide an undercurrent of stress—the sense of walking on eggshells—and is a reminder that you are ultimately at the mercy of a landowner.

* * *

Another key difference between renting in the industrial system and in the small-scale, localized system is ecological: to grow diversified, specialty crops on land that may be someone's backyard typically involves much more investment to build soil ecology and ensure healthy crops. This means more upfront capital per acre.

In my third year of farming, I realized that for both ecological and financial reasons, I needed to transition my farm to no-till. I was contracting out the tractor work that I needed on the farm, and my ability to turn over beds and maximize production was wholly impeded. Because my land is wet, I was missing a key production window on my main farm site, a window in which I would not even need to worry about irrigation infrastructure and timing. Furthermore, I came to believe that the ecological implications of tillage farming were contrary to my interest in building soil and landscape ecology, conserving water, reducing time spent weeding, and sequestering carbon. No-till systems, which are very resource- and input-intensive, require a hefty financial investment using thick layers of compost as a top dressing on beds to mulch weeds and provide nutrients; wood chips to do the same in the pathways; and high quality woven plastic and tarps to further provide weed suppression.

As farmers across the world are increasingly being looked to as an integral part of the solution to climate change, these kinds of highly ecological methods that sequester carbon in the soil will be key strategies. No-till farms operating at intensive, commercial levels earn more revenue than most traditionally-managed farms, but it does not make good financial sense for farmers who do not have solid land security to employ these methods because of the high financial investment. Ecological farming methods are like a farmer's investment portfolio: there may be an immediate return as the nutrient value of inputs quickly affects crop health and yield, but the real return is long-term. It is deep, complex soil systems, established habitat and insectaries, healthy waterways, and beautiful and biodiverse landscapes that feed into a smoothly functioning agricultural system. For this reason, I only transitioned the land on my main farm site, the three-quarters acre field that my family owns, to no-till. I continued using low-till methods on my secondary site, getting significantly less production off these lands.

I continue to see increases in production and revenue from my no-till site, indicating the ways in which ecological and intensive farming, made possible in this scenario by high financial and resource input, results in significantly higher output. These consistently high levels of production make farming viable on a small commercial scale. The land must be farmed ecologically in order to maintain these levels, and that requires constant investment in the land.

Here is the place where renting land in small-scale diversified production systems becomes problematic. Nowhere else in our neoliberal, capitalist society would we expect individuals or businesses to make short term, high cost, high risk, low financial return investments (bearing in mind that even an increase in revenue does not mean farmers are getting rich). This kind of high input, high-risk investment structure simply does not make sense. With the pressure we are putting on farmers globally to be the solution to climate change and to be the foundation of a revolutionized food system, we need farmers to invest in their land for the long term—and we need farmers to keep farming. However, even small-scale, community-centered farms are still businesses, and farmers must survive economically within the contexts of the society we are a part of even as we seek to change that society. This means that our agricultural practices cannot always meet our ecological ideals, particularly if we are at risk of not realizing the long-term benefits of those practices on leased land.

It is with this in mind that we must consider if we are focusing on the right question. All over the US, farmland organizations are working to help aspiring farmers access land, usually with a focus on the development of strong, legally binding lease agreements with land-rich community members. The goal is for farmers to have some degree of land security, so leases for less than three years are generally not recommended. But even these formal leases often contain clauses that allow the farmer to cancel the lease at any time or the landowner to end the lease with a six month warning. Thus, even within legally binding lease structures, farmers work within an unstable and insecure system. Moreover, even relatively long-term leases put farmers in the position of ultimately losing the time and money they have put into making the land productive, and eventually having to start anew. Therefore, projects to support long-term leases are important steps toward increasing farmland access, but considering their limitations, are they the best place to put in so much effort?

Leasing land has been part of the framework of the American agricultural system for generations. However, it is important to remember that the agricultural system of past generations is responsible for resource depletion; soil degradation; the poisoning of land, air, and water; inhumane labor practices; the proliferation of genetic engineering; and significant contributions to climate change, among other things. In the industrial model, the ecological investment is proportionally small compared to small-scale, biodiverse systems, and so the loss of per acre investment for industrial farmers is also proportionally less than what most small-scale growers face. Nevertheless, even in the industrial system there is less incentive to ecologically invest in rented land.

Reinstating that model by focusing on lease structures in smaller-scale, local food systems means that we are reinstating dominant structures within the food movement itself. We are building into our new models the concept that those stewarding our land—those we hope will help reverse climate change, build healthier communities, manage our natural resources, and provide a key foundation for our lives—should not also be those owning our land. We may be given access to land if we have the necessary "bundle of powers," but do not possess real power by right. Even long term leases, providing some degree of security to farmers, harbor extreme risk. Over five, ten, or twenty years a farmer will certainly see production results related to the ecological investment they make. However, the longer that lease, the more investment is made and the more will be lost should that lease not be renewed. That farmer then not only loses the financial investment they've made, they also lose the time it took for that investment to build something deep and rich on that landscape, and they are in the position of having to start the entire process anew.

In assuming that new farmers should accept the precariousness of their situation, we are also inherently building a precarious food system, a house of cards. It is a system in which most of the young farmers I know not only question, on a very regular basis, if and when they should get out, but because they are all highly educated and have off-farm work experience, they actually *could* get out.

According to the USDA:

> Farm real estate (land and structures) is the major asset on the farm sector balance sheet, accounting for 84 percent of the total value of U.S. farm assets in 2009...in addition to being the

largest single investment in a typical farmer's portfolio, farm real estate is the principal source of collateral for farm loans, enabling farm operators to purchase additional farmland and equipment or to finance current operating expenses and meet household needs. (Nickerson et al. 2012, iii)

In the industrial system, farmers usually rent land to add to the assets they own. Young farmers in the local food movement, however, often accept that we should not benefit from trends of private accumulation. We are often expected to accept the challenging trends of the dominant system (those associated with renting) without benefiting from the individually helpful ones (associated with owning). New land stewards live in tents, converted garages, little houses, and studio apartments. They wonder if they can afford to have families. If they do not have otherwise employed spouses, they rely on subsidized health care and joke about the last time they visited the dentist. They live simple and bohemian lifestyles that, in an age of consumption, should be celebrated but are nevertheless out of step with their broader communities. How this will create and sustain deep social transformation and commitment to the work is uncertain. At a moment in history when, according to Agrarian Trust, 400 million acres of American farmland are due to change hands, perhaps it is time that we think about pushing these questions further (Agrarian Trust 2016).

Towards New Models: Possible Solutions for Change

In a conversation with Edward Thompson (2016), founding member of American Farmland Trust, he emphasized to me that we must understand this struggle to build a stable place for new, small-scale, diversified farmers not just within the food movement, but also in society at large. The food system and food cultures weave together not just individuals, but also our society and our world. Txetxu Nuñez of the Basque Farmers Union explains that the deepest and most foundational change we must make is in breaking down this false binary between "consumers" and "producers" (2015). In fact, our connections are not that simple. Instead, we are all part of a complexly interwoven agricultural system whether or not we farm. When that is more broadly realized, the necessary value of those directly tending our land and water systems and the need for not just individual-level investments (i.e. vote with your fork), but actual *community*-level investments, will become clearer (Thompson 2016).

In a country founded on market economics and private property rights that rarely categorize agriculture as a highest and best use, institutionalizing the concept of community-level investments in land for farmers will be challenging. We are, however, beginning to see more institutionalized value being placed on new and aspiring farmers themselves, including a variety of programs focused on increasing new farmers' access to land and resources. These programs are somewhat limited in that they continue to rely on and perpetuate systems of renting. However, the concerted focus on new farmer success may provide a key first step to deeper transformation.

One example includes the increase in programs aimed at training the next generation of farmers. These programs are meant to fill the knowledge-gap resulting from several generations having moved off the farm. They are often connected to either incubator farms—which equip new farmers tending parcels on a larger plot with access to shared tools—or to land-linking programs that aid new farmers in finding access to land. The New Entry Sustainable Farming Project (NESFP) in New England, for instance, provides a Farm Business Planning Course and allows graduates to lease land at an incubator/training farm in Dracut, Massachusetts, where they can benefit from access to established infrastructure, additional trainings, and one-on-one technical assistance (NESFP 2016). Programs like California FarmLink work with aspiring farmers to connect them with landowners interested in renting land to a farmer. In all of these cases, the focus is primarily on temporary and/or leased land arrangements.

Federally, a small amount of funding in the Farm Bill is directed to beginning farmers and ranchers through the Beginning Farmer and Rancher Development Program. These funds are primarily geared toward helping aspiring farmers with education, training, outreach, and mentoring.

Additional farmland-focused land trusts are working to conserve farmland. The American Farmland Trust (AFT) began conserving farmland across America in 1980 under the leadership of farmer Peggy McGrath Rockefeller (American Farmland Trust 2016). More locally focused, the Marin Agricultural Land Trust (MALT) also began in 1980 and has preserved what amounts to 47,000 acres of farmland throughout Marin County, California (Marin Agricultural Land Trust 2016). Increasingly, smaller private land trusts—traditionally focused on environmental conservation—are also becoming interested in working with the agricultural community. In all cases, it becomes a question of what land gets preserved, and who has access to that land. In most cases, the focus is on preserving pre-existing farmland and farming communities, rather than on making land newly available to lower income, underserved, young, or new farming populations.

Beyond these rent-focused models, there are a growing number of projects that are beginning to shift away from traditional land ownership structures and toward new systems. Community Land Trusts (CLTs) have their roots in affordable housing movements and have historically used the concept of land trusting to help lower income individuals acquire owner- ship. Typically, in CLTs, the trust owns the land and individuals own the buildings on the land. Individuals have the ability to sell their homes, but at limited prices that will keep them accessible to low income communi- ties. This model is increasingly being considered with regards to agricul- ture. For instance, as farmers seek not just land, but also a place to live, the CLT model can provide a subsidized housing opportunity coupled with a 99-year, inheritable ground lease. This ensures that the land stays in agri- culture, while also ensuring that farmers not only have access to it, but can build equity from it as well.

Additionally, there are public agencies whose role it is to preserve ag- ricultural land and open space. Such an agency exists in Sonoma County: The Sonoma County Agricultural Preservation and Open Space District. This agency's primary work has been in the development of community separators and open space.[2] However, there is increasing dialogue around making public land available to farmers and developing an incubator farm on open space land. Again, this dialogue currently focuses heavily on leasing and incubating, but it is a crucial step and even hints at the ideas of *com- munity-level* investment in the food system and of developing some form of commons—land that is held publicly and used by and for the community. While this model may not yet build assets and equity for individual farmers, it could be a step in challenging the private property norms on which this country was founded. Were this to become a more institutionalized frame- work, it—coupled with incentives for farmers to participate—could be a step toward more transformative change in our land system.

Together, projects work to create some form of access, indicating a community-level awakening to the land struggle sitting at the center of ef- forts to change our food system. However, most of these strategies are still not pushing the question toward ownership or development of a commons. They are still isolated programs, primarily focused on leasing systems for individual farmers. They still unknowingly rely on the willingness of the farming population to accept precariousness and enjoy a bohemian life- style. They help create access, but not security or ownership. They are a part of the path, but do not represent a deep structural change in which farmers are acknowledged and valued as the stewards of landscapes, cornerstones of healthy communities, and individuals who deserve to live in equal step with these communities despite the embedded, structural devaluation of

---

[2] "Community separators are lands designated by the County of Sonoma to serve as greenbelts between towns and cities to protect rural character, prevent sprawl and maintain community identity." (Shore 2015)

the raw products they provide. This kind of necessary structural change will put farmers, as the caretakers of the land, toward the center of land ownership systems in society. It will necessarily take portions of farmable land off of the open market and redistribute it to those who build from it our food system, the foundation of our lives.

* * *

Like my farming colleagues, I am committed to the work, but always questioning whether or not it can actually sustain me. I am privileged to have access to a small piece of land from within my family. I am also privileged to farm at The Permaculture Skills Center, an educational center where I manage some land as part of Red H Farm and teach aspiring farmers the ecological farming techniques I employ. They financially co-invested in the initial inputs required to transform the land to no-till, recognizing the benefits that investment would bring to their land and their school. This kind of landowner commitment makes ecological farming increasingly viable and reflects the importance of community-level investment in the land and our local food system.

Nevertheless, I dream of a day when I can look across the land and know that I can be there forever.

If, as a social movement, we seek a true change in our food system, we must collectively push the solutions we are developing further. If we do not, these innovations will represent moments of gentle reform, but will not actually act to foster a more general and deeply rooted transformation. They will further institutionalize the struggles that have plagued the farming sector and the instability of our food system in general instead of building something long-standing and strong. The time is ripe.

References

Agrarian Trust. 2016. *About*. Accessed February 15, 2016. http://www.agrariantrust.org/about/.

American Farmland Trust. 2016. *Mission and History*. Accessed February 20, 2016. www.farmland.org/mission-history.

Forcey, Hal, Mark Gregg, Mike Pipkin, and Russ Forsburg. 2015. *2015 Trends in agricultural land and lease values: Region Two - North Coast*. California Chapter ASFMRA.

Marin Agricultural Land Trust. 2016. *Founding Story*. Accessed February 20, 2016. www.malt.org/founding-story.

New Entry Sustainable Farming Project. 2016. "Incubator Farm Training Program." Accessed February 20, 2016. http://nesfp.org/farmer-training/incubator-farm.

Nickerson, Cynthia, Mitchell Morehart, Todd Kuethe, Jayson Beckman, Jennifer Ifft and Ryan Williams. 2012. "Trends in U.S. Farmland Values and Ownership." *Economic Information Bulletin Number 92*. United States Department of Agriculture Economic Research Service.

Nuñez, Txetxu. 2015. Presentation. Food First Food Sovereignty Tour.

Ribot, Jesse, and Nancy Lee Peluso. 2003. "A Theory of Access." *Rural Sociology* 68(2): 153-181.

Shore, Teri. 2015. "Sonoma County Community Separator Backgrounder." Greenbelt Alliance. Accessed February 20, 2016. www.greenbelt.org/wp-content/uploads/2015/10/Greenbelt-Alliance-Community-Separators-Backgrounder.pdf.

Sonoma County Department of Agriculture/Weights and Measures. 2015. *Sonoma County Crop Report 2014*.

Thompson, Edward. 2016. Personal Communication with Author. January 8, 2016.

United States Department of Agriculture. 2014. *Farms and Farmland – Numbers, Acreage, Ownership and Use. 2012 Census of Agriculture Highlights, ACH 12-13*.

CHAPTER 7

Settler Colonialism and New Enclosures in Colorado Acequia Communities

Devon G. Peña

The "land grabs" unfolding across the globe are a major issue confronting the food justice and food sovereignty movements. Much of the recent critical research on changes in land tenure, associated with the advent of what Hardt and Negri (2009, 3-29) call the "Republic of Property," focuses on processes of accumulation by means of dispossession (Harvey 2004). I consider land grabs to be new enclosures of settler colonialism in the latest phase of globalizing, neoliberal capitalism. Because discussions about dispossession and enclosure are largely focused on the Global South, ways in which this process has unfolded in the context of North American *settler colonial* history are largely erased from the discourse. In reality, this history continues to provoke sharp conflicts over indigenous land and water rights in the United States.

The US, Mexico, and Canada are settler colonial regimes established via the enclosure and dispossession of indigenous peoples' ancestral territories. Today, these processes continue in ongoing acts of enclosure. Affected communities include both Native Americans (whose ancestors lived in what is now the US) and the diverse native peoples of Mexican-origin (Chicana/o). From the vantage point of indigenous, decolonial epistemic and political standpoints, the US private and public domains are the largest land grab in the history of colonial and imperial expansionism. The public lands alone comprise approximately 70 percent of the territories within the Intermountain Western states (see Table 7.1 on next page). These are rightly viewed by many indigenous peoples as illegally occupied or *unceded* territories, as they include large tracts of traditional subsistence territories that were never surrendered under treaty (see Blackhawk 2006; Correia

TABLE 7.1. Total Federal Land Administered by Five Agencies, Intermountain Western States, 2013.

State	Total Federal Acreage *in of millions acres*	% of all State Land
Arizona	28.064	38.6
California	45.864	45.8
Colorado	23.870	35.9
Idaho	32.621	61.6
Oregon	32.614	52.9
Montana	27.003	29.0
Nevada	59.681	84.9
New Mexico	26.981	34.7
Utah	34.202	64.9
Washington	12.176	28.5
Wyoming	30.013	48.1

Sources: For federal lands, see sources listed in Table 2. Total acreage of states is from U.S. General Services Administration, Office of Government-wide Policy, Federal Real Property Profile, as of September 30, 2004, Table 16, pp. 18-19.

Notes: Figures understate federal lands in each state and the total in the United States. They include only BLM, Forest Service (FS), Fish and Wildlife Service (FWS), National Park Service (NPS), and Department of Defense (DOD) lands. Thus, they exclude lands managed by other agencies, such as the Bureau of Reclamation. Also, figures do not reflect land managed by the agencies in the territories; FWS-managed marine refuges and national monuments (totaling 209.8 million acres); and DOD-managed acreage overseas. Federal land figures do not add to the precise total shown due to small discrepancies in the sources used.

2013; Capuder 2013; Vollmann 2002, 4). An example of this is the originary one million-acre Burns Paiute territory, a very small portion of which was the target of the recent Malheur occupation by armed militias.

This chapter presents a story of resistance to new enclosures in the Chicana/o land grant and *acequia* (communal irrigation institution) communities of Colorado. It begins with an historical account of the theft of common lands in one Mexican-era land grant (*ejido*), and then moves to examine the long term consequences of the original enclosure. This history serves as the context for understanding new enclosures that masquerade as "anti-government" politics by contemporary settler colonists.

The first part of this chapter provides background on *colonias*, defined here as subdivisions lacking access to water, electricity, and other utilities. Part two presents historical background on the Sangre de Cristo Land Grant and the acequia community's land and water ethics, which have shaped our place-based county land use regulations. The third part focuses on the backgrounds, leadership, ideology, and motivation of the newcomers. It also describes how unscrupulous land speculators have privatized large swaths of the land grant to lure unsuspecting and financially precarious buyers to an ecologically marginal, remote desert.

From *colonias fronterizas* to settler colonialism?

The popular image of *colonias* involves the unregulated subdivisions of vacant, desert-like lands that began to appear in the 1950-60s along the US-Mexico border, especially in the borderlands of Texas and California. The border *colonias* are largely non-metropolitan, unincorporated, rural enclaves that lack basic infrastructure (water, sewage, electricity, paved roads). In this context, they are also destinations for displaced populations fleeing violence, repression, poverty, and hunger, which is produced in no small part by US foreign and trade policies in Mexico and Central America. The largest concentration of *colonias* is along the Texas border, with more than 2,294 communities and a population in excess of 400,000 (Secretary of State, Texas 2015). These communities are the legacy of structural violence unleashed by decades of neoliberal policies and capitalist wealth accumulation at the expense of humanity and the planet (Hanna 1995-96; Garcia 1995; Peña 2005).

Precarious border *colonia* residents have proven resourceful; over decades, they have cooperatively built homes from recycled materials and engaged in limited self-provisioning of services. They are doing the best they can under conditions Michelle Tellez (2014) has described as the "spaces of neoliberal neglect." One factor bedeviling most efforts at sustaining the health and wellbeing of these communities is water. There usually is none, or very little, and certainly insufficient sources for sustainable health, sanitation, and general community wellbeing. It is unsurprising that the potable water crisis in *colonias* is a result of unsustainable extension of subdivision sprawl promoted by legislators' demagogic regard for developers' right to profit from the misery produced by neoliberal *mal*development.

Acequias, land grants, and new settler *colonias*

A new class of *colonias* is emerging in the desert prairies of Costilla County in Colorado. Unlike the *colonias* discussed above, these are located 300 miles from the border—in the heart of the southern Rocky Mountains—and their residents are not of Mexican or Central American origin. Costilla County, in Colorado's San Luis Valley (SLV), is a heartland of indigenous Chicana/o culture in the Southwest (see Figure 10.1 on page 128). This unique bioregional culture is the focus of conservation work initiated four years ago under the Sangre de Cristo National

FIG. 10.1. San Luis Valley. In this perspective, S is on top. Costilla County is along the edge of the southeastern side of the Valley between the Sangre de Cristo sub-range known as the Culebra Mountains (on the E) and the Rio Grande (on the W); upper left quadrant within SLV on this map. Source: geogdata.scsun.edu.

Heritage Area (SCNHA) that was established under former Interior Secretary Ken Salazar to protect the area's history, culture, and ecology as significant aspects of our national heritage.

The mostly nontribal, indigenous *acequia* villages along the Culebra River are widely celebrated as exemplars of sustainable adaptation to the arid conditions of life in a high altitude, cold desert environment. Costilla County is located within the historic boundaries of the Sangre de Cristo Land Grant, issued in 1844 when the area was still part of the Republic of Mexico (more on this land grant later). The area's multigenerational acequia farmers embrace an intense attachment to the watershed. The hydro-ecologist Robert Curry once wrote that:

> The farmers of the San Luis Valley depend upon the runoff to keep their alluvial basins full to sub-irrigate their meadows, and to supply the very long-standing system of irrigation ditches [*acequias*] that provide, in essence, the socio-political focus of

their entire culture . . . community interest [in watershed pro-
tection] is high and the public is well informed. These farmers
know their watersheds . . . (1996).

In 1996, Dr. Curry told me that the *acequia* farmers could be described
as having a uniquely deep "watershed consciousness," and that he believed
this was rooted in multiple generations of living and working in a high
altitude, cold desert environment. The indigenous and mestiza/o cultures
of this region established proven patterns of habitation based on respect for
the ecology of place, and these customs are an enduring source of material
livelihoods and spiritual watershed consciousness (Peña 2012). The *acequia*
farmers embody what I have called an "arid sensible way of life," with note-
worthy achievements in the provision of invaluable ecosystem and economic
base services. Costilla County *acequia* farms comprise 23,000 acres of field
and row crops, including many unique heirloom varieties of corn, bean, and
squash (see Peña 2016). Here, our flood-irrigated agroecological methods
have created an additional 10,000 acres of wetlands and uncounted areas
along *acequia* riparian edges. These are vital wildlife habitat and movement
corridors. *Acequia* methods also maintain high water quality, promote soil
regeneration, and preserve indigenous land race crops, among other ecosystem and economic benefits (Hicks and Peña 2003; Peña 2003, Peña 2005:
81-7; Fernald et al. 2007; Fernald et al. 2014). While these ecosystem and
economic base services are gradually being recognized and celebrated by
law and public policy makers, they actually remain undervalued in practical terms. For example, as *acequia* farmers, we have long proposed revisions
to the quadrennial Farm Bills by demanding a shift away from subsidies to
large corporate monoculture growers for "conservation reserves" to a system that rewards and invests in traditional and indigenous farmers through
direct payments for the provision of ecosystem and economic base services
that sustain us in unique bioregional pockets of ecological resilience.

Recently, a class of mostly white settlers has moved to the area and
become the residents of the new *gringo* (Anglo) *colonias* of Costilla County.
Some have proclaimed themselves "sovereign citizens." Others are wrapped
in the virtuous garb of the sustainable "off-the-grid" movement, and seek
ecological legitimacy by co-mingling sovereign citizen property rights ideology with a professed commitment to sustainable lifestyles. From this location, the new settler colonists disingenuously accuse local government of
"violating private property rights" when county officers enforce the legitimate land-use and subdivision regulations that *acequia* farmers and other
local citizens enacted over decades of study and struggle to protect the
cultural and ecological landscapes of our historic communities.

The original 1860 enclosure of the 1844 Sangre de Cristo Land Grant is at the root of this conflict. This was the last common land to be established under Mexican law, and also the last to be lost to enclosure after the end of the US imperial war against Mexico (Peña forthcoming). When the US acquired the territories comprising New Mexico and Colorado in 1848, they incorporated these into the national structure of privatized (and later public) property without the approval of the inhabitants who held legal rights and relations to the land. This community grant was approved ("patented") by the US Congress in 1860, and assigned to a land speculator, William Gilpin, who became the first Territorial Governor (1861-62). Despite this spurious enclosure, a long line of absent landowners could not prevent the *acequia* farmers from continued residence and inhabitation involving the use of the common lands and *acequia* water rights. We still administer these rights today through collective governance, using principles of, for instance, "one irrigator-one vote" and "shared scarcity." As noted above, the grant comprises all of Costilla County and this includes the desert prairies sprawled across the western half of the county. Under land grant law, which recognizes ecological limits, the dryland prairies and mesa tops were never intended for home-sites or farming, although some local ranchers did use the dryland pastures as fall and winter grazing range for sheep and, later, cattle. Water is extremely scarce on these desert prairies because there are no creeks or lakes, and the groundwater aquifer is many hundreds of feet below the surface.

By the 1970s, the Colorado state legislature adopted laws that allowed for the rampant subdividing of this land into small five-acre lots (Riebsame et al. 1996), and this imposed the legal grid space of private property over the open spaces of the land grant. This was before *acequia* farmers asserted their voice in shaping more modern land use regulations and the protection of *acequia* water rights. This gradual enclosure of the land grant common lands resulted in more than 40,000 subdivision lots. Most remain vacant, but clusters of ramshackle homes are now being built by the new settler colonists along the edge of the Rio Grande, and in the open prairies between the Rio Grande and the eastside *acequia* communities. There are also higher-end second homes in the subdivisions created by Malcolm Forbes in the 1960s, but that is another story (see: Peña and Mondragon Valdez 1998; Draper 2001).

The current conflict started when county code enforcement officers inspected newcomers' lots, found code violations, and issued fines for failures to obtain required permits to construct and install septic tanks. One disgruntled settler threatened an enforcement officer by calling her "a dirty Mexican." This set in motion a series of escalating events that revealed the settlers' racialization of indigenous people and disrespect for our deeply-rooted traditions of local governance. Confrontations escalated in July and August 2015, when settlers and locals faced off outside the County Commissioners building on Main Street in San Luis after a meeting to discuss these violations and the land use code. Local residents expressed anger that the settlers were stealing scarce water resources from *acequia* farmers and multigenerational resident families.

The acts of water theft were photographed and videotaped by locals when they confronted settlers who were filling 400-500 gallon tanks resting in pick-up truck beds with "poached" water. They used gas-fueled water pumps to draw from Culebra Creek, its tributaries, the *acequias* themselves (during irrigation season), and even from the Rio Grande, in order to sustain their own lifestyles and also—in some cases—the unauthorized production of marijuana. Locals viewed this theft as a consequence of the newcomers' cultural ignorance and arrogance, and as evidence of disturbing disrespect for the local environment, culture, and indigenous citizens of the county.

Great Recession refugees, "off-the-griders," and sovereign citizens

> We are residents who have come to live off the grid. It's all our land. . . These are harsh economic times. We have nowhere to go.
>
> - Paul Skinner in Colorado Public Radio interview as cited in Syrmopolous (2015)

> [We are]. . . modern day pioneers and Pilgrims. [A]merican[s] once did this. [L]oad up the wagons and head west. [I]t's just modern with the rvs [RVs]. [E]veryone is leaveing [sic] the "left coast" and "sleaze coast" to find new independent land...I lived in CA [California], UT [Utah], TXS [Texas]. lost my job in TX and came back to UT but I want to go back to TX and live independently. [J]ust need a bit of money.
>
> - Scott Allen, Comments. Michael Morris interview.
> YouTube clip posted by Alex Ansary

A deeper history of profound structural violence underlies the presence of sovereign citizens in our watershed. Many of these settler colonists are, themselves, displaced persons. Most are cash poor and desperate to find an escape from perceived governmental oppressors. They have arrived because federal and state neoliberal policies created the greatest wealth inequality the nation has seen since before the days of the Great Depression. These are economic refugees of the "Great Recession."

From an indigenous vantage point, deep irony prevails, since native peoples have been resisting governmental forms of structural violence and genocide unleashed by the white settler colonial state for hundreds of years. The threat of violence being articulated by sovereign citizen activists against the indigenous people of Costilla County—on display in the YouTube clips referenced in this chapter—compels us to refer to a constant state of war against local government as part of a nation-wide, white nationalist psyche tied to well-funded and organized political projects for the reassertion of white racial privilege and class domination. This occurs at a time when, in many native spaces, disenfranchised people are finally asserting their constituent power to enact more equitable, indigenous forms of local self-governance.

The various Patriot, Militia, Three Percenter, and Sovereign Citizen projects are part of a movement targeting "under-populated" states and regions where new wave pioneers and Pilgrims [sic] can "find new independent land" to colonize, with New Hampshire as the showcase (see Murphy 2011; Doherty 2016). The groups in Colorado enunciate extremist Christian identity rhetoric resulting in the subtexts of such popular refrains as, "We need to take our country back," presumably in order to restore it to an imagined, original, pristine state as a white, Christian nation forged by the rugged individualists who first killed and then later swept aside questions asked about the dead. This is part of a deeply-embedded, racist mythology of white, popular, working-class culture and it is the latest version of a very old, white, Christian, patriot identity formation that is xenophobic, nationalistic, misogynist, and dominionist.

From a demographic vantage point, the settler colonists are a diverse group. Their regional origins are quite varied and include people from cities like Atlanta, Los Angeles, San Diego, Portland, and Colorado Springs, while others left homes in smaller towns and cities like Logan, Utah and Meeker, Colorado, or fled low-waged jobs in places like Montrose, Colorado. Still others hail from the Deep South, including rural and small town locales in Georgia, Alabama, Mississippi, Arkansas, and Texas. A few are military veterans from the wars in Iraq and Afghanistan. A scant few of the newcomers claim to be "natural born" Colorado "natives." I have met two African American men; Internet trolls and right-wing pundits feature them as evidence that the newly-arrived Patriots and off-the-grid advocates are not racist, and that the county is the guilty party for attacking innocent people whose only crime is an honest search for "intentional" community and property rights.

There are young, middle-aged, and older adults; single persons, partnered, and married; some have arrived with families and have children who are attending local district public schools. The newcomer settler colonists fall into four distinct subgroups: refugees of the "Great Recession;" off-the-grid, alternative lifestyle advocates; patriots and sovereign citizens; and internet trolls, pundits, and social media activists.

The economic refugees

Most of the settlers are largely apolitical persons and families facing great economic and social distress who offer largely untold stories of material precariousness. For instance, one displaced family moved from Arkadelphia, Arkansas to the Costilla County desert prairie in 2007 after a catastrophic illness left the family bankrupt and in deep material poverty. I befriended them in Ft. Garland well before the latest wave of settlers arrived. They sought refuge from a world they view as cruel, chaotic, and punitive. The Arkadelphia family had acquired a five-acre sagebrush lot in northeastern Costilla County during "good times" (2005); their homestead was in the vicinity of the southern approach from San Luis to the Sangre de Cristo Ranches subdivision. After a series of catastrophic illnesses among family members, this lot was their only asset and the sole place left for them to go. On arrival, they lacked resources to build an adequately insulated home or to even install indoor plumbing or a septic tank, a requirement of state health regulations, which counties are now delegated to enforce. They could not afford the cost of installing a badly-needed domestic water well, and bought what water they could from local businesses, or occasionally took it directly from the creeks and agricultural canals against my advice. Access to vital health care involved long and costly travel to a clinic in San Luis or a more distant regional hospital in Alamosa.

The family suddenly left in the early spring of 2010, but not because of over-zealous land-use code enforcement officers. Like most people who share their abject circumstances, they left after environmental conditions were more than they could weather. The only imprint the Arkadelphia family left—strewn across an illegal garbage dump not far from their abandoned lot—is the broken shards of a harshly disrupted attempt at domesticity and the discarded yellowing paperwork of lives wrecked by neoliberal economic and social policies.

Since the 1970s, the unsuspecting have bought land in Costilla County, usually sight unseen. Most of these lots end up resold in county tax sales. Buyers keep coming, perhaps harboring dreams of a home in the Rocky Mountains with antelope and elk herds, but the herds seldom appear and the mountains are remote and elusive, located some 10 to 20 miles away and largely inaccessible due to private higher-end foothills subdivision inholdings and our own common lands. The newly "landed" arrive to find very little water to be acquired, unless they have the $20,000 average fee required to pay a private company to drill a well into the San Luis Valley unconfined aquifer and secure a well permit from the State Water Conservation Board. They are lured here by the misleading and perfectly legal advertisements for the sale of "dirt cheap" land by speculators and unscrupulous realtors. Internet realtors are currently at the center of this chaos, since land gets deceptively sold to people unaware of the very substantial hidden costs to the owners, neighbors, and environment.

The settlers are casualties of the neoliberal dismantling of the welfare state and the de-industrialization of the Northeast and Midwest. The newcomers represent 80 percent of all new cases for food stamp and family support assistance in Costilla County.[1] The Sheriff's Department also reports that, for the first time in the history of the county, people from outside the Town of San Luis and the surrounding *acequia* villages comprise the majority of the county jail inmate population. There are reports from concerned parents in the school district that the children of some of the settlers are bullied at school because they are unwashed and local students find the odor offensive and disruptive to coursework and social interaction. Some concerned parents are now pressuring the superintendent and school board to expand the number of showers available to these children so they can attend more regularly to their personal hygiene and perhaps end this harassment.

Costilla County is an economically distressed area, and is often cited as the "poorest county" in Colorado. Most locals reject this characterization by noting how the area is rich in land, history, and culture even if it is "cash poor." Regardless, the 2007-08 market failures of neoliberal capitalism produced the largest mass of displaced, newly precarious, poor, white, working-class families since the era of the Great Depression. Many of these people have had little choice but move to an area that is already economically distressed and marginalized.

The off-the-grid alternative lifestyle advocates

A second group of new settlers consists of mostly white young adults who envision intentional communities and sustainable lifestyles following an off-the-grid ethic. They seem limited by naiveté and a lack of sufficient knowledge, skill, or resources needed to establish a viable alternative

---

[1] As reported to the author by Costilla County officials in June-September 2015.

community in an arid environment constrained by the politics of the over-appropriation of water rights.

One of the genuine off-the-grid advocates is a 33-year old white woman from Portland, Oregon. Her partner is an Afghanistan War vet and originally from Logan, Utah. The couple was featured in an article published October 1, 2015 by Colorado Public Radio, with the misleading and inaccurate headline, "Off-Grid Residents Claim Victory As Costilla County Backs Off Proposal." The county did not back off; it decided that clarification of the code was unnecessary and that authorities have sufficient legal standing to enforce existing code regulations that reasonably require newcomers to, for example, install septic tanks to protect public health and sanitation, as required by state law.

I've seen the young woman at the Ventero Open Press, our local coffee shop, art press, and gallery. She has the look of someone lost in a new place, and lacks familiarity with local history, culture, ecology, and especially, our long tradition of environmental justice struggles, which have defined our community's special relationship to place. This naiveté is troubling because this segment of the settlers could be welcomed accomplices of the *acequia* community in relations of mutual aid, which is, after all, our tradition with newcomers. At this point, the newcomers exhibit a lack of knowledge of, or respect for, the local ecology and culture. Living off-the-grid in a manner that embraces social justice and not just ecological sustainability requires respect for place-based ecology, culture, and history. This can quickly become another exercise in complicity with the arrogant dispossession of a native peoples' sense of place by white settler colonists, which is exactly the agenda of the third group.

The 'Sovereign Citizens'

The smallest subset of settlers is the most vocal and "networked." They use an active, nation-wide social media campaign to escalate confrontations with local, state, and federal authorities as a test case for sovereign citizenry. These activist newcomers, who claim to be struggling to live among others in the hardscrabble terrain of Costilla County's *colonias,* embrace a distinctly resurgent thread of white settler colonial ideology that legitimizes itself by invoking the need for volunteer militia mobilization, and the possible use of violence in the name of freedom.

A former Army Ranger, claiming acreage in the Sangre de Cristo Mountains, discussed the idea that "sometimes the going gets rough in negotiations with governmental authorities." After the arrest of this sovereign citizen activist for ties to the same group involved in the Malheur occupation in Oregon, the clip was removed from the YouTube channel created by one of the Internet pundits promoting this mobilization (Alex Ansary). I transcribed the statements made by various unidentified "Patriots" and the others present during an impromptu meeting that took place in August 2015 after the Costilla County Commissioners monthly public meeting:

EX-ARMY RANGER: I am an ex-Ranger. . . here to fight for your rights. . . Now nobody wants to see this place turn into a Bundy Ranch. . . [Groans of agreement; nervous laughter]. . . Now here's what I want to know from each and every person standing here . . . do you believe in your constitutional right to do what you want with your own land? [Wide crowd agreement]. . . Now sometimes those solutions come easy through negotiation, sometimes they come a little rough . . . Everybody I am sure knows about Bundy Ranch and the stuff that happened there. Ah, we need to try and avoid those kinds of situations but at the same time you got to stand up for your constitutional rights. What are your constitutional rights. . . ? A lot of people don't understand that 'code' is not 'law.' Code is code; law is law. . . It is illegal for an officer of the law to enforce code on your property, okay. . . ? If you guys are willing and ready, Operation Patriot Rally Point is willing and ready. . . Now last night I received a message, an urgent message, on Facebook. . . I was advised to contact a United States Supreme Court judge, who wanted to speak to me, on this issue. . . Apparently Costillo [sic] County has. . . the attention of the U.S. Superior Court and he notified me that US marshals are going to be brought in on this. . . This is not going to be easy; any time you try to take on local government or federal government, anything like that and any kind of issue, it's not going to be easy. You have to be ready for a hard fight. You got to ruck up, balls up, get 'er done. . . That's how it rolls. . .

SECOND MAN: . . .I'm a Three Percenter; I'm a Patriot. They will not run me off my property without me being dead first.

Recurring in these video clips is the trope of absolute private property rights, a central tenet of sovereign citizen ideology. This ideology holds that "fee simple" ownership conveys a divine right to do as one pleases with the land, and that this right is older than the U.S. Constitution and antecedent to governmental authority at the county level. The reference above to "superior court judges" and "US marshals" is to the self-anointed officers of this movement. The most notorious recent example of direct action (before Malheur) was the Bundy Ranch in Nevada, which is frequently invoked by the Patriots and Sovereign Citizen activists in Costilla County. Advocates of this ideology proclaim the idea that individual sovereignty constitutes liberty from taxation and from regulation of private property rights when vested in fee simple ownership.

Internet Pundits and Trolls

Alex Ansary fits the mold of an obscure freelance writer and video documentarian trying to make it as the next Internet sensation. Ansary started as an irregular contributor to online conspiracy theory zines and unfiltered information clearinghouses, bot operators, and fake news agglomerators that span the whole spectrum of political thought, from "conspiracy theory" to UFOs, chemtrails, and mind control. His specialty, before becoming a champion of private property rights in Costilla County, was conspiracy theories and the New World Order, the police state, and mass media indoctrination of the masses.

Ansary seeks to apply his conspiracy theory approach to the case of Costilla County by asserting that land use administrators secretly and maliciously engineered a nefarious attack on the private property rights of the settler colonists. Ansary follows the right wing's notorious practice of using fabricated documentary evidence to serve selective libertarian, neoconservative, and anti-democratic agendas. One of the advocates of sovereign citizen ideology promoted by Ansary's YouTube channel is Vince Edwards, a white male in his mid-30s. Edwards' particular narrative revolves around the familiar sovereign citizen misunderstanding of the concept of "fee simple" in property rights:

> The problem that we're facing in this country and in this county is that most of the people just don't know their rights, and the fact of the matter is that our rights preexist the Constitution, eh, eh, preexist the forming of this county, ah, preexisted the regulations that they are trying to put together now. Every single warranty deed that I've ever looked at has the words 'fee simple' on it. Fee simple means absolute unconditional use of your property. That means I don't have to pay taxes on it, I don't have to get permission to do anything, I just exercise my rights.

This is more than a misunderstanding of the legal concept of fee simple or the status of English or Anglo common law in the US. It reveals a great deal of ignorance about the constitutional nature of this Republic of Property, a matter of urgent attention, but is the realm of the settler, colonial capitalist system and the enclosure and commodification of indigenous territories, which remain beyond Edward's ideological horizons.

Conclusion

This chapter on white settler-colonists in Costilla County reveals that land grabs inside the US today are a continuation of settler enclosures that privilege narrow, self-centered, and individualistic concepts of property rights. These form the ideological underpinning of attacks on local, democratic self-governance and institutions of collective action created by the indigenous *acequia* community. Endemic among the sovereign citizens is the absence of a sense of community obligations or respect for established principles of indigenous co-inhabitation of ancestral territories. While the economic refugees and off-the-grid settlers are less aggressive in their ideology, they too are products of neoliberal, colonialist culture, and their respective economic desperation and cultural ignorance also inhibits their ability to live in agreement with our traditions. These groups are an immediate threat to our everyday lives. We see this as a selfish, overbearing presence coupled with a complete lack of respect for the indigenous culture. There is also a profound lack of humility before the ecological realities and limits of our valley. Since the 1860s, our *acequia* community has endured repeated disturbances caused by settler-colonial violence and enclosures. The new instance of "gringo" coloniality is also being met with effective resistance, grounded in the resilience we have earned through more than a century of continuous environmental, land rights, and social justice struggles, efforts deeply informed by our respect for the original instructions of an arid-sensible way of life.

References

Blackhawk, Ned. 2006. *Violence Over the Land: Indians and Empires in the Early American West*. Cambridge: Harvard University Press.

Capuder, Karen Marie. 2013. "Forked Tongues at Sequalitchew: A Critical Indigenist Anthropology of Place in Nisqually Territory." Ph.D. diss., Anthropology. University of Washington, Seattle, WA. Chair, Devon G. Peña.

Correia, David. 2013. *Properties of Violence: Law and Land Grant Struggle in Northern New Mexico*. Athens: University of Georgia Press.

Curry, Robert R. 1995b. Interview on the History and Ecology of the Culebra Watershed. Interviewed by Devon G. Peña. Rio Grande Bioregions Project: Upper

Rio Grande Acequia Farms Study. National Endowment for the Humanities Project #RO-22707-94 (Interpretive Research Grants). Archived at the Acequia Institute, San Pablo, CO.

Doherty, Brian. 2016. "Free State Project Participants: It's Time To Move to New Hampshire For Real!" *Reason Magazine*, February 2. Accessed April 1, 2016. http://reason.com/blog/2016/02/02/free-state-project-participants-its-time.

Draper, Electa. 2001. "Forbes ranch offers picturesque haven." *The Denver Post*, January 28.

Fernald, Alexander G., Terrell T. Baker, and Steven J. Guldan. 2007. "Hydrologic, Riparian, and Agroecosystem Functions of Traditional *Acequia* Irrigation Systems." *Journal of Sustainable Agriculture* 30(2):147-171.

Fernald, Alexander, S. Guldan, K. Boykin, A. Cibils, M. Gonzales, et al. 2014. "Hydrological, ecological, land use, economic, and sociocultural evidence for re-silience of traditional irrigation communities in New Mexico, USA." *Hydrology and Earth Systems Sciences–Discussions* 11(2): 1821–1869.

FBI Counterterrorism Analysis Section. 2011. "Sovereign Citizens: A Growing Domestic Threat to Law Enforcement." *FBI Law Enforcement Bulletin*. Accessed July 21, 2015. https://goo.gl/cBi84D.

Garcia, James E. 1995. "Bills Would Improve Conditions in Colonias." *Austin American Statesman,* March 4, p.B5.

Hannah, David L. 1995-96. "Third World Texas: NAFTA, State Law, and Environmental Problems Facing Texas Colonias." *St. Mary's Law Journal* 27:871-927.

Hardt, Michael and Antonio Negri. 2009. *Commonwealth*. Cambridge: Harvard University Press.

Harvey, David. 2004. "The 'New' Imperialism: Accumulation by Dispossession." *Socialist Register* 40:63-87.

Hicks, Gregory A. and Devon G. Peña, 2003. "Community Acequias in Colorado's Rio Culebra Watershed: A Customary Commons in the Domain of Prior Appropriation." *University of Colorado Law Review* 74(2): 387-486.

Murphy, Tim. 2011. "Meet the Libertarian Utopians Trying to Take Over New Hampshire." *Mother Jones* September/October. Accessed April 1, 2016. http://goo.gl/HFJDQ0.

Peña, Devon G. 2003. "The Watershed Commonwealth of the Upper Rio Grande." In James K. Boyce and Barry G. Shelley, eds, *Natural Assets: Democratizing Environmental Ownership*, 169–185. Washington, DC: Island Press.

Peña, Devon G. 2005. *Mexican Americans and the Environment: Tierra y Vida.* Tucson: University of Arizona Press.

Peña, Devon G. 2012. "On Acequias: Water, Place, Resilience, and Democracy." *New Clear Vision* (Nov. 2). Accessed June 12, 2016. http://goo.gl/Is2HRd.

Peña, Devon G. 2016. "Deep Seeds and First Foods: Centers of Origin and Diversification of Maíz in the Río Arriba Bioregion and the Survival of Heritage Cuisines." *Green Fire Times* 8(5): 7-8. Accessed August 21, 2016. http://goo.gl/olx4nr.

Peña, Devon G. Forthcoming. *The Last Common: Endangered Lands and Disappeared People in the Politics of Place.* Invited submission to Environmental History of the Borderlands Series, edited by Thomas A. Sheridan. Tuscon: University of Arizona Press.

Peña, Devon G. and María Mondragon Valdéz. 1998. "The 'Brown' and the 'Green' Revisited: Chicanos and Environmental Politics in the Upper Rio Grande." In Daniel Faber ed., The Struggle for *Ecological Democracy: Environmental Justice Movements in the United States,* 312–348. Democracy and Ecology Series, v. 7 (James O'Connor, Series Editor). New York, New York: Guilford Press.

Riebsame, W. E., H. Gosnell and D. M. Theobald. 1996. "Land Use and Landscape Change in the Colorado Mountains I: Theory, Scale, and Pattern." *Mountain Research and Development* 16(4):395-405.

Secretary of State, Texas. 2015. *Texas Colonias: A Thumbnail Sketch of Conditions, Issues, Challenges and Opportunities.* Accessed August 2, 2015. http://goo.gl/cWjQ3S.

Southern Poverty Law Center. n.d. *Sovereign Citizens Movement.* Accessed July 21, 2015. https://goo.gl/R5Cn6L.

Syrmopoulos, Jay. 2015. "'Camping' on Your Own Land is Now Illegal — Govt Waging War on Off-Grid Living." *The Free Thought Project.* Accessed June 12, 2016. http://goo.gl/vwnXsj.

Tellez, Michelle. 2005. "Globalizing Resistance: Maclovio Rojas, a Mexican Community *En Lucha.*" Ph.D. Dissertation. College of Education, Critical Community Studies, Claremont Graduate School.

Vollmann, Tim. 2002. "Recognition of Traditional Forms of Ownership of Land and Natural Resources by Indigenous Peoples in the Jurisprudence and Legislation of the U.S.A." *Working Group on the Fifth Section of the Draft Declaration on the Rights of Indigenous Peoples (November 7).* Organization of American States Washington, DC. Accessed June 14, 2016. http://goo.gl/s5bwTy.

CHAPTER 8

We are all Downstream: Land Justice, Standing Rock, and Indigenous Sovereignty

Hartman Deetz

*A*round the country, native leadership is rising to defend land against commoditization and extraction. In the first section of this chapter, Hartman Deetz describes his Mashpee identity, and his people's struggle to defend their land and water through self-determination. In the second, he recounts his journey to Standing Rock, where he joined together with other native and non-native peoples to resist the construction of the Dakota Access Pipeline, defend the sovereignty of the Standing Rock tribe, and protect all of us who are intricately connected to the waterways the pipeline threatens.

Part One. More Than a Bingo Hall

Buddy Pocknett had been fishing the canal that day, pulling up lobster pots like he had been doing since he could walk. Like his father before him and the generations before, Buddy lived from the land. Like Buddy, his father Vernon was one of our beloved men, a fisherman and a hunter who, I imagine, may have never bought a pound of meat from a store. When electricity came to Mashpee, the Pocknett home didn't want none of it; Vernon's father thought it would make them dependent on the outside world. Vernon was raised with kerosene lamps and a wood burning stove – with game meat and a vegetable garden. Vernon raised his kids the same. So that day, Buddy had been out fishing the canal. When he came in to the docks, the fishwarden was there waiting.

Mashpee people have aboriginal fishing rights, but local officials often-times resent when tribal members exercise their right to fish, unregulated by the county or state. The fish warden decided to measure the lobsters and found one that, in his estimation, was too small. He told Buddy he was going to take his entire catch for the day because of this slight infraction, but Buddy said if he was not going to eat what he caught, the fishwarden was certainly not going to feed them to his family that night, either. So he dumped the lobsters back into the canal. The fish warden then pepper sprayed, beat, and arrested Buddy for fishing the way he had been doing since he learned to walk.

The legal process took some time, but eventually Buddy was vindicated by the courts and cleared of all charges. As he arrived home from court, the paperwork for the case in his back pocket, three police cruisers pulled into his driveway behind him, lights flashing. The officers didn't even question him; they simply attacked Buddy, beating him to the ground and stomping on his knees in front of his wife and small children. They beat him in his own driveway for harvesting a lobster that may or may not have been too small over a month before. The whole time, Buddy pleaded with the officers to look in his back pocket to read the release of the warrant issued from the court less than an hour before. Old wounds were torn open; that night, the community found itself gathered in resistance in front of the police station in a town that has sought to displace our tribe from our ancestral land for many, many years.

So often native people in the Americas are defined solely by their relationship to the colonizer's story. Rarely are we defined in terms of our own story. As Wampanoag people we share in the very origin stories of this country, the United States. We are "the Indians" who saved the Pilgrims from starvation and taught them how to grow corn. But our particular tribe is not important to the colonial narrative, though for us our distinct Wampanoag identity is very much a part of our story. The story of the first Thanksgiving for my ancestors in the 17th century is just one part in a complicated, interwoven tale of alliances, deception, war and betrayal.

We are the Mashpee Wampanoag. Our tribe is building a casino. To do that, we need to establish a federal trust. To the white residents of Taunton, Massachusetts our effort to establish a land trust is just a political maneuver to build the casino. But they have our story backwards: the only way for us to recover our land and the sovereignty to fish and hunt as we have always done—without fear of being beaten—is by building a casino.

I first fell in love with my homeland at age fourteen. I had come to visit my father in Mashpee, Massachusetts from California where I had lived since age two. We were driving along a dirt road when my father told me, "This is Great Hay road, an ancient way. This road is older than America." This dirt road that winds through the woods of Mashpee follows the Mashpee River from the Mashpee Pond out to the Bay at South Cape Beach. For thousands of years my relatives used this road to walk from the central village out to the coast. This old dirt road was literally made by the feet of my ancestors, and I could walk in their footsteps. Walking down to the Bay has been central to Wampanoag life for all eternity. The Bay is where we gather seaweed, clams, mussels, quahogs and scallops. It is where we fish for crabs, blue fish, or scup. The coast is also where we planted our crops: corn, beans, pumpkin, Jerusalem artichokes, sunflowers and wild onions.

For Mashpee people our life has always been about the land. When I was born, my grandfather Russell Peters was tribal council chairman. His administration had fought a land suit against the town of Mashpee that failed when the tribe was dismissed as a viable plaintiff after our identity as native people was brought into question. This finding in our land case brought our tribe to file one of the first applications for federal recognition in 1974. For 33 years, our federal recognition case languished in the courts where it was systematically backlogged as other cases moved past us. Finally, in 2007 we won our recognition as a tribe, and in 2015 – after eight years of intergovernmental negotiations – we established our land into trust.

I was born in 1976, and many changes have come to Mashpee in my lifetime. Mashpee peaked as the fourth fastest growing town in the US. In the 1960s our people were the majority of the town at 800 tribal members. Today, even at 2,000 tribal members, we make up less than one percent of the town of Mashpee. The waterfront is full of mansions; many of the ancient trails are now paved roads. Attempts by private landowners to block access to water have come in the form of parking restrictions, blocking roads, and building fences. "No Trespassing" signs are abundant in new developments that cut Mashpee tribal members off from their traditional fishing places. Now, tribal members buy their meat from a supermarket where my uncle's favorite hunting spot once was.

Mashpee is the name of the pond; "great pond" is the translation. Mashpee Pond flows out through the Mashpee River and the Mashpee people take their name from these waters. My grandfather used to say that the Great Depression never came to Mashpee, because people in Mashpee didn't use money anyway. They lived off the land – hunting, fishing, and farming as our people had for all of time. However, the last 40 years has seen this change. People who used to make a living fishing the waters have now turned to building the houses for the people that have pushed them out of their fishing holes, and pushed Mashpee out of their income bracket. Unlike the Great Depression, the housing crash of 2008 is driving Mashpee people out of Mashpee, myself included. But Mashpee people are Mashpee—the pond, the river, the land. Is our federal recognition and putting our land into a trust about a casino? It is, but it is much more than that. When we depended on our merits to make the case of our tribal status, we languished in courts for 30 years. When casino investors hired lobbyists, our case moved forward to active consideration. When the case was finally heard, the merits were said to be the strongest to ever come before the review board, with documentary evidence going back to 1621. So yes, it is about casinos, because merit alone is not enough. We may have won our case on merit, but without money we could not be heard.

For my people, casinos are about economics, sovereignty, and jurisdiction. For the citizens of Taunton it is a job creator. Some would argue that there are other industries that the tribe could invest in to create jobs, and it is true. We could invest in restaurants, fishing boats, museums and retail shops, creating jobs to help people stay in Mashpee. However, this approach would not be possible without the financial ability of the tribe to actually invest, and none of these create the kind of profits that a casino does. A casino can be the economic engine that funds our tribal government programs, such as small business grants, housing assistance, education, cultural and historic preservation, natural resource management, courts and legal and political representation.

We have a long history of members of the tribe asserting their rights to hunt, fish, and gather, as well as to access water in all of our usual and accustomed places. These rights have been used to defend against parking violations, trespassing charges, hunting without a license, fishing without a license, and tree poaching, among others. Asserting our rights was a part of what made our federal recognition case so strong. We have a case history of tribal rights beginning in 1833, with letters of complaint to the state – and even to the old colony of Massachusetts. Opening the doors of a casino would be an additional act of exercising our sovereign jurisdiction over our economy.

When we can assert our own laws on our own lands we can do more than assert economic rights, we can assert our legal jurisdiction. For the Akwasasne Mohawk tribe of New York, this has proven to be effective for environmental protection; the tribal council has set environmental standards for land contamination and water pollution that are among the most stringent in the nation. The Akwasasne have asserted the need for higher standards based on their cultural connection to the land. Because their people depend on hunting, fishing, and gathering from the environment, they reject false solutions such as eliminating local fish from their diet. For Akwasasne people, much like many other native people, eating from the earth is about more than diet; it is about cultural continuity. It is about the recipes, methods of harvest, the cycle of the seasons, and holidays. It is identity.

For Wampanoag people such as the Mashpee tribe, our new year is tied to the return of the herring. In the late spring there is always a buzz of excitement waiting for the first herring to be taken from the river. When the first catch is made, word spreads through town. *"You hear Buddy caught the first herring? ....yeah down past the meeting house."* To be the fisher who takes the first herring will draw both jealousy and admiration. It is still an honor among our people. After the news spreads, the medicine man, the chief, elders, and members of the community at large will gather at the herring run, throwing hands full of corn meal into the water, singing songs, and passing general blessings to the waters and to this fish that has brought the return of life after winter. Traditionally, herring were smoked and preserved the previous year, and what's left could now be turned into the soil to fertilize the fields. This year's herring would be smoked and preserved for the lean times of winter, where they could be eaten dry or reconstituted into a soup or stew.

A week after the fields are fertilized with the herring, the corn can be planted, followed by the beans and squash. Traditionally, our lives depended on the success of these crops to get us through the winter. Without the herring there is no corn, beans, squash, or pumpkins. How can we have live as Wampanoag people today without our new year? How do we have our green corn festival, our strawberry thanksgiving or our cranberry day without these fruits of our land? How do we call ourselves Mashpee Wampanoag without herring swimming up the Mashpee River to the Mashpee Pond?

In today's world, protecting the river that we belong to is no longer about controlling the hunting grounds now paved over by parking lots; it is no longer about defending the fishing holes from neighboring tribes when the water is being contaminated. To defend our river, our land, our mother Mashpee, we must be able to leverage the legal power of jurisdiction, environmental standards, and land use approval. We must have the resources to leverage political power to enforce these. This is power that comes with economic strength. Economic strength for a whole community comes from projects and businesses the size of a casino.

For some people, Mashpee is where they live or where they own a house or some land. For the Mashpee Wampanoag, we *belong* to the land. For the people who see the world as something that belongs to them, the river, the fish, and the land is a commodity to be used. For those of us who belong to the land, we must defend it as our mother. The fish and trees as our brothers and sisters. If we are not here in Mashpee, who is left to defend our relatives? Who will be here to speak for those who cannot speak for themselves? Is our land trust about a casino? You could say it is, because a casino provides the resources for our people to stay in Mashpee, to have sovereign control over our land. For Mashpee people, it is a means to an end, a means to care for our mother land.

Part Two. Everyone is Downstream: Resisting the North Dakota Access Pipeline

I left California late at night, later than expected. My friend arrived outside along with another woman whom I was meeting for the first time. I jammed my duffel bag and camping supplies into a car that already seemed full to the brim, and we left for Standing Rock.

We drove Interstate 80 across Nevada, Utah, and into Wyoming. I was struck, once again, by the beauty of the land in this country – great salt plains, rocky mountain faces, multi-colored hillsides, pine forests. We are truly blessed to live in a land of such grand, diverse landscapes.

The weight of the earth and sky particularly impressed me in the great plains of Dakota prairie land – sparsely accented with small rolling hills, occasional trees along creeks, and streams that then feed into mighty rivers. The world is cut in half by a flat horizon, reflected by the scale of the nighttime sky with the stars, Milky Way, and the Northern Lights. Or in the day, under the shifting pillars of clouds. This is quintessential farm land of mythical, Americana proportions. Of tornadoes and Dorothy, beef ranchers, wagon trains... and Indians. The shrieks, the panic, the disdain, the hatred instilled in that Hollywood line still lingers on for some in the Dakotas.

The Dakota Access Pipeline, also known as the Bakken Pipeline, is an oil infrastructure project planned to bring fracked oil from North Dakota through South Dakota, Iowa, and Illinois, where it will then connect with existing rail and pipeline networks, transporting highly volatile crude oil to the Gulf Coast.

In May 2014, a "not in my back yard" group of concerned citizens in Bismark successfully moved the initial pipeline route out of their region, citing concerns that it could potentially impact drinking water for the city, as well as other environmental considerations. These same issues did not seem to be a concern to regulators when a new route was approved in September of 2014 that cut across Standing Rock Reservation, which are treaty lands, without consultation or approval from the Standing Rock tribe (Dalrymple 2016).

This is a violation of the sovereign standing of a tribal government; the Standing Rock tribe has not and will not give approval for this project. It is a threat to their ability to live on what they have left of their ancient homeland. *Mni wiconi*: water is life. In fact, the tribe has taken every measure to ensure that this project is not approved - pursuing the case in federal court, seeking to redress their grievances through government, participating in negotiations, and more. However, the project approved by the state of North Dakota's government has been actively moving forward with construction despite ongoing objections from the tribal government.

A group of 30 youth ran on foot from Standing Rock to Washington DC to communicate their resistance (Houska 2016). Sadly, President Obama has yet to respond. People set up an opposition camp in the path of the pipeline; many are using their bodies to block construction and halt operations. Tribal Council Chairperson David Archembault was among those arrested for trespassing when tribal citizens and supporters flooded into an active construction site (Talisman 2016).

On September 2, 2016, the Friday before Labor Day, the tribe found a new method of resistance – the Native American Graves Protection Act. The tribe's historic preservation officer submitted a stop work order, showing the presence of grave sites in the path of the proposed pipeline route. The following Saturday, the situation came to a head as tribal citizens and their supporters arrived to plant their tribal flags and lay down their tobacco ties, prayers, and offerings to mark grave sights – but a team of bulldozers had arrived before them, 20 miles away from any active work zone, in order to bulldoze any evidence of graves in the pipeline route (Goodman 2016; Bernish 2016).

Tribal members occupied the active construction zone while bulldozers plowed the graves of their ancestors. Private mercenary security forces hired by Dakota Access attacked unarmed tribal citizens with pepper spray and dogs. A pregnant woman and a child were among those who suffered dog bites; both went to the hospital. The attack dogs were so out of control that one of the mercenaries was even bitten by their own attack dog.

The video went out across the web, as did the call for support. Like many people, Native and otherwise, I answered.

"It's an affront to our culture to bulldoze burials [sic] purposefully, women and children were at the forefront when the dogs attacked and they don't care," said Erin Strongheart Ford. "If there was [sic] crosses or headstones there do you think they would have done that?" Erin is a woman of mixed descent identifying herself as "from Chaktaw, Cherokee, African and Celtic lineage." She is active in the food justice and organic farming movement in the Driftless region of Wisconsin, where she now lives. She has travelled back and forth between Wisconsin and North Dakota, in all bringing between $10,000-15,000 of food donations to the camp. As a farmer, she helps bring a broader perspective to the issue. The risk of contaminating the Missouri River could impact the water supply for a significant portion of the nation's farmland. "If you are an organic farmer making a stand against GMOs [genetically modified crops] and pesticides, this is the same fight," she explains.

On the way to Standing Rock, I stopped in South Dakota where I spoke with farmer Jim Keller. Keller lives on a farm just a few short miles from the banks of the Missouri River. Just like the Standing Rock Sioux in North Dakota, the state of South Dakota would also bear great risk from a pipeline spill without reaping any of the meager economic benefits. Keller has been involved with social movements around water in the region since the 1980s, when he worked with Families Against Radioactive Mining (FARM). He finds much in common with the pipeline fight of today. "This affects the entire Missouri from here to the Mississippi, and the whole Mississippi south of St. Louis." Keller told me, "The river feeds into the aquifer [Oglala Aquifer], and that's where we get the water when we turn on the tap." From Standing Rock to Keller's farm, to South Dakota, Iowa, St. Louis, and all the way down to New Orleans, Keller says, "everyone lives downstream."

While many Native people stand in opposition to this pipeline at Standing Rock, the resistance reaches far beyond Standing Rock tribal members alone. Many people have seen the opposition, and have recognized parts of themselves in the people who have travelled to Standing Rock. Bill Hill of Tucson, Arizona said, "If we don't band together as human beings, then why are we here?" Hill brought a 30-foot bus from Tucson full of people and supplies. Some had money, some had material donations, others had only themselves. Hill said, "It's important to get people out of their comfort zones, because most Americans... we are too comfortable. Indigenous people have nothing; we have taken everything from them and now we want to put an oil pipeline through their water?" Hill reminds us of the importance of water and life, "Separation is what destroys people. We are all here together to stop the pipeline."

Michael Tinter traveled from Putnam Valley, New York, where he does permaculture education at Eden Village Summer Camp. He said: "I knew there was some way I could help." Taking the teaching of permaculture that states, "the problem is the solution," Tinter was put in charge of dealing with food waste, and started the camp's composting program. He went on to describe how the camp is about more than stopping the pipeline, "This is the fight to stop something bad and hurtful, but it has taken the bad and turned it into something good by bringing the people together."

Taking the problem of food waste and turning it into compost seemed like a no-brainer. However, the state trumped the rights of the Standing Rock Tribe once again – the North Dakota Environmental Protection Agency insisted that composting amounted to burying waste and would be considered illegal dumping. "If we have to compost above the ground we will have to shut down," said Leigh Salway, one of the two women leading cooking at the Wild Oglala Kitchen. Every day, this camp kitchen starts the morning by cooking breakfast. After breakfast Leigh and the rest of the team starts cooking lunch, and after lunch they start cooking dinner. As the sign says, everyone is welcome - to food that flows all day, but also for a sense of home. Leigh is a quiet, soft-spoken classic Native matriarch whose hospitality has gathered a whole camp around her kitchen. "These people are out here to help us. I come from Oglala, but we have a lot of family up here," she told me. "We want people to know we appreciate them being here, so we feed them and invite them to visit with us by our fire."

I helped dig the compost pit with her partner, a man alternately introducing himself as John, Frank, Billy, and Richard. He is a man full of jokes. When he was told to remove the compost from the pit, he used the old Indian weapon of humor to strike back. "They say we can't dig up the ground for compost, so we should just tell them that it's for a pipeline... What could go wrong? Thirty inches of crude oil?" He continues on, shovel in hand, working the soil out of the pit. "What if we told them we found some graves eh? They would send the bulldozers over and dig it for us." Like the others digging the compost out of their pits, Richard is using his shovel to work; however, I notice in classic trickster fashion he is digging a new compost pit right next to the old one.

That spirit of resistance is fed and supported by women like Salway. The morning of the Labor Day action, many of those flooding into construction sites first came through the wild Oglala kitchen, or the Hoopa or Navajo camp, picking up fry bread, bananas, peanut butter and jelly, or other travel food along with bottles of water. The camp rallies, and a caravan heads to the construction site. This happened three times during the week I was at Standing Rock: 300 or 400 tribal citizens and their allies rush through corn and soybean fields, and each of them are supported from coast to coast and around the world by donations of food, clothing, money, and skills. The camp is alive with volunteers at the medical clinic, the legal aid tent, and media hill. People splitting wood, working, and serving as security. There is a constant procession of speakers, singers, and poets coming through the main circle. These people go to the work zones and stop the construction that continues in spite of mounting opposition from federal agencies such as the Bureau of Indian Affairs, Department of Justice, Department of the Interior, and the Army Corps of Engineers (United States Department of Justice 2016).Numerous tribal nations have issued support and solidarity statements, as have cities and states across the country and the world. The UN has even weighed in, saying the tribe has been treated unfairly (Germanos 2016).

Despite this support, pipeline construction has [up until the time of writing, Fall 2016] continued – and so have the direct actions. A recent action resulted, once again, in turmoil as witnesses came back reporting that police had thrown an elder woman to the ground, guns with live ammo were pointed at crowds of unarmed tribal citizens with children and elders present, armored vehicles blocked both ends of the road, and a crop duster sprayed the crowd with unknown chemicals (Pember 2016). The determination of the water protectors reads clear in a social media post from Amber Knudson,

> "There were military tanks, guns possibly loaded with projectiles or tear gas, and guns loaded with bullets brought by the police.
>
> Many water protectors are arrested weekly, and yet... we are still here.
>
> [...]We will still stay, we will still fight for our water, because oil is a privilege and water is life."

References

Bernish, Claire. 2016. "Oil Company Takes Dozers on 20-Mile Detour to 'Deliberately Destroy' Ancient Native American Sites." *The Free Thought Project*, September 06. Accessed November 30, 2016. http://thefreethoughtproject.com/dakota-pipeline-destroy-native-sites/.

Dalrymple, Amy. 2016. "Pipeline route moved south of Bismarck partly because of drinking water contamination concerns." *Inforum*, August 19. Accessed November 30, 2016. http://www.inforum.com/news/4097616-pipeline-route-moved-south-bismarck-partly-because-drinking-water-contamination.

Germanos, Andrea. 2016. "UN Experts to United States: Stop DAPL Now." *Common Dreams*, September 25. Accessed November 30, 2016. http://www.commondreams.org/news/2016/09/25/un-experts-united-states-stop-dapl-now.

Goodman, Amy. 2016. "Bill McKibben: Dakota Access Pipeline Resistance Powerful Enough to Overwhelm Fossil Fuel Industry." *Democracy Now!* September 30. Accessed November 30, 2016. http://www.democracynow.org/2016/9/30/bill_mckibben_dakota_access_pipeline_resistance.

Houska, Tara. 2016. "Native American Youth to Obama: 'Rezpect' Our Water." *Indian Country Media Network*, August 11. Accessed November 30, 2016. https://indiancountrymedianetwork.com/news/native-news/native-american-youth-obama-rezpect-our-water.

Pember, Mary Annette. 2016. "Water Protectors Rounded Up After Prayers at DAPL Construction Site." *Indian Country Media Network*, September 29. Accessed November 30, 2016. http://indiancountrymedianetwork.com/news/native-news/water-protectors-rounded-after-prayers-dapl-construction-site/.

Taliman, Valerie. 2016. "Dakota Access Pipeline Standoff: Mni Wiconi, Water Is Life." *Indian Country Media Network*, August 16. Accessed November 30, 2016. http://indiancountrymedianetwork.com/news/native-news/dakota-access-pipeline-standoff-mni-wiconi-water-is-life/.

United States Department of Justice. 2016. "Joint Statement from the Department of Justice, the Department of the Army and the Department of the Interior Regarding Standing Rock Sioux Tribe v. U.S. Army Corps of Engineers." September 9. Accessed November 30, 2016. https://www.justice.gov/opa/pr/joint-statement-department-justice-department-army-and-department-interior-regarding-standing.

Cross-Border Implications

CHAPTER 9

Unbroken Connection to the Land: An Interview with Farmworker Activist Rosalinda Guillen

David Bacon

Large tracts of agricultural land offer farmers the opportunity for increased production and profit—but not without a cost. While soy, corn, and other grain farmers can purchase agricultural machinery, genetically tailored seeds, and chemical inputs, farmers of fruit, vegetables, herbs, and livestock still rely on human labor and skill. Most often, they find it in migrant and immigrant farmworkers.

The same markets that compel the intensification and consolidation of agricultural land in the United States have also pushed farmers off their land, depressed local economies, and driven massive out-migration across Latin America. For generations, displaced peasant farmers have come to the United States seeking work. They often find it on farms, where they bring extensive agricultural knowledge and appreciation for the work of growing food. However, in many cases they are confronted with dangerous working conditions and poor pay.

This interview with Rosalinda Guillen highlights the interlocking destinies of farmers and farm workers, and the ways in which the land and its people can resist the exploitation and discrimination of migrant farm work while offering a deep, restorative land ethic. And it reminds us that the knowledge and skills that farmworkers have gained over lifetimes and generations of farming is a precious resource essential for a new food system.

David Bacon (DB): Tell me about the history of your own family. They worked as farmworkers, but did they ever own land?

Rosalinda Guillen (RG): Not in my lifetime. My dad identified himself as a Tarascan indigenous person from Zacapu, Michoacan. The Guillens from Zacapu were *ejido*-type farmers and farmworkers. It appears from listening to my father's stories that the Guillens were always in leadership. My father's father, my grandfather Panfilo Guillen, was a migrant farmworker. He was part Irish. His mother was half Irish and half indigenous. I have a photo of him —he was beautiful. He ended up being a forest ranger type of person in his community, his municipality. He worked the land but he was also in charge of protecting the forests. A lot of indigenous people were cutting wood in the forest to sell, to use for themselves. It was his job to try and stop that, and they were not happy with that. So when my father was eight years old, several of the men in the village murdered my grandfather because they needed the wood.

That had a huge impact on my father's life. The family was living in Zacapu, and his mother came from a landowning family in Texas. Not by any means as big as *hacendados*. I think they were at one point, but after the Mexican-American War, they lost their land and ended up with a small piece where they grew cotton. Still, they had their own land. At the time, in the 1920s, Mexicans from the United States were considered *gringos*. My grandmother could not speak Spanish and she was in this indigenous village in Zacapu. So she was marginalized in that community.

DB: Did they speak Purépecha in that village?

RG: Yes, they did. They spoke Purépecha and Spanish, and she could speak neither. My father spoke English and Spanish. They also saw her as a very upper-class person. I have photos of my grandmother, and she was a very elegant woman. She looks very humble and like a peaceful, calm woman. She was marginalized because she was a *gringa* and of course she was with my grandfather and there was a lot of jealousy among other women that he had gone and married a *gringa*. And so when my grandfather was killed, it became very difficult for my father. He became the head of the family.

My grandmother had several brothers who were still in Texas, so her brothers arranged a marriage for her. They brought the man to Mexico. He came and got her and they married her off in Texas. That's how my father left Michoacán and came to Texas with his siblings. Her new husband was a farmworker in the United States, and there the family began the migrant circuit. My father, at the age of 10, became a farmworker, working as an adult male with his stepfather. The whole family travelled all over the United States working in the fields.

At 14 or 15 my father left the family to work on his own with other young men in similar circumstances. He travelled the migrant circuit, but with another group. In those years, they travelled in groups—families and car caravans. He made money and helped support the family. He would send money to his mother and his sisters to make sure they had what they needed, because the stepfather controlled the family's money.

Mom was 21 or 22 when she and dad got married. She first met my father when she was 14, although he didn't pay attention to her then. But then he met her again when she was 18 or 19 and they fell in love and ended up getting married in Coahuila. My mother grew up in Coahuila, on the other side of Mexico, basically as an orphan. Her mother died when she was 4 years old and her father abandoned her and her siblings. She lived on the streets in Rosita, a coal-mining town, until she was 11 years old, taking care of her brothers and sisters. Then an aunt took her in. That traumatized my mother a lot. She was already homeless, and then she was forced to abandon her brothers and sisters. Here story is very similar to dad's. He was forced to abandon his family in order to take care of them. And my mother was forced to abandon the brothers and sisters that she'd cared for all this time.

We've grown up seeing the effects of that kind of orphan childhood. My Mom has been working as an adult since she was 4 years old, and she was abandoned. Her father was in and out of her life. He, my grandfather, was Basque and my grandmother was very indigenous. We have a photo of her, and she looks like she's Kickapoo or Apache or something like that—very, very dark, with straight hair: a very indigenous woman. She's got my mother on her lap because she's the oldest. My grandfather is standing next to her, and she's sitting. He's a Spanish-looking man. They're a very different couple.

When my mother and father got married, her whole family disowned her because she married a *gringo* from Texas. They bought a piece of land in Coahuila, and they tried the migrant circuit. My dad continued working in the fields while married to mom, but he wanted her to go with him. She didn't want to, but one time she went with him in the migrant circuit that goes up into Minnesota and Wisconsin. It was a disaster. But she did live with him in Texas several times when he was working in the railroad, and that's where Elida and I were born.

DB: Why did he buy a piece of land in Coahuila? To live on or to farm?

RG: It was land to live on, and he bought it for my mother. After their disastrous experience when she went with him on the migrant circuit, she said there was no way she was going back to that country again. They had worked picking apples and cherries, tree fruits in Wisconsin. They made good money, and with the money they made they bought a car. They had driven up with other families, but they ended making enough money to buy their own car. Then they headed back to Coahuila. Mom wanted to visit her family in Texas, on the border. They were headed back and had all their money and belongings in the car. Before they left Wisconsin, they stopped at a gas station in a rural area. And I don't know what happened, but their car burst into flames. Elida was an infant then, and dad ran into the car. I was in my mother's arms. He grabbed Elida out of the car, and it exploded. They lost everything. They were left in this town with nothing except their two babies.

It was 1952 or '53, and they were scared because of the racism. Dad always talked about that. No matter where they went they encountered the racism, the attacks. When they saw large groups of white men they would all hide because there were beatings and things could happen. He talked about hangings, lynchings of Mexicans. So they were really scared. So the guy in the gas station of course came out running to them. Mom and dad didn't know what to do, how they were going to protect us. But the guy wanted to help them, and he took them inside and got on the phone. Dad thought he was going to call the police, and he told Mom, "Let's get out of here. We don't want to be with the police." But he called other people in town, and they came and helped. They put [us] up, they fed [us] and gave [us] money and clothes. They gave [my parents] enough money for a bus to get [us] to the border. It was amazing. Dad said he'd never encountered white people that were so nice to them.

Dad always told us that story to try to guard us from being racist. Racism exists. It's bad. It's almost all over the place. But every once in a while you find these white people who are not that way and you have to learn how to get along with them, because it's not 100 percent. You have to understand what racism does to people, but you have to have friends who are white, because there are good white people. That was his story to show he didn't think it was going to turn out good, but it did. Well, kind of good. But after that mom said, "No more! I'm not going back. It's too risky and we've got our daughters with us." He knew life on the road, with the labor camps and no living spaces, so they gathered enough money together—I don't know how. I have to ask mom where they got the money. But they bought a little piece of land in Coahuila for mom to live on while he was working in the fields in the United States.

She ended up farming that piece of land. It was like an *ejido*, now that I understand what an *ejido* is. She planted corn, beans, squash, and tried lots of other vegetables, once even watermelons. I remember eating them. She became quite the gardener and farmer. To keep us fed we had chickens, and of course we had a dog. It was a really cool way for us to grow up. It was her own little place, situated between two creeks, so she had access to water. Dad dug a well, and they built the house together. I remember the smells and the sounds of them working. The bricks being piled, and the cement . . . dad letting me throw the cement on the bricks. Dad built a fireplace. That's not something you have in Mexico, but she had this beautiful big fireplace, kind of pioneer style. It was big and domed, and I could walk into it. It was for cooking, and mom cooked on it a lot. We had a bookcase—something nobody else had. People used to come just to look at it.

DB: How long did you live there?

RG: Until we left, when I was 10 years old. Dad always said we were going to leave. Apparently he always told mom that as soon as he found a place for us to live in the United States, we were going to go to the United States. Dad was hardly ever there at our place with mom. The long distance connection we had to dad was a money order that arrived every week. He would show up around Christmastime or winter with gifts. Every time he came it was like a big holiday. And then he would leave. It was fine. Mom was there and she was great. She was a very easygoing Mom. She grew up as an orphan, with nothing, treated really bad by people around her, and then a very strict Catholic upbringing by her aunt who adopted her. So she never believed in religion or going to church. She allowed us to be free. We pretty much could do whatever we wanted, as long as we didn't kill ourselves. And we helped her in the garden. But then one day dad showed up. There were long conversations into the night between the two of them. And two days later we're all being packed into a car and we drove away. And that was it. First we went to Idaho where dad and mom worked in the potato [fields]. From there we went to La Conner, Washington, into the labor camp at Hulbert Farms.

There we were in Skagit County. We showed up in March, which was horrible because it was raining and wet. I was 10 years old, and that summer I was in the fields picking strawberries, just like my dad. I'm the oldest of eight, and every one of us was in the fields at 10 years old, working. Perhaps not as hard as some of the other farm working families. We lived there year around, and dad didn't believe we should work that hard, but we had to work because there were so many of us.

DB: So you'd work after school and on weekends?

RG: Sometimes not after school, depending on what was going on at school. But me and Elida and Angelica, because we were the oldest, did work weekends in the spring and sometimes in the fall if there was work. As the other kids grew, they didn't work as much as we did. But in the summers we started working the minute school was out, and we worked all summer long. That's how we bought our school clothes—coats and things like that.

DB: So you lived in the labor camp for a while and then you got your own place?

RG: Mom and Dad were saving the whole time they were in the labor camp to buy a house in town, in La Conner. So in 1967 or '68, they bought a house in town. But we lived in that labor camp even beyond that, because the house needed a lot of work for us to live in it. Dad was fixing it up a little bit at a time. We would go and live in the house in La Conner for a couple of months in the summertime when we didn't need heating. But it was a pretty old house. In fact, now it's a registered historical building.

So it was an old house. It needed insulation. It needed a foundation. It needed a new roof. All of that my father and mother fixed up, and it took years to do that. They continued living in camp into the late '70s, for 17 years.

DB: They lived in the labor camp for 17 years?

RG: The whole time dad worked for them. Dad was eventually fired from Hulbert Farms and the labor camp after 18 years working there. So they lived in that labor camp while they were working on the house. They owned the house but they would go back and forth. I left the labor camp at 17 to marry a farmworker who had come on the migrant circuit. I ran away with him. But it broke my father's heart, because he had big plans for me. He always talked about all of us going to the university. He would ask, "What are you best at? Do what makes you happy. Think about what makes you happy and that's what you will do. That's what you should do, not something that doesn't make you happy, because no matter what happens, if you're doing what makes you happy and keeps you healthy, you will make money. Because that's just the way of nature." His idea of money was not vast amounts, but enough to live well.

DB: Why did they give up the farm in Coahuila? Was it that they didn't think that owning land and having a farm was important? Or that the money in the US was better? What made them decide that it was better to be a worker for wages than a farmer on their own land?

RG: It was always a conflict because my mother wanted to stay on the land and farm. She believed that after all the time she'd been there she had been creating a life for us. We were living off the land and living well. Of course, dad was also sending money to us. But she liked the farming. My father had been a worker all his life for white growers in the United States. He was also an artist. His goal was to settle in the United States where he could work as a farmworker and paint. That's all he knew how to do, and he liked it. He liked working as a farmworker. In La Conner, he was offered a year round job and free housing, in a place close to Seattle where there was a big artistic community. La Conner in the '60s was becoming an avant-garde artist community, an avant-garde intellectual center. There were writers, poets, and artists living there. My father met them and became part of their circle, and he liked that. I think he opted for the art rather than the farming.

DB: Why did he like being a farmworker?

RG: He loved being a farmworker. He could not have been an artist or a good father if he wasn't on the land. That's what kept him sane and complete. He loved growing food, growing plants. He talked to us about it and kept journals about it. In those journals he would write, "Today I sat out in the fields. I was getting ready to go out, and the smell of the soil was this way. The birds sounded this way . . . the clouds . . . the air. Touching the soil makes me feel happy. It makes me whole." He was a person of the earth. He said, "We are people of the earth. There's no getting around it. We are people of the earth and we have to be in it." My father was a self-educated man.

DB: That's very romantic.

RG: It was very romantic. And he talked to us that way. He would say, "You are children of people of the earth. You are farmworkers. Don't let anybody make you ashamed for being that."

DB: After a lifetime spent organizing farmworkers, do you think that the way he felt is shared by a lot of other people? Or was he a unique individual in that way?

RG: When I talk to farmworkers, I think it's shared. Industrial agriculture has taken the farmworker's voice away, so we don't hear them identifying themselves as people of the earth. We have been identified as machines, as beasts of burden. It's convenient for people to identify us that way because then it's easy to exploit us. But if you're talking about a human being who can express herself or himself as a person of the earth, with this intellect and wisdom about the right way to grow food, then it's not as easy to exploit. A lot of the family farmers and growers know that the way they're growing food and treating the earth is wrong. They feel guilty, and want a buffer between them and the reality of what farmworkers will say if you give them the opportunity. You're looking at that human being every day, knowing that you are doing wrong.

My father was very vocal, and he talked to other farmworkers about it. He made them feel proud of the good work they were doing. And he made us feel proud. He would say, "This is special. What you do is a work of grace, because what you do will make somebody else healthy and whole. You are feeding humans, and nobody else is doing that except for the person growing the food or the animal." In Spanish we say *don*. It's like a big gift that you have to give. I was the oldest and I don't know if he spoke to my other brothers and sisters at length as much as he did to me about this. I have to say that when I was in the fields working, I liked it. My father would say when the soil was ploughed, "Just stand here, *mi hija*, and smell. Take a deep breath." And we would. And he would say, "This is the only time you can smell that smell." Then when you irrigate it's another different smell, but it's the same earth. It's nourishing itself. Every time is different. You know the smell of the plants when they grow and the different types of plants by touching, sitting in the fields. I've said this to many people who think of farmworkers as different, or beasts of burden or machines. "Let me explain something to you and you tell me if you're different from me. When we drive up to the field, you hire us to work and we sit in the field. We watch the sun come up, and the mist comes out of the soil, and the smells change, and the breezes come up, and the earth comes alive. And you feel an energy. Nothing else can give you that energy. And you want to get to the hoeing or whatever it is you're doing. It makes you feel good—the beauty of the earth around you, with the birds flying and the bees buzzing. There is nothing like it in the world. You know it, and I want you to know that we know it and we feel it, too. And it's wrong that you will not recognize that we are the same as you."

DB: Farm work is also exhausting and dangerous, especially if you're doing it in 105-degree heat. There are a lot of aspects to the work that are not so great. How do you reconcile that with the vision that you just painted?

RG: I reconcile it by organizing. There has been a shift in how food is grown, how the work is done, and the way we are treated. That exhaustion takes away our ability to be able to recognize Mother Earth as her own living soul that connects with us. So my personal reconciliation with it is organizing for change, to bring some balance. When I was growing up and working in the fields, I remember the exhaustion at the end of the day. I remember being so exhausted that even at the age of 16 I couldn't get the energy up to go to a dance. The only thing I could do was read, so I would stay home and read. Not because I didn't want to go to the dance, but I was too tired. Your whole body is aching and your hands are swollen from picking berries. They're black. When I was 12 or 13 years old, my 12-year-old school friends from La Conner would irritate the hell out of me. They'd come on their bikes, in their shorts—little blonde girls—and call me: "Rosalinda, Rosie, come on let's go bike riding!" And I was exhausted. "I don't want to go bike riding with you! How can you even think of going bike riding? I just worked 12 hours. I'm tired." I could see that something's off here. Something's not right. And I would talk to my dad. "There's something screwy. We're not living in the right place. Why are we in the labor camp and everybody else is in town?" So my Dad told me to read, and that's when I started reading: *1984*, *Animal Farm*.

DB: Is that also why you oppose piece rate and think that people should be paid by the hour—because of the exhaustion?

RG: The exhaustion and the pace! You have to have a pace where you can actually enjoy your work. The piece rate is all about the money. Farmworkers look at it as the way to make money. These farmworkers are recent immigrants who were family farmers in Mexico. We have to capture that feeling of loving the land before it's gone. One more generation and it's gone from these people like it's gone from us. If the piece rate doesn't end, a whole tradition is going to be lost. I know what it's like to push your body to exhaustion to earn what you should be earning anyway by the hour while enjoying the work.

Living in the labor camp, nothing there was ours. Nothing! We were landless. In Mexico, we had our place. The first thing that we realized when we got to the labor camp was that nothing was ours. We couldn't go anywhere, do anything, touch anything... It was made very clear that nothing belonged to us. That's a very dislocating feeling. You're nowhere. That had a huge impact on me. Being taken away from our land in Mexico was huge. My mother went into a deep depression and we, as children, were stunned. We refused to accept that the labor camp was a reality.

DB: Well, just to play devil's advocate here for a second: autoworkers don't own the auto plant. Longshoremen don't own the container cranes. But you don't hear people feeling alienated from the worksite— from the tools of their work and from the factory—in the same ways

you describe people feeling alienated because of not owning the land. Is there something different about working as a farmworker?

RB: Farmworkers in the United States are the largest landless workforce in the food system. We're not just landless in that we don't own the land we're working. We don't even own our own homes. The biggest issue for many farmworkers is that people expect us to live in farm labor camps. Labor camps are like a slap in the face—throwing in our faces how really landless we are, how little we count for in every way. When you live in a labor camp, the people in town know that you live there. Therefore you're something less than everybody else in the community, because you don't have a place. Some of these other workers own their homes. When you go into even rural towns there are parks named after somebody, buildings named after somebody. That's like a recognition that you're a human being that owns something in the community. For farmworkers, we're nowhere. We're not seen anywhere. We are so invisible, except for the value we bring to some landowner.

You have to have land to produce food. You have to have land to package it. You have to own the land where you put the coolers. Some landowner is receiving the value of your work. What you're getting is the opportunity to give him value, and that's it. That's what I found out. And that's wrong. I'm better than that. My father was better than that. I think about the contributions he made in spite of all of these obstacles, what he could have done, given an equitable chance in a community. To this day the museum in La Conner will not recognize him as an artist. The last fight my sister put up was trying to get him recognized at the museum in La Conner. They just courteously tell us that, well it's not the time. Our family has been in that town 50 years. They recognize us now as being members of that community, but they will not recognize my father as an artist.

As farmworkers that happens over and over again everywhere, in every community where you go. The value of what we bring to a community is blatantly waved aside. We're invisible. Our contributions are invisible. That's part of the capitalist culture in this country. We are like the dregs of slavery in this country. They're holding onto that slave mentality to try to get value from the cheapest labor they can get. If they keep us landless, if we do not have the opportunity to root ourselves into the communities in the way we want, then it's easy to get more value out of us with less investment in us. It's as blunt as that. We need to look at farmworkers in this country owning land, where we can produce. That is the dynamic change we need in the food system. We all know Cesar Chavez talked about owning the means of production. I think a lot of farmworkers talk about that. John Steinbeck's book was all about the land that they had to leave and the fact they had to work on other people's farms. That book is about the change in their value of themselves, to themselves, and to their communities, with the Great Depression and being displaced from their land. I recognized that when I read it when I was 12 years old. When I finally read *Grapes of Wrath* I understood what the labor camp was.

I told my father, "Dad! This is just wrong. Living in this labor camp is wrong. Don't you see that?" And of course all he cared about was, "I'm supporting my family. We're surviving." When he worked in the field, it was brutal, and he didn't want us to have to work like that. That's why we didn't migrate. We never migrated. We stayed on that farm and we worked on that farm.

I didn't migrate until I got married at 17 and started migrating with Danny, my husband. And then I got it. Holy crap, it was hard! Moving from town to town working, finding the labor camp. Walking into these dirty, stinky wood cabins and trying to cook and clean, and then go back to work . . . it was exhausting, and I was only 17, 18, 19 years old.

DB: How long did you do that?

RG: I spent five years migrating, and then five additional years working in the fields in Walla Walla and living in a labor camp. After that I had an opportunity to work in a bank. Through affirmative action they were forced to hire another Mexican. When I started working in the bank, I just focused on making money and building a career. I didn't think about farm work or farmworkers until I started organizing with the Rainbow Coalition. Then everything started coming back—the way conditions were for farmworkers when I was a farmworker, and the way they are now. It's really worse now than what it was then in the lack of respect. I was ridiculed because I was a farmworker and a child of a farmworker. You know the looks people give. "Oh that's just his daughter." I know what it's like. It's much worse now because it's more overt—the racism and disdain and the invisibility, and still we're landless. It's more direct, and easier to do now. Couple that with the lack of regulation—there's just no enforcement. Anything to do with farmworker policy or rights is a huge joke. We're a joke and the growers have total control. Piece rate wage rates are legal. The fact that the dehumanization and exploitation of farmworkers through the piece rate process has been institutionalized through the legislative process is a perfect example.

DB: In California, there are many *colonias*, or communities of people, where farmworkers, who were mostly farmers in Mexico, are living out of doors under trees. People don't even have a labor camp, let alone

an apartment or other kind of housing. Yet they are working. I think this is growing. It wasn't nearly this bad 30 years ago when I was an organizer for the farmworkers union. In Washington State do you see people living out of doors like that?

RG: Yes, there are places like that in Washington, but it's seasonal here. It hasn't gotten to the point that is has in California because the labor camp system is still prevalent here. It's easier to be homeless in California because of the weather. Weather here prevents that from happening as much. But I know that in the '50s in Washington state many farmworkers had to live outdoors. My first husband, Danny Torres, told me this story once about his mother, who had a baby in a hospital in the Walla Walla area while they were working. I believe they were cutting mint in a field in eastern Washington. After she had the baby she had to come back from the hospital to a tent by the field where they were living. His father was alcoholic, so the kids were working to support the whole family. Danny was 6 years old. The baby starved to death in that tent. A year later she had another infant that died of the flu because they didn't have the money for a doctor, and again they were living in a tent. For many years his family lived in those canvas tents.

Farmworkers being a landless people in the United States leaves them in a much more vulnerable position, and in the US this is easily ignored. It doesn't even come into a discussion on a policy level or a social level. And we can go all the way back to our land being taken from us in Texas, Arizona, New Mexico, and California. It's a legacy of that conquest, and we've accepted it. We don't talk about a way for us not to be landless. What would that look like? I went to the World Social Forum in Brazil and met with the leaders of the landless workers' movement. We've had ongoing conversations since then, and they've come to visit us.

I think we need to occupy. Farmworkers need to take land. We need to start getting a taste of that. We need to start occupying farming land, agricultural land, and farming it. Land that is not being used, that's just sitting idle. We're thinking about that. What would be the pushback, and is the pushback worth it? Because we've tried everything . . . We've tried doing the right thing and earning enough money to buy land. USDA has programs supposedly so that Latino farmers can own land. But you end up with maybe a few Latino farmers farming the traditional conventional way. Latino farmworkers become Latino farmers who hire Latino farmworkers and exploit them. That's wrong. That's not what we want. We want to change the whole system. So what's it going to take?

DB: You've now spent over 30 years as an organizer, essentially organizing farmworkers into unions—United Farm Workers, Chateau Ste. Michelle, Sakuma Bros. Farms, and *Familias Unidas*. In other words, fighting over the actual conditions that people are working in, as well as the housing that people are living in. How does that relate to this problem of being landless? On a day-to-day concrete level, you really are organizing people more in terms of their existence as wageworkers.

RG: That's right, and I think that's the big recognition. I didn't start organizing until I was 40 years old. Now I'm 65, so that's 25 years. I don't think that's very long. I don't think I can say I'm an organizer, and then run a campaign, win a union contract like Chateau Ste. Michelle, and then I'm done. That is just barely touching the surface. What's clear, even with Chateau Ste. Michelle, is if you don't own the means of production in some way, you're always under attack. You always have to fight for that contract renegotiation. It's like an election campaign. Every two years you have to win the votes again, convince the workers again, you have to always be wary about the employer.

I think what I've learned is if you're an organizer, you have to evolve with the political moments that keep coming at you. If you continue organizing then you know that the longer you do it, the more you're digging into the fundamental causes of the oppression your people are under. If you don't address those fundamental causes there is no way organizing is going to change anything. To me, that is the crux of the matter. Just what are we doing as organizers? Are we enabling systems to continue the way they are? If I'm going to be a lifetime organizer, what fundamental change has been made? It's not enough to say we've got X number of union contracts. Because you know what? Those workers are still in a fight. They're fighting every day for their existence. It's a little bit less of a fight. Maybe it's easier. Maybe their children are moving away from the fields and learning that we don't want to be people of the land anymore.

I don't think that should be our goal. Our goal should be to be proud of a tradition of growing food with dignity. That's the next step. As an organizer, I can't see continuing to do the type of organizing we're doing if we're not going to have fundamental change. And there can be no fundamental change if we are not taking the land to show what the possibilities are. We have no chance to show it otherwise. They want us to fit into the mold, with these huge mortgages, high interest rates—lots of money. And they know that's not possible. Farmworkers can't sustain that. We are poor people. It becomes another slap on the face. "It's not our fault, it's your fault. You just can't seem to get it together."

So how do we take the land?

DB: You talk about farmworkers having to become the owners of the land or the owners of the means of production as workers. What does that mean?

RG: I'm specifically talking about land ownership. And when I talk about production, it's about owning your work and your time—developing alternatives that will change the system. But we know we can't develop those alternatives in small numbers. One of the things I've learned from the Landless People's Movement is the way they own their means of production by developing worker-owned cooperatives for everything that they need: services, materials, products. What they use they make themselves in worker owned cooperatives. They become the consumer, but also sell these things outside of their solidarity economy circle. They're looking for ways to develop that solidarity economy. They've done a really good job developing a large model in Brazil through those efforts.

So we're looking for a way to do that. How do we make it possible for farmworkers to own their means of production, and what does it take to get to that point? The first thing we have to do is to take away the fear that exists in the farmworker community. People fear something other than working in the fields as hired workers for farmers. That's where the organizing comes in, and the fundamental education or *formación*, as we call it—the consciousness of looking at other options. What I'm finding in talking to farmworkers is they actually have alternatives in their heads. They know ways to create those alternatives, but they're just afraid to try. They have not been given the opportunity and the resources.

How can farmworkers begin to develop alternatives as worker-owners of whatever enterprise they want to take on? We're looking at different options for land ownership through community land trusts. How we can buy 500 acres, for example, for food production and homes and facilities for farmworkers to work on that land. How do you govern something like that? How do you set it up? Through existing structures or developing new structures? If a group of bold workers say we want to farm this land, can they just to take it and occupy it and farm it? See what happens? That's what we're learning from the Landless Workers' Movement—that's how they started in Brazil. They started that process during a dictatorship. But when I look at the conditions they were in, and the conditions we're in in the United States, they're really not much different.

In Brazil they were working with millions of people. We're talking about a more manageable number of farmworkers in the United States—maybe two-and-a-half to three million max. For me the saddest thing is that there isn't enough unity among the few farmworker leaders across the country.

Farmworker leaders in the United States today are like an old guard. We're from another generation. We each have our own ideas, and we come from different organizing models that have certain demands we've learned from those organizing models. Some of the older farmworker leaders are very comfortable with what they're doing. They have been validated by a lot of people who tell them that they did the right thing. I'm not saying they're wrong. What I'm saying is, is it enough? Is it going in the right direction? Is it time to change our tactics and our strategies?

What some farmworker leaders call changing tactics and strategies is actually conforming to what the corporate food regime wants us to do. For example, recruit workers in Mexico and bring them up here as H-2A workers. That supposedly alleviates the pain and the suffering of farmworkers because they don't have to run and hide from Border Patrol. But there are already three million farmworkers in the United States, who are mostly undocumented. They're already here and they need to work. It's the system that's keeping them back, so why capitulate to the system to end pain and suffering? We don't want to just reduce pain and suffering—we want to change the system and stop it. We don't want to create another system that will lead to more pain and suffering in the future.

We need bold tactics. That could be occupying land and testing that tactic, to see what happens. Would it make people pay attention, to see that we are a landless workforce and deserve better than what we have? It wasn't Felimon's (a farmworker and Vice President of *Familias Unidas Por la Justicia*) fault that NAFTA (the North American Free Trade Agreement) took effect and he was displaced. He can no longer farm his land in Oaxaca. So now he's here, and by God, now he sees a piece of land and he's going to take it. This way we call attention to some of the fundamental causes of farmworker suffering and exploitation in this country.

DB: Out of those, say, two-and-a-half million farmworkers in the United States, a third—or probably almost half of them—work in California, and land there is monopolized. California agriculture is based on huge tracts of land that belong to private owners. Unless you can find some different land to occupy, you're talking about the land that already belongs to somebody else. Even if you pulled those workers out of that system and found some other land, as you say yourself, those growers would simply start an H-2A program[1] or find some other farmworkers. There we would be again, with another 750,000 farmworkers in California in the same conditions.

---

[1] The H-2A visa allows US agricultural employers to bring in foreigners for temporary or seasonal work.

RG: I see this change being a process of challenging the status quo. There can be no development of solutions or answers with clarity that consumers will understand, and that family farmers in the US can understand, without those solutions being manifested in some way. Maybe the first manifestation is not going to be a solution, but a drastic demonstration of the current exploitation and a demand that people listen. It's calling out these corporate agricultural giants about what they have done—not just to the farmworkers, but also to the rest of the communities around them. It isn't just farmworkers who are suffering from the corporate takeover of the food system. They taint everything. Food is grown with toxic chemicals and slave labor. It's going to have to be a very public challenge. Like anything else, it will depend on the support we get from consumers and people of good conscience, and how strong that support is. We have to take a chance. I've learned this from farmworkers themselves across the years. The strawberry campaign was a good example. If the union had done what the farmworkers wanted, we could have won. But the majority of the leaders hold back because we think we know the system more, or we know the danger that's coming. We think that gives us the right to hold back.

DB: What did the workers want to do that they were being held back from?

RG: They wanted to keep organizing, to keep the campaign going, to keep having elections whether they won or lost. They wanted to constantly challenge the agricultural industry, and we didn't sustain it. I don't know that we could or couldn't have, but I feel like we didn't try. If farmworkers are willing to lead that effort, we should stand by them. That's the one thing I've learned from my years of organizing at Chateau Ste. Michelle. We did it to a certain extent, just because they were leading and we were there to support them. They had enough support and we won. What was missing with the Chateau Ste. Michelle campaign was broader education about the food system, about corporate exploitation. Without that, what you got was a union contract for less than 200 families, and it was neatly contained to that.

Meanwhile, everything around them is going to shit. Farmworkers are worse off. We have more pesticides and more exploitation. But that contract is there. That's not good enough. With Community to Community and our alliances with the US Food Sovereignty Alliance, the Domestic Fair Trade Association, and others, we are expanding our vision of where we are as farmworkers. Why do we keep losing? It's not our fault. It's not because we're not good enough or not brave enough or not smart enough or not strong enough. It's because the system is created so that we can't win. So what new system do we have to develop for ourselves that we know works for us? And how can we make it grow? It's like a virus or a disease. If we grow it and we get it out there to enough farmworkers, people will be attracted to what's good and safe, and will help them live a good life. I firmly believe that if we have those options out there, people will gravitate towards them and will fight for them.

I've seen it in *Familias Unidas por la Justicia*. They say *"hasta el fin."* They know that where they are now is bad. They will fight to fix it until the end. And what is the end? To them, winning is fighting with dignity. So as long as they're fighting with dignity they don't see a loss. They've told me that. *Hasta el fin*. That means you're standing up with your dignity and you keep looking for another option, because in their minds there's always something else out there. If we stand true and we have our dignity, we will find that way. The only other *fin* is death. If they're killed, that's ok too because they tried. You talk to Felimon Pineda, president of the *Familias Unidas* union, and it's Zapata[2] all over again. He's actually reading the history of Zapata and taking strategic ideas from what they did then. All sorts of things can happen if you just take action. You can't over-analyze, over-predict, or be fearful that if we do this, people are going to get hurt. No matter what we do, if it's not part of the status quo, people are going to get hurt.

DB: Do you think that private ownership of land in big chunks by big corporations is part of the problem?

RG: Yes, it is totally part of the problem. This country no longer has a family farming system because of that. Family farmers did not fight hard enough to stop the monopolization of land ownership in this country. There are groups, like the National Family Farm Coalition and Family Farm Defenders, which are very militant. They're fighting to keep the land they have, and trying to protect land taken away from other farmers. Farmworkers are not the only ones who understand this problem. Many family farmers could be our partners in this fight to break up the ownership of land. People have broken up banks and stopped the monopolization of other businesses in this country. They should do the same thing with land. Land should be broken up. African Americans are talking about reparations. Land should be given back to the Native Americans, and restored to their traditional growing areas.

We've got to restore our food system to what it needs to be. People are dying because the food we're eating is shit. When I think about the way sausages are made, with the meat that's used and chickens and bones,

---

[2] Emiliano Zapata was a leader of the Mexican Revolution and of a peasants' movement for land reform.

it's just disgusting the way processed food is made and sold today. There's got to be a big change. So who's going to lead that change? You can say whatever you want about the United Farm Workers, but it was a group of farmworkers that were fearless. They went out in their rickety old cars and stood in front of grocery stores and said, "Don't buy those grapes because I'm the one getting exploited." That created a big shift in people, in people's minds, about the food they were looking at, even if it was just a grape. We can do that again.

That's what *Familias Unidas* is doing. Ramon was standing in front of Whole Foods in Bellingham just this last Wednesday telling people, "Don't eat those strawberries because when you eat them you're hurting me and my people. You see that family right there? They picked them. They're being exploited." Some people were really offended, because they can't take it. But they need to see it. They need to see the fact of the exploitation that goes into the food they're eating. It's going to take us farmworkers to do it again.

Maybe that's what we need to do to wake up a lot of family farmers. Ramon said he recognized several Whatcom County farmers there. They were shocked, but they didn't oppose what he was saying. They were just totally stunned by listening to the farmworkers. They're used to having farmworkers in their fields be submissive and quiet, doing exactly what they want. Here was a group of farmworkers standing up for themselves and being very strong. That's the only way you can change things. And it has to be changed in people's minds first, before you can go out and really do something that will change a system.

DB: What do you think the connection is between the movement for food justice and immigrant rights?

RG: In our minds it's the same movement. You can't separate the two. During the hunger strikes at the detention centers we get reports from the immigrant workers inside about the way their food is doled out to them by calorie count. The food is this horrible processed food, with no salt, no pepper, and no seasoning. It's the cheapest, most easily prepared processed foods they can give them.

Everybody eats. In the United States the immigration system is fed by the displacement of landowner-workers. They were landowners in Mexico and South America, and because of the trade agreements that started in 1994 with NAFTA, workers in South America and Mexico were displaced and moved to the North. Now many are sitting in detention centers. A lot of these workers are professional farmers; they know how to grow food with no chemicals, how to conserve water, how to take care of the land. We desperately have to find a way to change this system now, and to organize these family farmers from South America before they lose that knowledge. Their children are already losing it. We are one generation away from losing that knowledge of how to grow food. It's a big challenge. No more thinking that we have a lot of time. The corporate food regime is poisoning the earth and the water to levels where we may not be able to grow food on some land for a long time, in some places never. So we have to challenge the status quo in ways that people may think is not appropriate, or is offensive. But it is what it is. And we can only take so much.

DB: When you say changing the system, are you talking about capitalism?

RG: Yes. You cannot look at producing food simply for the profit that it's going to make. That's where we are right now. The production of food is based on how much money a farmer or a corporation can make from the food they're growing. Farmworkers are a liability in their financial statements. There is no investment going into us because they don't believe we're worth investing in. In the capitalist system we are disposable and easily replaceable, and have been especially because of the trade agreements. The guest worker program is a good example. We're disposable. You can bring people in and ship 'em out and make money off of them. It's time to end that. We're human beings and we're part of the community. We eat too, like everybody else. Cesar [Chavez] said it: we can't afford the very food we grow. Like these organic carrots. A farmworker can't come and pay the price for these fresh carrots, and they grow 'em! It's totally off balance. It's unsafe, unsustainable, inhumane, and unhealthy for everybody—for people, for animals, for the earth.

Farmworkers are the first ones to feel that unhealthy situation, with the pesticides and the broken backs and bones because of the production standard set by the piece rate wage process. We have to be the first ones to speak out because we're the first ones to die. The average lifespan of a farmworker is 49 years. Two years up from what it was in year 2000. Then it was 47. Yay. We're up to 49.

DB: Are organic farms better places for farmworkers to work?

RG: They are better places because the farmworkers are not exposed to chemicals. But that's it. There are very few farmers we know who treat their workers with respect and pay decent wages. There's no job security. There are no benefits.

There's maybe a little more respect, because the worker can use the skills he already knew about how to grow food without chemicals. Many small- to mid-size organic farms have improved their production because they've let farmworkers use their skills. But they're not recognizing the workers for those skills or paying them more for them. Workers get a little more pleasure because they get to maybe farm a bit more than they would in an industrial production farm. But the vast majority of organic farmers do not treat workers any differently than conventional farms.

Driscoll's has organic agriculture. It's just industrial organic. The only difference is the worker is not exposed to chemicals. I don't think worker safety is any better because the production standards are still there. There's no relief and no benefits. Farmworkers still injure themselves to try to earn a little bit more than minimum wage by pushing their bodies faster, so it's not any better.

I'm running out of time. I'm 65. Do I have enough organizers ready to take on the tough work that I know I can't do because of my age? Yeah, it's tough. Some people think I'm crazy because of what I think. That's alright! I accept that because it's the right way to think, I'm a farmworker!

CHAPTER 10

From US Farm Crisis to the *Cerrado* Soy Frontier:

Financializing Farming and Exporting Farmers

Andrew Ofstehage

Is the US Exporting Its Farmers?

"Is the US exporting its farmers?" read the headline of the August 2002 cover story of *The Progressive Farmer*. The article covered three Mississippi Delta farmers who migrated to Brazil in response to chaotic farm policy, high land and production costs, and a lack of security in the United States farm sector (Shute 2011). On an agricultural tour of Brazil, they saw thriving rural communities, cheap land, and boundless fields of soy. They decided to join the Brazilian soy boom; just months later, they were landowners in the Brazilian *Cerrado*. By acquiring land in foreign countries, taking it away from local use, and incorporating it into the global agrifood economy, these migrant US farmers are part of the global land grab. But in contrast to many instances of land grabbing, these farmers are individuals, not corporations. While they are economically privileged in relation to local Brazilian landowners, they are not wealthy elites on a global scale. Moreover, they are not focused exclusively on return on investment. Rather, they are farmers interested in agricultural production and continued engagement with farming.

Soy production in the Brazilian *Cerrado*—like the mono-production of other commodities carried out on grabbed land around the globe—causes indisputably negative social and ecological impacts. However, this chapter argues that the migrant US farmers are not only perpetrators of the destructive expansion of soy production in Brazil, but also products of a farm crisis in the US. This crisis, spurred by the financialization of agriculture, has limited farming opportunities for young, beginner, and under-capitalized farmers. Thus, the migration of US farmers to Brazil underscores both the difficulty of farming in the United States, and the negative ramifications of the global tendency towards financialization.

Since the early 2000s, dozens of US farmers have followed the same path as these three farmers, from the US to the Brazilian *Cerrado*. Prior to purchasing land in Brazil, the migrant soy farmers I encountered were primarily young (25 to 35 years old at the time of migration), did not own land in the US (with some exceptions), and had little financial capital. One Idaho farmer, for instance, chose to migrate to Brazil after realizing he could "go broke farming in Idaho or go broke farming in Brazil," so he might as well give Brazil a shot. An Illinois farmer toured the Brazilian *Cerrado*, where he saw cheap land, productive fields, and a much better labor to profit ratio; he subsequently invested in several thousand hectares of *Cerrado* farmland. Some saw a chance to live out a page from *The National Geographic* by "roughing it" in Brazil, and a few perceived a spiritual calling in the plowing of *Cerrado* land and in the preaching to Brazilian farmers. Still others migrated to turn a quick profit. Regardless of their religious zeal, sense of adventure, or nose for profit accumulation, migrant farmers shared a view that they could no longer fulfill their vision of farming in the United States (Ofstehage 2016). Each migrant farmer's story is different, but *crisis* is the common thread in their narratives.

Taken at face value, US farmer migration to Brazil is the triumph of American-style farming and agrarian entrepreneurship. A deeper analysis, however, suggests that their migration is a response to and continuation of a twenty-first century farm crisis characterized by agricultural financialization (Ofstehage, In Press). While the flight of American farmers to Brazil is not a dominant trend, it is indicative of the extreme land access and economic challenges that young US farmers are facing, and

FIGURE 1: Is the US exporting its farmers?

of the profound ramifications it has on both US and international agricultural systems. This chapter begins with a discussion of farm crisis in the US, offers two profiles of migrant US farmers to Brazil, and concludes with a discussion of necessary political changes needed to rethink land access and stop the negative social and ecological ramifications of agricultural financialization. It is based on fourteen months of ethnographic fieldwork I carried out in the Brazilian *Cerrado*.

Since the 1980s farm crisis, agriculture in the United States has undergone profound social, economic, agronomic, and cultural changes. While these changes have allowed a niche of well-resourced, established farmers to flourish, they simultaneously make it difficult for farmers to succeed on small pieces of land and push land prices up. This creates a high barrier of entry for beginner and young farmers, and poses a challenge to farmers who do not have the resources to scale-up. The National Young Farmers' Coalition found in 2011 that three major obstacles to beginner farmers are capital, land, and healthcare (Shute 2011; see also Hachmyer this volume). This chapter outlines how land access, in particular, constrains farmers' decisions and has global implications. To understand the extent of agrarian change in rural America, and the emergence of transnational farmers, I return to the 1980s farm crisis.

1980s Farm Financial Stress

The term "farm crisis" often brings to mind 1980s instances of farm loss, along with memories of the Reaganomics that produced it, and Willie Nelson's Farm Aid, designed to counter it. However, the current situation of farming in the US in many ways mirrors and extends the 1980s farm crisis. The innocuous term "farm financial stress" characterizes the 1980s farm crisis as marked by increasingly heavy debt loads, decapitalization of agriculture, and low commodity prices (Buttel 1989). The debt load of the US farm sector nearly doubled from 1972 to 1982 (Buttel 1989) and debt/asset ratios (see Figure 2) skyrocketed in the mid-1980s (USDA Economic Research Service 2016) as debt increased and farm assets such as land and machinery lost value. Farmland value in Iowa, Illinois, Nebraska, Indiana, Ohio, and Minnesota decreased by more than 39 percent from 1981-85. Reduced inflation and rising interest rates further compounded the high debt burden and declining asset value of US farmers (Buttel 1989).

Farm financial stress led to bank foreclosures on farms throughout rural America, particularly in the Midwestern states of Illinois, Indiana, Iowa, Wisconsin, and Minnesota (Buttel 1989). The liberal lending policies of

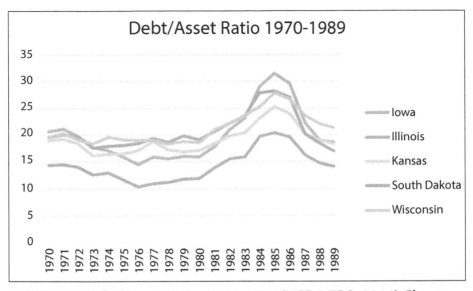

FIGURE 2: Debt/Asset Ratio 1970-1989 (USDA ERS, 2016) Chart created by author.

the 1970s Farmers Home Administration (FHA) abruptly ended in the 1980s as the administration tightened lending and substantially raised interest rates. Faced with low crop prices and high interest rates in the early 1980s, many farmers took out mortgages on their farms through FHA, the lender of last resort. Continued farm financial stress coupled with stricter enforcement of loan repayment led to a rash of foreclosures. Kathryn Dudley recounts how one family, the Porters, descended from the prosperity and security they experienced during the 1970s. Rising interest rates and poor harvests in 1982 and 1983 led them to take out a new loan to cover seeds and inputs in 1984. The loan consolidated their new debt with the mortgage on their farm. Over the years, their interest rates climbed from an initial six percent to 11 percent in 1984, then to eighteen and nineteen percent in 1985. With weekly debt payments reaching an untenable $1000, they turned to the FHA to alleviate their debt. The Porters were able to continue farming, barely breaking even, but they did so under the strict supervision of the FHA, who required approval for all seed, fertilizer, and pesticide purchases (Dudley 2000).

Many families were not as fortunate as the Porters. Farm foreclosures became the sites not only of economic insolvency, but also personal and community trauma. Farm sales auctioned away farmers' means of production alongside relics of family farming traditions. Communities fractured as foreclosed farmers blamed predatory banks, and surviving farmers blamed their neighbors' lack of frugality. In the worst of cases, farmers took their own lives (Dudley 2000).

Studies in Wisconsin, Georgia, North Dakota, and Texas found involuntary farm exit rates of 2 to 3.4 percent (Bentley et al. 1989). The incongruous term "farm loss" also meant the loss of a desired occupation, farm property, steady income, and even a home. While the farm crisis did not lead to a mass exodus of farmers (Buttel 1989), it did redefine the work, values, and relations of farm families as farmers changed management styles, became part-time workers, and engaged with government farm support (Barlett 1993). Farmers forsook agrarian values of autonomy from the state and market, connection to nature, deep religious beliefs, sense of accomplishment derived from farming, and occupational identity in favor of industrial values of personal success, financial security, engagement with the market and state, and conspicuous consumption. The economic pressures of the farm crisis on households resulted in a clash of industrial and agrarian values as families took on increasing debt, which in turn required many to participate either in part-time wage labor and/or state-directed credit programs to pay it off (Barlett 1993). Farmers in Barlett's study de-emphasized community, stewardship, and religion, while financial security gained greater importance.

Agricultural crises are a re-occurring aspect of modern agriculture, but the nature of the 1980s farm crisis is unique. It was not associated with a plant disease, like the Irish Potato Famine, or a drought, like the Dust Bowl. It was a financial crisis. Decapitalization of agriculture, rising farm debt, and low commodity prices led to the farm crisis and farm financial stress. However, while farmland regained value, commodity prices rose, and farm debt and debt/asset ratios fell, the socio-cultural changes of the 1980s farm crisis have proved lasting. Wendell Berry feared that businesspersons and technicians would replace farmers; the farm crisis of the 1980s accelerated this process (1977).

Farm Financialization

The 1980's farm crisis accelerated changes in American agriculture, which granted the market a profound role in everyday rural life. It also spurred the creation of Farm Aid; a trio of Hollywood films on the plight of US farmers (*Country*, *Places in the Heart*, and *The River*); and a number of proposed Congressional farm relief acts. The current farm crisis, characterized by financialization, has also continued to deepen the role of the market in rural life, but it has received little public attention outside of farming communities and academic circles. On its face, the US agricultural economy is strong for family farmers. Ninety-six percent of US farm entities are family farms, and their production accounts for 87 percent of US crop production by value (MacDonald, Korb, and Hoppe 2013). However, the loose definition of "family farm"—"any farm where the majority of the business is owned by the operator and individuals related to the operator, including relatives who do not live with the operator" (Hoppe 2014, p. 56)—belies the vast difference in small, medium, and large-scale farms. The US agricultural sector had a net income of $118 billion in 2011, and large- and very large-scale family farms accounted for 35 percent of the value of production while accounting for only 2 percent of total farms. Midsize family farms accounted for 5.7 percent of farms and 24.8 percent of value of production, while small-scale, sales-based farms accounted for 31.5 percent of farms and only 11.9 percent of value of production (Hoppe 2014). Small-scale farmers are facing great challenges, and this is particularly true for young and beginning farmers. Like all farmers, young and beginning farmers face the everyday agronomic difficulties of weather, soil health, and pest management, but their biggest concerns, as mentioned above, are capital, land access, and health care. The financialization of farming has limited their access to land and their opportunities to farm profitably or to farm at all.

Financialization, following Greta Krippner's definition, is "the tendency for profit making in the economy to occur increasingly through financial channels rather than through productive activities" (Krippner 2011, p. 4). In the context of agriculture, financialization is experienced in terms of value, social relations, and practices, as well as profit accumulation. There is a tendency for capitalist value to take precedence over other forms of value (i.e. the preference of profit over land stewardship) and for a stronger tendency towards commodification of land and labor. We also see financialization of social relationships, in which the family is no longer the primary unit of production.

Financialization has been critiqued as fuzzy and ahistorical—Ouma (2016) argues for a greater focus on "the situated modes, processes and practices of financial economization that have reworked organizations, economic relations, labor and nature at specific historical conjunctures" (p. 83). Financialization is neither entirely new nor a force in itself, however, I make use of the term to identify a *process* of insertion of finance into agrarian life. It is the process of financializing practices, land, and value on which I focus here, not financialization as an outside force acting upon agrarian life.

In the face of increasing worries regarding the fate of Wall Street in the years leading up to the 2008 financial crisis, investors added agricultural land to their investment portfolios. Encouraged by high commodity prices and the perception that agricultural production was "safe," investors purchased land to lease out to farmer-renters or to operate themselves via hired farm managers and workers. Each strategy hinged on the principle that land operates simultaneously as a financial asset and a means of production, and therefore contributed to the historical financialization of land (Fairbairn 2014). Wall Street investments can negatively affect farming realities by disrupting farmland markets, and raising floor prices for land. Moreover, land acquired as an investment can be securitized and sold in markets instantaneously for financial gain, decoupling an illiquid asset from production and making it a liquid asset ready for rapid sale and resale (Fairbairn 2014).

Family farming has persisted in the US despite repeated crises and the current financialization of agriculture. Self-exploitation by farmers (responding to low farm gate prices by reducing compensation), the inherent riskiness of agriculture, and lack of short-term profit opportunities generally make farm production an unappealing investment, even while farmland purchase remains appealing to investors. They profit from farmland rent, while deferring the most severe risk to farmers until they can sell the land for speculative profit. Further, private farmland investors are re-framing the meaning of land, production, and farming:

> Based upon the logic that small family farms are backward and inefficient, financial actors frame their activities as socially necessary investments that will modernize agriculture and solve the contemporary food crisis. . . they consider the concentration of family farms into larger industrial operations as a solution to Malthusian scarcity and a positive contribution to society (Isakson 2014, p. 768).

Farmland financialization is not expressed via disrupted land markets and inflated land value, but in re-appropriation of the meaning of land for finance. The financialization crisis of agriculture is twofold. First, it is an economic crisis in which beginning farmers with less access to capital have less access to farmland. Second, it is a cultural crisis in which farmland loses non-capitalist value (e.g. as a site for carrying out preferred occupation or as the location for producing desired—or even nutritionally- or socially-necessary—food products), in favor of capitalist notions of value (e.g. efficiency, profitability, and modernity).

Even as the number of small farms grows, reversing a decades-long trend of small farm loss, farmland continues to be consolidated in the hands of a few large holders. The long-term decline of small farms reversed trends in the 2000s as the number of farms with 0-49 acres of cropland grew from 43.7 million in 2001 to 51.5 million in 2011. During the same time, mean farm size shrank only from 235 acres per farm to 234 acres per farm. However, the share of farmland held by large farms rose sharply. The percentage of farmers with greater than 2000 acres of cropland grew from 1.7 to 2.2 percent, and their share of US farmland grew from 24.1 to 34.3 percent (MacDonald et al. 2013). MacDonald and co-authors argue that higher rates of return, labor-saving technologies, and federal farm policies support farm consolidation, while the growth of small farms is probably due to the growth of "lifestyle farmers" who farm small acreages but primarily generate income from off-farm work (2013). Appropriation of land by large-scale farms limits land availability, especially to under-capitalized beginner farmers. Iowa farmers reported in 2012 that, despite average farmland values near $9,000/acre, one of the main limits on purchasing land was not cost but availability (Duffy 2013).

Farmers experience financialization through decreasing land accessibility as well as changes in crop specialization, technology, and government policy. Farmers shift away from integrated crop-livestock operations and complex crop rotations towards simplified rotations and crop-livestock separation and specialization. Technology, including genetically modified seed and GPS-guided machinery, and changes in farming practices (herbicide use and no-tillage) have controversial impacts on farmers and agro-ecologies, but reduce on-farm labor requirements, and thus encourage farmers to expand acreages and pursue off-farm work. Federal policies that inject capital into the farm sector and reduce financial risk for crop production may have also encouraged investment in farmland (MacDonald et al. 2013). While consolidating, family farms are taking on corporate business forms. Forty-three percent of US farm production in 2007 originated from corporate farms and farm partnerships, up from thirty-four percent in 1982 (O'Donoghue et al. 2011).

While farm consolidation and corporatization limit land availability, farmland value increases have accelerated (Gunnoe 2014). Average farmland prices plummeted during the 1980s farm crisis and have steadily risen since, reaching nearly $2,000/acre in 2009 (Nickerson et al. 2012). Farmland values are considerably higher on highly productive land. Poor-quality land in Indiana, for example, sold for an average of $5,750/acre in 2013, while top-quality land sold for an average of $9,177/acre, up 19.1 percent from 2012 (Dobbins and Cook 2013). Iowa farmland registered a state average of $8,296 in 2010. Iowan agricultural producers cited high commodity prices, low interest rates, cash/credit availability, and lack of land availability as key factors in the rising cost of land (Duffy 2013). Tellingly, rent-to-value ratios are falling and farmland value increases have exceeded increases in farm income (Nickerson et al. 2012). Rent-to-value indicates the time necessary for farmland rental to pay for the cost of land—a lower rent-to-value suggests that farmland value is not in line with income from agricultural production and thus, likely to be influenced by non-agricultural factors. In other words, farmland value is becoming priced beyond the reach of production farmers because it is increasingly unrelated to farm income.

The financialization of farming is not limited to farmland. Labor is increasingly hired out, minimized, and simplified. Financialization entails a distancing of farmer from food and land (Clapp 2014), as complex socio-physical systems are broken down into abstract financial components (e.g. wage labor, land price, commodity price, etc.). Changes in farming practices have reduced on-farm labor requirements: today, 91 percent of soy, 70 percent of cotton, and 52 percent of corn is herbicide tolerant. Fifty-one percent of cotton and 49 percent of corn is insect-resistant (O'Donoghue et al. 2011). Each of these genetically modified traits reduces labor. It also simplifies agricultural work and expertise. Farmers have also shifted towards reduced tillage systems, which greatly reduce labor requirements. From 1982 to 2007, operator labor fell by 40 percent and hired labor fell by 37 percent (MacDonald et al. 2013). The operator and spouse conduct three-fifths of labor on "small" farms, one-half of labor on "medium-sized" farms, and 11 percent of labor on farms with sales exceeding $1 million (MacDonald et al. 2013). In addition to farm labor, 40 percent of US farmers worked off-farm for at least 200 days per working year; indeed many rely on this labor for financial survival (MacDonald et al. 2013).

In summary, farm financialization is a trend taking activities away from production and focusing on financial channels. Inflated land prices better reflect their status as speculative assets than means of production. Family farms are re-organizing as corporations and partnerships in which farmers hire out farm labor in favor of office or off-farm work. Even values of agriculture are shifting as farmers adopt industrial and capitalocentric values of farming (Barlett 1993; Gibson-Graham 2006). Financialization extends beyond the means by which people pursue profit—it affects the very meaning of work, land, and social relations. The reality of farming imagined by Wendell Berry includes a farm family unit conducting farm work while maintaining the land and community as stewards. This vision is ceding as work becomes wage labor, land becomes commodified, and value becomes simplified from many values to capitalist value. Returning to Brazil, we can see both the response to this process and its continuation.

Farm Crisis and Soylandia

US farmers have been migrating to Brazil for decades. A group of US Mennonites migrated to Goiás, Brazil in 1968 to pursue greater cultural autonomy and economic security. In Goiás, they were able to find cheap land and, more importantly, autonomy in educational curricula and exemption from military service. The more recent migration of farmers, from 2001-2005, however, is a disarticulated collection of family farmers hailing primarily from the Midwest, but also Idaho and upstate New York. They report migrating for a number of reasons, but all refer to the difficulty of accessing land and farming profitably in the US. Two migrant farmer career histories demonstrate the situation of farmers in the US farm system prior to their migration, as well as the changes they have made since migration:

Leon

Prior to moving to Brazil, Leon was a young, small-scale edible bean and sugar beet farmer in Idaho.[3] Unlike many other migrants to Brazil interviewed for this study, he had land, but his 600-acre farm suffered through four consecutive years of financial loss from 2002-06, and he found that he could not continue to farm at a loss. Improving the economic situation of his farm would have required an expansion of his acreage, but land prices were high, and Leon did not want to incur an unmanageable debt load. Unable to sustain his farm, but uninterested in leaving the farming lifestyle, Leon went on an agricultural tour of Bahia, Brazil. In 2007, impressed by wide-open landscapes of soy and cotton, productive land, and cheap prices, Leon, then in his early 30s, purchased 2,300 acres in Bahia with capital from the sale of his Idaho bean and beet farm.

Leon's soybean farming began inauspiciously, as he optimistically expected to begin production at a large scale from the start. Delays in paperwork, difficulty in obtaining farm machinery, and poor weather delayed his first planting, which dampened his first harvest. When he did start producing soy, Leon implemented "American style" production on his farm. This entailed living on his farm, rather than in nearby Luís Eduardo Magalhães; doing his own farm work; making farming decisions as a family; owning all of his production land; and self-financing. These decisions came partly out of Leon's passion for the American farming lifestyle, his disinterest in distancing himself from the actual labor, and also from his relative lack of capital, which was a barrier to hiring farm labor. His choice to live on the

---

[3] Leon is one of the two farmers interviewed whose family did not migrate from the US Midwest (the other was from Upstate New York).

farm was a natural one for Leon, but it drew attention from neighboring farmers (both Brazilian and American), who preferred to live in nearby Luís Eduardo Magalhães.

Within years, Leon had gone bankrupt in Bahia. His rough start and lack of capital severely limited his operation's room to maneuver and allowed agronomic and financial problems to compound on each other. Farming in Brazil without incurring greater debt became infeasible, and debt avoidance had been among his original reasons for migration. Unlike investors, speculators, and wealthy elites who have come to represent the global land grab, Leon was driven to Brazil by his joy of farming, desire to escape the US farm crisis, and hopes of returning to "normalcy" in Brazil. What he found instead was that farming without capital to invest was increasingly difficult not only in the US, but also in Brazil.

Dennis

Another farmer, Dennis, followed a similar pathway to Brazil, but employed a different approach. He began working his family farm in Illinois in 1979. After finding he "worked his butt off to make fifty dollars an acre" on his 160-acre corn and soybean farm, he decided to quit farming in 2000, and he turned to real estate, with a special focus on farmland sales. Before he quit farming, Dennis had toured Brazilian farming regions as a participant of a farm leadership program. In 2003 he went again. On his successive trips he saw the rapid growth of the agricultural economy in Brazil, and he heard from consultants that in a year or two, Brazil would be out-producing the US.

Not having given up his interest in farming, Dennis saw an opportunity to re-enter the profession while making a greater profit in proportion to his work efforts. He bought a small plot of land in Tocantins in 2004. After yielding well, he purchased a 1,010-hectare farm in 2005. By 2012, Dennis owned 650 hectares of land, rented 700 hectares, and managed 280 hectares in Tocantins. He was able to accumulate land rapidly, thanks to a number of Illinois investors. He readily adopted the "Brazil model" of farming (Gudynas 2008), which includes a set of agronomic practices such as no-tillage, GMO seeds, and high fertilizer and pesticide use, as well as a particular set of farm organization characteristics. Brazilian farms are often managed by a landowner who lives in a town or city, either nearby or far away. The owner visits the farm regularly, but depends on managers and farm workers for day-to-day operations. Dennis managed his Brazilian farm from Illinois, visiting several times per year. He hired a trusted agronomist to manage daily activity and farm laborers. After several years of "farming" successfully in Tocantins, Dennis has recently offered his Brazilian farm for sale. He does not plan to farm again in the US. His and his investors' decision to sell was based on finance and politics. Expanding the farm in Tocantins had become difficult due to increasing land prices, as an influx of Brazilian and foreign farmers increased competition. Equally troubling for Dennis and his investors is the possibility of enforcement of limits on foreign ownership of land (though this policy has since been reversed following the fall of the Dilma administration).

Both Leon and Dennis saw Brazilian land as a means of farming despite the farm crisis and impacts of financialization. Because they could not purchase more land at home, they sought out cheaper land and better returns on labor in Brazil. However, their paths then diverged wildly. Leon migrated to maintain his farming lifestyle and to avoid incurring greater debt. He rejected seeking wage labor, incurring debt, and courting investors in an effort to preserve his way of farming (family decision making, family capital, family labor units). To Leon, land was a means of production and a connection between him and farm production. Dennis preferred a different tactic. He responded to farm financialization not by fighting it, but seeking success within its terms. He became a manager of labor, rather than a laborer himself, and added capital by courting outside investors and adopting a more finance-ordered value of work. In contrast to Leon, Dennis has adopted a financialized sense of land value, mirroring the dual-values of land described by Fairbairn. As long as he was producing soy on his land, it existed both as a productive asset, which enabled him to profit from soy production, and as a speculative asset whose potential value could be realized at the next opportunity.

Leon and Dennis's moves to Brazil may be extreme reactions to circumstances in the US, but the farm crisis is driving other farmers to take related, if less drastic, efforts at home. Landless beginning farmers must often choose between continuing traditional production practices and strategies, or adopting the tools of finance along with their associated practices and organizational strategies. The first option can be risky, requiring them to take on high debt loads to acquire expensive land, with doubtful options for paying it off. The second accelerates the movement of US agriculture towards financialization.

Slowing Financialization

Financialization and associated high farmland values make farming exceedingly difficult for young and beginner farmers. Slowing this process can lessen barriers to young farmers' entry into agriculture. Changes in the

US Farm Bill are necessary to stem the trend towards financialization, and changes in the means of land access can improve the way farmers respond to financialization.

Farm subsidies support the over-production of commodity crops by directing funding toward these crops, rather than diversified vegetable, fruit, or livestock production, without setting quotas. The 2014 Agricultural Act (US Congress 2014) eliminated direct payments to farmers, but increased price and revenue protection, as well as agricultural risk coverage. Counter-cyclical price and revenue protection provides cash benefits to farmers if commodity prices fall below a reference price. In addition, the Farm Bill offers agricultural risk coverage (farmers choose between price and revenue protection or agricultural risk protection) to farmers when revenue falls below 86 percent of benchmark revenue. While cash payments provide benefits to farmers as insurance against weather and market forces, landowners accrue primary benefits. A 2011 working paper (Goodwin, Mishra, and Ortalo-Magné 2011) reported that each dollar of farm policy benefits raised land values by $13-30 per acre, leading the authors to conclude that landowners factored in these benefits when determining land value and planned to continue to accrue benefits. Market returns, being more volatile, are less associated with land value increases due to their unpredictability. Agricultural subsidies reduce risk for all qualified farmers, but proportionally benefit landowners. Further, this benefit is then accrued in land value. This guaranteed minimum return on investment is likely to encourage financial investors to see farmland as a safe, long-term investment.

Farm subsidy restructuring would benefit young and beginner farmers by dispersing funds more equitably. The 2014 Farm Bill provides $100 million for beginning farmers and ranchers, and reduces premiums to crop insurance programs for farmers' first five years of production. More needs to be done to direct funds towards young and beginner farmers. Uncoupling of subsidy payments from land ownership would limit the relationship between payments and farmland value, and perhaps improve land access for young tenant farmers. Incentivization of renting to beginning farmers can improve land accessibility. Nebraska and Iowa provide tax benefits to landowners who sell or rent to beginner farmers; state-by-state or federal adoption of this policy would reduce financial barriers to beginning farmers and intervene in the land market on behalf of farmers with fewer economic resources.

Young farmer advocacy organizations, including the Young Farmers' Coalition, argue for the re-negotiation of land tenure and democratization of land access via land trusts (Rippon-Butler et al. 2015). Land trusts are non-profit organizations that protect designated resources (e.g. land, water, habitats) from development. They can also be used to protect farmland from financialization by valuing land according to agricultural use, rather than developmental or speculative value. By keeping land in trusts, communities can protect farmland from over-production and development, but also restrict access to farmers who have certain characteristics. A trust could rent land preferentially to beginner farmers, young farmers, or farmers who live and work on their farms. Besides simply increasing land access to beginner farmers, land trusts may be a tool in addressing financialization of farming as a whole. In valuing land according to given characteristics such as conservation, stewardship, and supporting young farmers, land can be protected from trends towards financialization and the collapse of multiple forms of value into the singular value in terms of capital (however, see Hachmyer, this volume, for a discussion of issues of access equity related to land trusts).

Conclusion

Financialization of the US farm sector is visible in high farmland values, changing farm organization, changing values of farming, and changing goals of farming. High land prices drastically limit farming opportunities for young and beginner farmers, leading them in many cases to abandon the farming lifestyle and career, or to migrate to find cheaper land elsewhere. As the case of US farmer migrants to Brazil illustrates, the impacts of financialization are not limited to the US. This process pushes both individual farmers and investment groups to seek cheaper lands in frontier regions, which in turn increases prices there, continuing the cycle. Both at home and abroad, the US farm crisis prompts farmers to scale-up and adopt ecologically destructive practices as they struggle to survive in economies in which small- to mid-scale production no longer finds value. The answer to financialization is not—as some might believe—found in increasing subsidies. Rather, to give farmers like Leon and Dennis the option to stay at home and even pursue more ecologically sustainable methods of diversified production, subsidies should be limited, and alternative political and legal frameworks should be used to re-define land access and tenancy.

References

Barlett, Peggy F. 1993. *American Dreams, Rural Realities: Family Farms in Crisis.* Chapel Hill: The University of North Carolina Press.

Bentley, Susan E., Peggy F. Bartlett, F. Larry et al. 1989. Involuntary Exits From Farming: Evidence From Four Studies. *Washington, DC: US Department of Agriculture, ERS, AER-625.* Accessed September 28, 2016. https://naldc.nal.usda.gov/naldc/download.xhtml?id=CAT10411120&content=PDF.

Berry, Wendell. 1977. *The Unsettling of America: Culture and Agriculture*. San Francisco: Sierra Club Books.

Buttel, Frederick H. 1989. "The US Farm Crisis and the Restructuring of American Agriculture: Domestic and International Dimensions." In *The International Farm Crisis* (pp. 46–83). New York: St. Martin's Press.

Clapp, Jennifer. 2014. "Financialization, distance and global food politics." *The Journal of Peasant Studies 41*(5), 797–814.

Dobbins, Craig and Kim Cook. 2013. *Purdue Agricultural Economics Report (August 2013)*. West Lafayette, IN: Purdue University. Accessed June 1, 2015. https://www.agecon.purdue.edu/extension/pubs/paer/pdf/PAER8_2013.pdf.

Dudley, Kathryn Marie. 2000. *Debt and Dispossession: Farm Loss in America's Heartland*. Chicago: University of Chicago Press.

Duffy, Michael. 2013. *2012 Farmland Value Survey* (Ag Decision Maker No. File C2-70). Ames, IA: Iowa State University. Accessed June 1, 2015. http://www.extension.iastate.edu/sites/www.extension.iastate.edu/files/www/2012%20Land%20Value%20Survey%20Overview%20%20Final.pdf

Fairbairn, Madeleine. 2014. "'Like gold with yield': Evolving intersections between farmland and finance." *Journal of Peasant Studies 41*(5), 777–795.

Gibson-Graham, J. K. 2006. *A Postcapitalist Politics*. Minneapolis: University of Minnesota Press.

Goodwin, Barry K., Ashok K. Mishra, and François Ortalo-Magné. 2011. *The Buck Stops Where? The Distribution of Agricultural Subsidies* (Working Paper No. 16693). National Bureau of Economic Research. Accessed April 14, 2014. http://www.nber.org/papers/w16693.

Gudynas, Eduardo. 2008. "The New Bonfire of Vanities: Soybean cultivation and globalization in South America." *Development* 51(4): 512-518.

Gunnoe, Andrew. 2014. "The Political Economy of Institutional Landownership: Neorentier Society and the Financialization of Land." *Rural Sociology 79*(4), 478–504.

Hoppe, Robert. 2014. *Structure and Finances of U.S. Farms: Family Farm Report, 2014 Edition* (No. 132). USDA Economic Research Service. Accessed March 1, 2014. http://www.ers.usda.gov/publications/pub-details/?pubid=43916.

Isakson, S. Ryan. 2014. "Food and finance: The financial transformation of agro-food supply chains." *Journal of Peasant Studies 41*(5), 749–775.

Krippner, Greta R. 2011. *Capitalizing on Crisis: The Political Origins of the Rise of Finance*. Cambridge: Harvard University Press.

MacDonald, James M., Penni Korb, and Robert A. Hoppe. 2013. *Farm Size and the Organization of U.S. Crop Farming* (Economic Research Report No. 152). USDA Economic Research Service. Accessed March 1, 2014. https://www.ers. usda.gov/webdocs/publications/err152/39359_err152.pdf.

Nickerson, Cynthia J., Mitchell Morehart, Todd Kuethe, et al. 2012. *Trends in US farmland values and ownership*. USDA Economic Research Service. Accessed April 14, 2014. https://www.ers.usda.gov/webdocs/publications/ eib92/16748_eib92_2_pdf.

O'Donoghue, Erik J., Robert A. Hoppe, David E. Banker, et al. 2011. *The changing organization of US farming*. Economic Information Bulletin Number 88. Washington, DC: USDA Economic Research Service.

Ofstehage, Andrew. In Press. "Encounters with the Brazilian Soybean Boom: Transnational Farmers and the Cerrado." In *Food, Agriculture and Social Change: The Vitality of Latin America*, edited by Stephen Sherwood, Alberto Arce and Myriam Paredes. London: Earthscan.

Ofstehage, Andrew. 2016. "Farming is easy, becoming Brazilian is hard: North American soy farmers' social values of production, work and land in Soylandia." *The Journal of Peasant Studies 43*(2), 442–460.

Ouma, Stefan. 2016. "From financialization to operations of capital: Historicizing and disentangling the finance–farmland-nexus." *Geoforum 72*, 82-93.

Rippon-Butler, Holly, Sophie Ackoff, Eric Hansen, and Lindsey Lusher Shute. 2015. *Finding Farmland: A Farmer's Guide to Working with Land Trusts*. National Young Farmers' Coalition. Accessed June 1, 2015. http://www.youngfarmers.org/ wp-content/uploads/2015/01/NYFC-Finding-Affordable-Farmland.pdf.

Shute, Lindsey Lusher. 2011. *Building A Future with Farmers: Challenges Faced by Young, American Farmers and a National Strategy to Help Them Succeed*. National Young Farmers' Coalition. Accesed March 28, 2016. www.youngfarmers.org/re-ports/Building_A_Future_With_Farmers.pdf.

US Congress. 2014. *Agricultural Act of 2014*. Washington, DC: US Government Printing Office.

USDA Economic Research Service. 2016. Data Files: U.S. and State-Level Farm Income and Wealth Statistics. Retrieved May 26, from http://www.ers.usda.gov/ data-products/farm-income-and-wealth-statistics/data-files-us-and-state-level-farm-income-and-wealth-statistics.aspx.

Rebuilding the Urban Commons

CHAPTER 11

Land, Ownership, and West Oakland's Struggle for Food Justice

Excerpted from interviews with Brahm Ahmadi of People's Community Market

West Oakland, a historically working-class, African-American neighborhood with a rich cultural and industrial history, sits directly across the Bay from San Francisco. As average white-collar salaries and prices in the metropolitan area rise, West Oakland remains economically marginalized and underserved. This is especially so in regards to access to fresh, healthy, affordable foods. West Oakland is what is often called a "food desert." Nonetheless, the neighborhood has both a deep history of social activism and a renewed interest in community-based projects. Since many of the lots and buildings in West Oakland currently sit vacant, it would appear that the neighborhood is ripe for new and positive development. However, much of this property is currently held by real estate speculators who bought when prices were low, pay very little property tax, and now are only willing to sell for prices far above market rate. The struggle of People's Community Market to access land for a grocery-based community project in West Oakland underscores the long-term effects of land accumulation and dispossession on urban food justice. It also points toward potential ways forward.

Why West Oakland Needs a Community Market

West Oakland has no supermarkets. To access a grocery store, residents must travel to other communities. Because almost half of the households in this neighborhood do not own a car, they must walk or take public transportation to get there, requiring them to spend significant time, money, and energy on the trip. Moreover, without a car it is difficult to carry more than a couple day's worth of food home. This leaves residents with little option but to frequent local corner stores. West Oakland has an unusually high number of them: approximately one for every 300 people, according to the number of registered liquor licenses. Unfortunately, these stores carry fairly low quality, packaged, and—most often—processed foods. They offer very little fresh food, and what they do have is generally expensive: anywhere from 50 to 200 percent higher in cost than in a typical supermarket. The scarcity and price of fresh food contributes to significant rates of malnutrition and health crises in the community. According to research conducted in 2014, over half of the adults and a third of children living in Alameda County, where Oakland is located, are overweight or obese, and the rates are disproportionately high in West Oakland. Consequentially, rates of diabetes, cardiovascular disease, high cholesterol, and hypertension are also high (ChangeLab Solutions 2014).

Moreover, the lack of grocery stores results in major economic leakage from the community and lost opportunities for job creation. West Oaklanders spend approximately $58 million a year in grocery expenditures, with $45 million of this total being spent at stores in other neighborhoods.[1] This is money lost from the local tax and municipal bases. If put to different use in the community, it could create as many as 150 jobs at union-level, living wages, which would prompt additional growth and spending in the neighborhood.

People's Community Market (PCM) is a plan to address these issues. It is an outgrowth of People's Grocery, a non-profit founded in 2002. PCM is a for-profit C corporation[2] created in order to develop a full-service fresh food market in the West Oakland community. The mid-sized market will create quality jobs with living wages, benefits, and an employee-ownership program. We have developed a seven-year plan with the National Center for Employee Ownership to implement a training program and bonus model that will eventually evolve into stock options and grants.

PCM will also play a catalytic role for community development by serving as an anchor institute for community growth. West Oakland is currently experiencing a demographic shift as more whites and Latinos move into the neighborhood. This inevitably leads to various social and cultural challenges. We aspire for PCM to play a bridge-building role between

---

[1] According to research conducted in 2015 by Inalytics for People's Community Market.

[2] In a C corporation (as opposed to an S corporation or limited liability company), the business is considered legally separate from its owners. Income is taxed at the corporate level, and again when it passes on to owners. Though some corporations consider this double taxation a drawback, it allows money to be reinvested in the company at a lower corporate tax rate.

community members by providing a common ground and meeting space for residents to interact and build relationships. Our store plan includes a social hall, "the Front Porch," which will house various programs, activities, and events organized by our community partners. We will also have a stage where music performances, movie nights, dinner events, and poetry readings can be held. Currently, West Oakland lacks the type of large organizations or businesses that can serve as anchor-institutions to increase pedestrian traffic and spark additional local development. Because everyone in the community needs food, we believe that the market could serve this role, and we hope that it will lead to the development of a main street-style corridor while also supporting an emerging coalition of residents, organizations, and city government.

PCM has encountered many logistical challenges in the pathway to breaking ground on a new market, but the most significant challenge was securing a location. We wanted the market to be centrally located and within walking distance of most community members' homes. Only several corridors in West Oakland fit this description. Although many lots and buildings in them are currently unused or under-utilized, they are essentially inaccessible for new development. Years ago, real estate speculators purchased these pieces of land at very low rates, and they continue to sit on them in hopes that their value will continue to rise. In the meantime, they want to avoid complications with tenants, so the trend has been for these owners to either not lease the spaces out at all, or only to offer short-term leases for less than 15 years. Because the 1978 Proposition 13 set California property taxes to the incredibly low rate of 1 percent and prohibits them from increasing by more than 2 percent a year, the speculators can afford to own vacant property without experiencing financial burden. A 15-year lease is not enough time for a business like PCM to set-up and stabilize, so our only option was to purchase space. However, land owners in West Oakland are asking exorbitant prices—up to 200-300 percent of current market value—making it economically infeasible for new businesses—whether traditional or socially-minded—to buy.

A History of Dispossession and Speculation

This present economic geography emerges from a long and complicated history around land access and ownership in West Oakland. For 150 years, waves of immigrant populations have moved to the area. At one point, the immigrants were predominantly Polish; later, they were Italian. Beginning around the 1920s and '30s, African Americans from the South began moving to West Oakland in search of maritime, port, and railroad jobs, all of which were concentrated in the neighborhood.

These waves of change have always sparked tensions around land and ownership, but the most significant events to reshape land ownership and promote inequality began in the 1950s. At this time, government agencies began using what is called the right of "eminent domain" to seize land for the construction of the West Oakland Bay Area Rapid Transit (BART) station, elevated tracks, various freeways, and a central US postal facility. Eminent domain is the government's right to take private property for public projects. Although projects are legally required to serve the greater benefit of society in order to evoke eminent domain, these benefits are very often uneven. In this case, it was used disproportionately against African American communities to sacrifice their economic foundations for projects that would not benefit them.

Before the 1950s, there was a stable, middle-class of small business owners in West Oakland spread out across several thriving commercial corridors. The most famous of these was 7th Street, known to some as the "Harlem of the West," which was a bustling cultural center where famous jazz and blues musicians from around the country came to play. Many of the properties seized by eminent domain were Black-owned businesses located along these corridors. Some were homes. Their appropriation was not only traumatic at the time, but also has been destabilizing in the long-term. Many people say that West Oakland has never fully recovered. The same pattern has been seen in the effects of freeway/interstate construction across the country from Detroit, Michigan to Durham, North Carolina, once the home of the "Harlem of the South."

As West Oaklanders lost their properties, they lost their economic stability and, in many cases, spiraled into poverty. The problem was further accentuated by "redlining" practices. As white-flight from the urban core increased in the post-World War II period, realtors' associations, home-owners' associations and banks formed deeply-racist covenants to prevent African Americans from buying property in white suburbs, which they would delineate by circling these areas on maps with red pens. Thus, as public development projects disrupted West Oakland, African Americans with the interest and financial resources available to leave West Oakland did not have the same opportunities to relocate that their white neighbors had. Therefore, the poverty resulting from business-loss remained concentrated in the neighborhood.

By the 1960s, housing had become a major crisis for the West Oakland community. As families' economic situations worsened, they lost homes and had decreasing means available for paying rent. The Black Panther

Party, which emerged from this very neighborhood, created a strong base of activism in the community as it organized around social issues including food security and housing. This history gives roots to current West Oakland activism, and also offers important lessons. Though the Black Panthers demanded housing, they did not specify ownership as the central problem. Today, it is clear that land ownership—as opposed to access through fair rent—is what really provides the stability and resiliency to housing and any other land-related use. Contemporary activists are, for example, now evolving more creative portable housing projects and other means to create a pathway to home ownership for even the poorest of residents.

As West Oakland's local economy bottomed out, real estate speculation began to pick up. Beginning in the late 1970s and early 1980s, a small group of speculative investors saw a very long-term investment opportunity in West Oakland. Despite the community's deep economic problems, it sits in a very advantageous geographic location. After the West Oakland BART station was constructed, it became the closest point from which to reach San Francisco via public transportation, and the neighborhood is central to various trucking lines, railroads, and the Oakland port, making it a strategic center for both residential and commercial development. Nonetheless, few outsiders beyond this small group were paying attention to struggling West Oakland at the time, so the speculators were able to come in quietly and make purchases without attracting significant attention or concern.

Ownership in West Oakland Today

Fast-forward to the present and circumstances are very different. As housing prices in San Francisco have skyrocketed, many people who work in the city can no longer afford to live there, and are looking toward Oakland as an alternative. There is significant new demand in West Oakland, but speculators already own the most-desired commercial and residential properties. On the streets with the greatest potential to become small business corridors, there are six to ten block stretches in which everything is owned by speculators. Although the value of these locations has already increased significantly, the speculators continue to believe that if they hold out long enough, a wealthy developer will eventually offer them an outrageous price far above market rate.

As the vision for PCM came together, the project quickly built community consensus around the need for the store and a strong stakeholder network. We were able to demonstrate the neighborhood's aggregate spending power, and even attract powerful financial partners. Nonetheless, land access remained a bottleneck. The most recent transactions in Oakland, which are the base for market rate, were around $65 a square foot. PCM and an angel investor—who believes in the social impact and economic potential of the project—went above this and offered $75 a square foot to several owners, only to find that they were asking $95, $120, or even up to $250. These rates not only make purchasing difficult for small start-ups, they also provide complex financial challenges to traditional developers and economically sophisticated partnerships such as PCM. If PCM were to have taken out a loan for a property secured at the rate sellers were asking, it could not pay it off sustainably at the profit margin expected for the grocery store. This same problem is driving stagnation for all community development in West Oakland. Everyone in the neighborhood who is trying to advance community development—whether for affordable housing projects, market-rate housing projects, small businesses, or storefront operations—has been stymied in securing property. Even large, multi-national corporations that have considered moving into West Oakland have found it to be financially untenable. This has created a disconnect: what you see on the ground in West Oakland does not match the perception of value held by speculators. In other up-and-coming neighborhoods around the country—such as Brooklyn, New York—you see new construction and rehabilitation in the neighborhoods where prices are rising. Here, you see very little new activity.

Ways Forward: Policy versus Creative Capital

In recent years, both the federal government and various local government agencies have made commitments to eradicate food desserts, malnutrition, and obesity. For example, the Obama administration has created the Healthy Food Financing Initiative (HFFI) in order to fund Community Development Finance Institutions, which in turn can offer low rate loans for the development of grocery stores in low-income underserved communities. The idea has been to relieve the risk of starting out business in "risky" neighborhoods by supplying federal funds. Unfortunately, much of this money has gone unclaimed because grocery stores remain unwilling or unable to open in communities, even with these low-cost loans.

A huge part of this—especially in West Oakland—is the tremendously high cost of land and the difficulty in achieving tenable lease agreements. The local government in Oakland has claimed that it has no power or authority to intervene in property owners' actions in the real estate market, but the Oakland Food Policy Council (OFPC) believes that it could, if the right policy instrument was created. The OFPC, founded in 2008 to analyze and improve Oakland's food system, supports the development of urban agriculture. Like the PMC, it recognizes land access as a major barrier to food justice and community-based development. To improve this situation, OFPC is encouraging the city to develop "urban agriculture zones," which would allow Oakland landowners to access tax incentives (created under California Assembly Bill 551) if they put their land into agricultural use. This and similar tax incentives or penalties could be used to discourage speculative "squatting" behavior and push owners into either putting land into productive use, selling it, or making it available to others in the interim.

Ironically, one of the factors tying the government's hands is a moratorium on the use of eminent domain. After the property seizures and acquisitions carried out in the 1950s, the community felt that eminent domain had and could be abused again to target people of color. A major organizational effort came together in the 1980s to impose a ban on its use. This successful policy intervention, which protects the community from the fear that their past trauma could be repeated, now unfortunately also prevents the city from using it against real estate speculators. In response, there have been calls for write-in exceptions to the moratorium that would allow eminent domain to be used in favor of community development.

Unfortunately, there has not yet been a strong enough organizing effort or movement in place to push such policy changes forward. In the interim, community developers must enact creative financial solutions in order to buy back land. At People's Community Market, our solution has been to leverage our social mission and the impacts that we want to have on the neighborhood to attract more flexible and creative funding and financing, which essentially provides us with a partial subsidy. The investor that has come forward to support PCM's land acquisition is doing so because of his belief in the project's social mission, not for its profit-potential. We have also brought in financial institutions to provide construction loans, equipment loans, working capital, and other lines of credit at flexible and subsidized rates. Fortunately, we are beginning our project at a time when there is increasing support for social enterprises and the idea of using community businesses to create resiliency and address social needs through job creation. This fills in the gaps in access where traditional financial institutions have fallen short. These alternative partners include community development financial institutions, such as large banks with specific social mandates. For example, banks across the country are providing money to designated neighborhoods in order to meet the requirements of the Community Redevelopment Act (CRA), which requires regulated financial institutions to help meet the credit needs of the communities in which they are chartered.

Crowdfunding is also a viable and popular model that is emerging as an option for real estate acquisition. Some of these projects are still somewhat cutthroat, in that they come from a conventional business model and are working to make returns. However, there are a few examples of people using crowdfunding platforms for co-operative land purchasing. For instance, people can put in a few hundred or thousand dollars and buy shares and vetting rights in a larger-buying entity. This can work for housing projects or grocery stores. PCM did not use a crowdfunding platform, but implemented a direct public offering (DPO) in order to sell securities to small-scale, "unaccredited" community investors. As of July 2016, PCM has raised $1.5 million this way.

Capital raised through public offerings, crowdfunding, and socially-minded investors can be used in combination with federal programs. While traditional grocery chains may have trouble opening in low-income neighborhoods even with assistance from the Healthy Food Financing Initiative, community-based businesses can draw from multiple sources. Other federal programs, such as the New Markets Tax Credit Program, which provides subsidized capital to small businesses in underserved neighborhoods through a tax credit to investors, can also be utilized, as can donations from foundations, which are increasingly recognizing the importance of securing physical infrastructure in order to grow social projects.

In short, rather than taking on the real estate problem directly by enforcing re-pricing on speculators, government, community, and private sources are putting together mechanisms that we can use to pay outrageous land prices at a subsidized rate. Ultimately, this is not fair to community members and taxpayers whose contributions are helping real estate investors to make a killing through speculation. Nonetheless, these options ease the burden of doing so by spreading the cost over many people and institutions.

This is important to do because it is very possible that neither prices nor policy will change anytime soon. If we are able to leverage new forms of capital in creative ways, we may be able to get some land back in local hands. For any project to be sustainable and resilient in the long-term, ownership, whether collective or individual, but not by an external entity, is essential. This is the logic we've used with grocery stores. We have the evidence that food deserts are creating health problems, job loss, and other economic problems. We also have the evidence that the community food systems we are cultivating will not achieve longevity if we cannot get in now, before a developer comes in, accepts the exorbitant prices owners are asking for, and permanently shuts the gate. Therefore, there is pressure to act now. It is a question of reversing a decade-long trend, and also ensuring future opportunity for locally beneficial development.

Success for PCM

In March 2016, land access finally became a reality for the PCM. The company and its partners found an owner willing to sell at 50 percent above market rates. Although this price is still above what traditional lending agents would be willing to offer a loan for, it was better than what other sellers had asked. PCM's angel investor was willing to provide an interest-free loan to a third party partner—the East Bay Asian Local Development Corporation (EBALDC)—in order to purchase the property. As a 40-year-old community development organization, EBALDC has the resources and experience to take on a loan and acquisition of this scale. Because EBALDC shares the goal of systemic, community-based development, it agreed to a 30-year, rent-free lease with PCM, and will also allow the market to eventually buy-out the title to the property at no additional cost. This creative partnership is allowing the People's Community Market to become the first mid- to large-size retail business to come to West Oakland in many decades.

Organizing for Land Justice

The concept of land justice is fundamentally about equal access and opportunity—not only to land ownership, but to control and long-term land tenure. This is necessary in order to resolve the extreme stratification and disparities that we see both here in Oakland and globally. It is the wealthy who are able to own land, and everyone else can, at best, be a tenant, dependent on agreement from the land owner. It is tremendously problematic, especially when those land owners demand lease or rent rates that make it impossible for users to ever save enough to break the cycle. The classic capitalist view of land as a mechanism for generating return to land owners and investors is the problem. We have taken land and turned it into a commodity or an investment tool, rather than something of use value.

This connects to job creation because, in many cases, the ability to create jobs requires a physical place for those jobs to exist. At the large-scale, land is needed to create industry and manufacturing, but it is essential at the small-scale too. We know that small-scale businesses can collectively create more and more reliable jobs (Shuman 2007), but if business owners are expending too much money on rent or mortgages, they cannot hire the labor support they need.

To move forward in resolving the problems of land access, job creation, and a crumbled economic base, we need policy change and we need a real organizing campaign. In Oakland and many other cities, political leadership is aligned with investment's interests, and most often is facilitating development in a way that is not inclusive, that accelerates gentrification, and that displaces lower income, working class and moderate-income families. We need a strong organizing effort to push political leadership to align with the vision of inclusion and equity, and to be accountable to its constituency.

The challenge of building an organizing effort is two-fold. First, people who are struggling for day-to-day survival have all their time taken up by work and household responsibilities, so we must find ways to sustainably bring them together without infringing on these limitations. Second, currently there is not strong solidarity or alignment across class differences. Although middle-class families are also struggling with displacement and rising costs in Oakland, there is a division between middle-class neighborhoods and the truly underserved neighborhoods. We need to bring these communities together, bridge the economic divide, and work toward common goals.

If we are able to do so, we may be able not only to build more resilient food systems and economies, but also to preserve the cultural diversity, richness, and history of the city. Ironically, though these things are what attract newcomers to Oakland, they are being eroded through the homogenous path of non-inclusive development. As a result, cities like Oakland look more like the suburbs and less like the thriving urban communities they could be.

References

ChangeLab Solutions. 2014. "The Health and Economic Impacts of Obesity in Alameda County: Potential Policy Interventions." Oakland: ChangeLab Solutions.

Shuman, Michael H. 2007. *The Small-Mart Revolution: How Local Businesses are Beating the Global Competition*. San Francisco: Berrett-Koehler Publishers, Inc.

CHAPTER 12

Urban Land-Grabbing and a Movement for Community-Based Control in Detroit

Excerpted from interviews with Malik Yakini of Detroit Black Community Food Security Network

In 2012, the Detroit City Council agreed to sell over 1,500 parcels of land to a man named John Hantz, who is using it to construct a 140-acre "woodlands," or urban tree farm (Halcolm 2012). This land transfer threatens to set a dangerous precedent for Detroit: one of selling off chunks of the city's public land to wealthy investors, rather than undertaking the more difficult challenge of transferring it to local residents and community-based organizations or investigating how it might be used as a local commons. This chapter discusses the long, intertwined histories of racism, land, and geography in Detroit, and how these histories have simultaneously enabled the Hantz land transfer and inhibited community-based power and control. It also considers alternative ways to support equitable land access and food justice in Detroit.

A History of Land Racism in Detroit

To understand Detroit, one must understand that it is one of the most segregated metropolitan areas in the country. As in many other American cities, African Americans in Detroit have been segregated into specific locations throughout the city through a series of political processes marked by both structural racism and, at times, explicitly racist objectives. After World War II, city dwellers, mostly white, began an exodus to the suburbs. As their movement drained resources, services, and jobs from the city center, the government was making plans to build Interstate 75, which would cross directly through the city's east side. The government used the policy of "eminent domain" to seize land and property from the Black community's most important districts in order to make room for construction. These areas included the neighborhoods of Black Bottom, one of Detroit's oldest Black communities; Paradise Valley, a thriving entertainment district; and Hastings Street, which was a bustling business corridor. Thus, the seizure effectively dismantled many of the Detroit African American community's most important economic and cultural assets. Afterwards, it was difficult for residents to move to different and more thriving neighborhoods because housing covenants created by white homeowners, real estate companies, and banks prevented African Americans from buying homes in areas they had agreed to maintain for whites only. Over the next two decades, middle- and upper-class white residents continued their "flight" from the urban area. Between 1964 and 1966, an average of 22,000 white residents left the city each year. Between 1967 and 1969, another 173,000 residents, mostly white, moved away (Safransky 2014). Even as homes became vacant, the city failed to make affordable housing and land available to working class residents. As the once-prosperous auto industry declined and the city's tax base eroded, the city government had a difficult time providing basic services and amenities. All of these processes laid the groundwork for ongoing economic struggle, and for a geography of racism in Detroit.

Fast-forward to the present day, and the descendants of the same African Americans whose lives, business, and properties were interrupted by the interstate are still struggling to find a way to build healthy communities. Although Detroit is surrounded by relatively wealthy and predominately white suburbs, over half of Detroit's African American residents (who make up 83 percent of the population) reportedly cannot find jobs (Data Driven Detroit 2010). The median household income in the city is only $28,000. Now, a city that was built to accommodate a population of 2 million is home to only 713,000 residents (Safransky 2014). Nonetheless, we should not consider Detroit to be "vacant." The population continues to live, make communities, and struggle to maintain our city. Ironically, considering the amount of empty space available, residents are not granted easy access to the land and property that many strive to take care of.

An Emerging Food Justice and Urban Agriculture Movement in Detroit

Detroit has a strong community of food and economic justice advocates, many of whom emerge from decades of activism and community organizing experience through the Black liberation movement. We have learned from these experiences that we stand to be victimized when our communities are not organized or mobilized, and that we are in a much stronger position when we are working as a cohesive body to define our aspirations and collectively make and enforce demands. For instance, in the 1970s, the Detroit Police Department formed a unit called Stop the Robberies Enjoy Safe Streets (STRESS), which patrolled our neighborhoods and used many abusive policing practices. Residents mobilized, and after many hard-fought battles—including electing Coleman A. Young, Detroit's First Black Mayor (who ran on an anti-STRESS platform)—were able to have the unit eliminated. Today, as we turn our focus toward food justice as part of the larger struggle for economic and racial justice, we draw inspiration from history, as well as from many other historic struggles over housing, education, labor, and the environment in Detroit.

The Detroit Black Community Food Security Network (DBCFSN) was founded in February 2006. It grew out of work being done at the Nsoroma Institute, an African-centered charter school that I directed. Beginning in 1999, we had developed a food security curriculum and were practicing organic gardening with students on-site at the school. Eventually, we created the Shamba Organic Garden Collective, which consisted of about twenty gardens, located throughout the city in the backyards or vacant lots next to the homes of students' parents and school staff. As this group grew, we recognized the need for a larger container for this work.

The DBCFSN was also inspired by events that took place at the Community Food Security Coalition's (CFSC) 2005 annual conference in Atlanta. At the time, CFSC was the leading organization addressing community food security and food justice, and that year, race was the dominant theme of the conference. The coalition's board had contracted a group called Dismantling Racism Works to conduct anti-racism trainings for various members of the coalition, and there were a variety of workshops and lectures on the theme of race in the food system. The conference catalyzed my thinking about food justice, because it allowed me to see that what I observed in Detroit was also going on at a national level; work referred to as "food security" or "food justice" projects were largely being done in African American or Latino communities, but non-profit organizations staffed by mostly white employees were doing it. This was an eye-opening realization for me.

As a result, 40 of us came together in February 2006 to form the DBCFSN. From the beginning, we wanted to build self-reliance, food security, and food justice in Detroit's Black community. We saw several ways to do this. For one, we wanted to influence public policy. Although we do not think that grassroots communities should wait on the government or the corporate sectors to act, we do believe that we should hold the government accountable for behaving in a responsible manner. We also believe that if we can create a better policy environment, community organizations will be better able to do their work. Additionally, we wanted to take advantage of the unused land available in our communities to engage in and promote urban farming. Related to this, we were very concerned with promoting healthy eating habits in order to counter the crisis of dietary-related diseases that affect African Americans at disproportionately high rates. To support access to healthy foods, and to keep wealth circulating in Black communities, we also wanted to galvanize our economic power by encouraging cooperative buying. Finally, the DBCFSN wanted to direct youth toward food-related careers. Those of us that come out of the social movements of the 1960s and 1970s have learned that change does not occur immediately, but takes place incrementally over long periods of time. In order to sustain our food justice movement, we need inter-generational participation and ways to help young people see valuable and sustainable livelihoods in food careers.

These broad goals are now manifested in six program areas. The largest is D-Town Farm, a seven-acre urban farm in a city-owned park where we grow more than 30 different fruits, vegetables, and herbs using organic methods. We do large-scale composting, keep bees, use hoop houses for season extension, and engage in agrotourism. Additionally, we have two youth programs. The Food Warriors Youth Development Program works with young people ages seven through 12 at three locations throughout the city to teach food justice and raised-bed gardening, and to get them thinking about food access in their communities. The other youth-focused program, for teenagers ages 14 thru 17, is called Food and Flava. In addition to gardening skills, it teaches entrepreneurism to participants who preserve and sell produce from the gardens.

Our fourth program area is a lecture series called "What's for Dinner?" held four times a year at Detroit's Charles H. Wright Museum of African American History. The series is designed to raise people's consciousness about issues related to urban agriculture or the food system in general. Fifth, we are developing the Detroit People's Food Co-op, which will be a cooperatively-owned, full-service grocery store located in Detroit's North End. It is part of a larger project, called the Detroit Food Commons, which will include an incubator kitchen, café, community-meeting space, and the offices of the DBCFSN.

In addition to these program areas, we are periodically involved in community issues that relate to urban farming, land, and food justice. We took a lead role in authoring the Detroit Food Security Policy and were the lead organization in the initial formation of the Detroit Food Policy Council.

Land Speculation and Acquisition

One of the most critical issues that Detroit's food justice community has faced in recent years is the large-scale sale of land to a man named John Hantz. Hantz is an area businessman who says that, as he drove everyday through the city and looked out at its landscape, the idea came to him that what the city lacked was the scarcity that encourages entrepreneurs to buy. He professes to believe that if he could take the first step in acquiring a large piece of land, he would prompt others to do the same (Smith 2010). When he first approached the city about purchasing land, he said that he wanted to create the world's largest urban farm. Specifically, he proposed constructing a massive 5,000-acre farm and urban agriculture resource facility. City residents reacted strongly. They worried, among other things, that because the city had not yet created any ordinances to govern urban agriculture, an operation of this scale would put city residents in direct contact with pesticides and other farm chemicals. In response, Hantz scaled his project back and planned to build a 140-acre woodlands (tree farming) project. He's said it will help to beautify Detroit (Williams 2014). In 2012 the City Council agreed to sell him over 1,500 parcels (Halcom).

The largest threat posed to land and food justice movements by the Hantz sale is not the nature of the tree farm itself (although his claims that it will beautify the city landscape thus far have not been proven). The concern is that the sale sets a very dangerous precedent. According to a survey conducted in 2009, around one-third of Detroit's residential lots currently sit vacant or have unoccupied homes (Osorio 2010). Approximately 70,000 unused parcels are owned by the city (Detroit Future City n/d). The question of what to do with this land is of major importance to both city residents and the local government. In recent years, Detroit Mayor Mike Duggan has turned to the Detroit Land Bank Authority (DLBA) to manage sales, transfers, and leasing of these lots; DLBA now holds roughly one-fourth of the properties in the city (Gallagher 2015). The DLBA now allows neighbors to purchase lots adjoining their homes if they meet certain eligibility requirements. However, many individuals and community groups who have long tended to vacant lots, or started developing plans for utilizing them, still have not formally acquired access to the land they wish to purchase.

Hantz only paid eight cents for every square foot of land that he purchased, much less than some area residents and community-based organizations could bid for individual plots in their neighborhoods. However, Hantz's proposition was of unprecedented scale, offering the city a unique opportunity to shed responsibility for a large tract of land in one transfer.

After years of economic struggle, the city is eager to construe any business interest as a positive development. However, if this pattern continues, land will only be available to large-scale purchasers, and eventually to only the highest of bidders. Following this path, we could find ourselves a few years down the road in a situation in which one-third of the entire city—all of the once-vacant or abandoned lots—are owned by only a few wealthy individuals.

The Hantz deal included a particularly problematic clause that allows him the first right of refusal to purchase any city-owned land that goes up for sale within a mile radius of his property. This radius extends all the way to the Detroit River, so includes riverfront property that could potentially be extremely valuable, and also desirable for both private and public projects. The sale may have been framed as a way to counteract urban blight, but in our eyes it has always been a *land grab*, a calculated move to ensure that Detroit's land becomes privatized and re-directed to benefit the interests of Hantz and others like him. Hantz himself may never receive direct economic benefits from the tree production on his property—the trees he is producing will take decades to mature. However, he does stand to benefit tremendously from the privileged opportunity that he has been given to amass land during a time in which it is undervalued by market rates.

In Hantz's vision of forced scarcity, economic growth and urban improvement only occur when entrepreneurs are motivated to privatize and purchase land. City officials, following his logic, hope that his and other development projects will create "ripple" effects in the local economy, gradually spreading improvement to all city residents. But the reality of our society is that land is the basis for power, and not only allowing but encouraging large-scale acquisitions will only reinforce uneven and unjust power dynamics.

Hantz is the only person to have purchased such a large tract of parcels to date, but other businessmen have also acquired disturbingly large amounts of Detroit property. Through his Bedrock Real Estate Services, Dan Gilbert, founder of Quicken Loans, has acquired over 80 downtown buildings (Thibodeau 2016). Although he has paid as much as $142 million to acquire privately-owned buildings, the city has also transferred properties to him for under $10, in exchange for "major developments" (Aguilar 2016). Mike Ilitch, co-founder of Little Caesars Pizza, owns Detroit's hockey team, major league baseball team, and various Detroit properties including the historic Fox Theatre in downtown. To help him develop his Little Caesars Arena, the city sold him 39 parcels for only $1 (Gross 2016).

Already, the renewed interest in Detroit is driving up prices, just as Hantz has hoped. In some cases, prices exceed those that organizations with community-based interests can pay. For instance, the first piece of land that the DBCFSN considered for the construction of the Detroit Food Commons was priced in March 2014 at $850,000. By June of that year, the owner had raised the asking price to $1.2 million, and by August the price was $1.4 million. What the three people above, who *have* been able to purchase extensive property, have in common is that they are already wealthy, white, and male. This is worth noting because oppression tends to manifest itself in three powerful ways: through class, race, and gender. It is not a simple coincidence that the buyers who are successfully gaining access to Detroit's land and property—and have the economic and social capital to argue that it is for the "general" benefit—identify with these categories of privilege.

A Failing Government

As the owner of a significant portion of Detroit's "unused" land, the City of Detroit cannot ignore its responsibility to equitably steward and make land available to the city's residents. The Detroit Food Policy Council has invested much time to collaborate with the city government on achieving this goal. In some cases, the government has been helpful. For example, the city has entered into negotiation with the DBCFSN to sell city-owned land to the organization for the creation of the Detroit Food Commons. However, in many instances, it has failed to act responsibly or to respond to the desires and demands of the people it ostensibly represents.

For example, the Urban Agriculture Work Group, led by the City Planning Commission in collaboration with the Detroit Food Policy Council, assessed the needs and status of urban agriculture in the city and recommended that the city pass an ordinance to regulate urban farming before any agricultural or forestry land sales went through. The absence of a protective policy, in combination with other concerns, prompted, 400 people—almost all opposed to the sale—to attend a public hearing in 2012 and voice their concerns about the Hantz proposal to the City Council. Despite this opposition, five out of nine City Council members voted in favor of the sale the next day, demonstrating a clear disregard for their constituencies' opinions.

In 2013, an urban agriculture ordinance was eventually passed. It allows for the urban production of vegetables and fish, but made raising livestock illegal. It is expected that before the end of 2016, the Detroit City Council will vote on a second ordinance that will allow for sustainable, small-scale livestock operations of chickens, goats, and bees within city limits.

The city has thus far failed to create effective policies and mechanisms for small-scale land transfers. Whereas Hantz purchased his land for only eight cents per square foot, many individuals with intentions to set up small community gardens have not been able to get formal permission—neither through lease nor sale—to use the land they cultivate. The city is generally more supportive of efforts proposed by well-financed, non-profit organizations and corporate sponsors than it is of small community groups. We at the DBCFSN see this as problematic because we are generally more in favor of small-scale projects that families or community organizations can run, based on the idea that small-scale projects generally create more job opportunities and community empowerment than larger corporations.

The situation worsened in 2013 when Michigan Governor Rick Snyder appointed Kevyn Orr to act as emergency city manager of Detroit. Snyder took this action based on a law that he himself pushed through to give the governor (himself) the ability to legally appoint an emergency manager to oversee cities' financial operations. The law takes power away from cities' elected officials and places it in the hands of appointed counterparts who are answerable not to the public, but to the governor. During Orr's tenure, he was responsible for approving each and every land sale; these included not only large-scale acquisitions like Hantz Woodlands, but also any attempt by individuals embedded in the community to acquire land. This extreme act of appointing an emergency financial manager, thus, interrupted regular government operations, paralyzed city officials from making positive progress, and made it even more difficult to work toward just governance of land in Detroit.

Alternatives and Opportunities

If we hope to create a society with any possibility for justice, then the question of power distribution and land access is primary. To continue to amass land in the hands of the same individuals is the antithesis of freedom, and it must be struggled against. Traditional capitalistic logic would have it that selling land to the highest-bidder and waiting for "trickle-down" impacts to occur is the only way for Detroit to move forward from its current economic struggles. However, there are many alternative and better ways to build economic resiliency and equity.

Communities are built on the land, and we—as human beings—get most of our food, fibers and materials from it. In our present society, to be without land ownership is to be without power. However, the very concept of individual land ownership is problematic. If a person can own land, then it follows logically that with enough money they could own a river or even an ocean. It suggests that the earth is essentially up for sale. To consider and create the types of societies we would like to see in the future, I believe we must examine this concept critically and think about how we can create equal opportunities for land access without reinforcing conventional ideas about ownership.

It is difficult to imagine how land justice could be reached in the United States, considering the history of land theft and dispossession. How can we have true justice without returning land to the indigenous people that European settlers took it from? How could we find a solution that brings true justice to the people of African descent whose ancestors were enslaved and brought to this land against their will? Finding true "justice"—steps that make amends for these historical acts—is essentially impossible within current realities. However, there are steps that could move us forward.

In cases where the courts can prove that the United States broke treaties or acted in duplicitous ways, I believe that land should be returned by the US government to Native Americans. I also support reparations for the African Americans who are descendants of those Africans that were enslaved on this land and did much of the labor that created the nation's prosperity. Additionally, we must cease the confiscation of land owned by African American farmers. At the time of writing (2016), land is still being unfairly seized from local land-owners and government agents are complicit in the process. This must be investigated and stopped.

Additionally, I believe that community land trusts can be established to allow communities to exert their collective voice in what they want to see happen with land in their communities, and to play a role in decisions regarding green spaces, industrial projects, housing, or anything else that they, themselves, envision for the well-being of their communities. It is important to create policies that give the maximum number of people access to land, as opposed to policies that concentrate ownership in the hands of the few, and support for land trusts could play a role in this.

Finally, I believe that in order to create good analyses of land issues we must understand history. A real telling of the real history is important so that governments, non-profit organizations, and community organizations can have an understanding of how we've gotten to this point. To do this, we must continue lifting up stories of dispossession, disempowerment, resistance, and building power.

References

Aguilar, Louis. 2016. "Putting a price tag on properties linked to Gilbert." *The Detroit News,* April 29.

Data Driven Detroit, 2010. *State of the Detroit child: 2010.* Detroit, Michigan.

Detroit Future City. N/d. "Land & Buildings Assets." Accessed August 9, 2016. http://detroitfuturecity.com/priorities/land%20buildings-resources/.

Gallagher, John. 2015. "What's next for Detroit's vacant lots and who decides?" *Detroit Free Press*, June 1.

Gross, Allie. 2016. "The properties of one Dan Gilbert." *Detroit Metro Times*, April 29.

Halcom, Chad. 2012. "Detroit City Council OKs land sale to Hantz Woodlands." *Crain's Detroit Business,* December 11.

Osorio, Carlos. 2010. "Survey: A third of all Detroit lots are vacant or abandoned." *Associated Press,* February 20.

Safransky, Sara. 2014. "Greening the Urban Frontier: Race, property and resettlement in Detroit." *Geoforum* 56:237-248.

Smith, Eleanor. 2010. "John Hantz." *The Atlantic*, November.

Thibodeau, Ian. 2016. "Dan Gilbert's Bedrock tops 80 properties acquired in downtown Detroit." *MLive Detroit*, Jan 6.

Williams, Corey. 2014. "At Hantz Woodlands in Detroit, 15,000 holes to be filled with tree saplings this weekend." *Crain's Detroit Business*, May 16.

Lessons from and for Land Activism

CHAPTER 13

Occupy the Farm: The Legitimacy of Direct Action to Create Land Commons

Antonio Roman-Alcalá[1]

In 2012, hundreds of students, alumni, community-members, activists, and environmentalists marched to the University of California at Berkeley's "Gill Tract," broke the locks, and occupied this piece of urban agricultural land in order to protest and prevent its privatization. This struggle, known as Occupy the Farm (OTF), also strove to reclaim and rebuild a "land commons." Because land occupations are relatively rare in a United States, OTF attracted much attention, and soon became an emblematic example of food sovereignty struggles in a northern, urban context. In this chapter, I examine how OTF, which I both studied and was involved in, has used direct action in attempts to democratize land access, and I analyze the possibilities and challenges of this approach.

Struggles like OTF help to build "agrarian citizenship"—the active participation in and reflection on the social systems of land use and food production (Wittman 2009)—amongst its participants and supporters. This is an essential underpinning for successful food sovereignty struggles, and is particularly crucial in the US context, in which an industrialized society has meant lost and severed relationships to the land. However, as I will describe below, occupations to build a "land commons" in urban environments located within capitalist society are complex and sometimes contradictory. Occupy the Farm describes its own actions as efforts to "reclaim

[1] This chapter emerges from the author's active participation in and previous study of Occupy the Farm. The author is not currently an active member of the group, but maintains relationships with many of the organizers who have worked and continue to work with Occupy the Farm. Parts of the chapter are based on previously published papers for the Yale Food Sovereignty Symposium in 2013 and the journal Globalizations in 2015.

the commons"[2] by putting land access and decision making in the hands of the public. In OTF's work and in that of other similar struggles, reclaiming the commons is both a defensive and a constructive process; it seeks to protect democratic control of land access, while also improving upon it. However, existing social divisions—often based around race, gender, wealth, and other class factors—complicate the ideals of democratization.

Social divisions present in society at large can be reflected in groups like OTF, and bring up the reality that not all "commoners" are created equal. The process of reclaiming a commons raises the questions: who can make claims to a particular piece of land? Who constitutes the public? Whose claims do those with control over the land listen to? And, if the entire public cannot benefit from a public good provided by a government, who should benefit from it? Moreover, if the goal of action is specifically to advance democratized land access for more marginalized communities (a central demand for true food justice), what is the relationship of land activists to the communities in whose name they act?

As if these questions were not complicated enough, even more come up after a commons has been successfully reclaimed, and must now be managed. Are land occupiers the proper constituency to use and manage a commons once it has been reclaimed? If not, who? Elinor Ostrom (1990), well-known expert of "commons" management, described how "user boundaries," which delineate who is and is not included in a commons, are essential to a functioning commons management system. In the case of Occupy the Farm, these boundaries are unclear and contested. With this in mind, can direct action and land commoning be considered a useful strategy for the democratization of land for less privileged communities in the US (and the Global North more broadly)?

History of the Gill Tract

The University of California, Berkeley (UC Berkeley), the Gill Tract's legal owner, is a "land grant" college, founded in the mid-1860s in order to spread agricultural knowledge across the western frontier. In 1928, the Gill family sold the university their 104 acre parcel, located in Albany,

---

[2] Occupy the Farm organizers used "commons" language in many of the interviews I conducted, along with the frames of "food justice" and "food sovereignty." There are conceptual overlaps between each of these frames, the important aspects being combinations of ecological production, social justice, and democratic control. The goal of the 2012 occupation was to gain community access to the Gill Tract; the expectation was that "the community" would democratically manage the land as an ecological farm focused on education and providing good food to local people who lack food access. For purposes of simplicity I use the term "food justice" to describe the goals of the occupation, recognizing that food sovereignty, food justice, and commoning each provided specific goals and language that were incorporated into the organizing effort, but each frame is not equivalent.

California (near Berkeley), with the intention that it would be used for agricultural research.

From 1945 to the late 1990s, UC Berkeley's Division of Biological Control (DBC) used the Gill Tract for research in biological pest control. However, developments in biotechnologies and molecular genetics eventually caused funding for DBC to decrease and the university's use of the Gill Tract for agricultural purposes to be reduced (Jennings 1997). The university gradually sold off or developed most of the Tract for other purposes, primarily housing. Following a UC Berkeley research agreement with biotechnology corporation Novartis in the late 1990s, the DBC was entirely displaced from the Tract and defunded. This shift was reflective of an overall transition in the university away from ecologically focused farming research and toward investigations into microbiology with applications towards genetically engineered seeds (Jennings 1997; Kloppenburg 2005). At the time of the occupation (2012), all but one researcher using the Gill Tract worked in the field of basic genetics (a field that supports biotechnological applications).

In 1997, a coalition of Bay Area environmental justice organizations and urban agriculture groups approached UC Berkeley with a proposal to convert the remaining Gill Tract land into a site for urban and sustainable farming research and education. Collectively, they put forth the Bay Area Coalition for Urban Agriculture (BACUA) proposal, attempting to integrate the local community's interest in food security and economic justice with UC Berkeley's existing resources at the Gill Tract. While the University briefly entertained BACUA's proposal and allowed for a small community farming project to be maintained on the land for one growing season, it abruptly halted discussions with BACUA a short time later, and did not agree to open the Gill Tract up to community groups.

In 2004, the UC Regents moved to further develop the Gill Tract. They approved a "Master Plan" for what was called the University Village housing development. The plan allowed UC Berkeley's Capital Projects division to develop the remaining portions of the Gill Tract into baseball fields, grocery stores, and market-rate housing. At this point, BACUA had ceased to exist as a coalition, but many community groups, students, Albany residents, and urban farming organizations remained interested in the Tract. Many of these groups opposed the development plans on the grounds that they would displace all agricultural uses from the land, pose potential negative impacts (such as increased vehicle traffic) on the surrounding neighborhood, and result in the privatization of public land. They continued to petition the University to stop the development, but they were unsuccessful.

Nonetheless, the university had to complete various legal, political, and bureaucratic processes before it would be able implement the plans, and it was not until 2011 that the development seemed imminent. In that year, Occupy the Farm formed as an effort to use direct action to prevent the Tract's development and to achieve community access to the land.

Occupation: Events and Narratives

In late 2011, Occupy the Farm—initially a seven-person group of UC Berkeley alumni, students, and local political organizers—began organizing clandestinely to plan a coordinated illegal act of occupation. In 2012, they communicated with local food justice organizations and activists, and found support for the idea of occupation. On Earth Day, April 22, hundreds of participants (including UC Berkeley students and alumni, Occupy Oakland participants,[3] environmentalists, and other urban farming advocates) marched from a nearby park, broke the locks on the Gill Tract's gates, entered, and planted over 15,000 vegetable seedlings. Where the University had denied the potential of a community-based urban farm, they created one anyway.

The occupying group included some of the Gill Tract's immediate neighbors, but the majority came from other communities around the Bay Area.[4] The initial OTF organizers spearheaded a media campaign to spread information about the Gill Tract and its importance to food sovereignty and food justice, and they also supported lawsuits filed by Albany residents to dispute the Environmental Impact Report approved by the city council of Albany for the proposed Capital Projects development.[5] However, in the larger struggle over the Gill Tract, it was the occupation that received and sustained the most attention.

According to one OTF participant:[6]

> The story of how there is a higher use of the [Gill Tract], that it is a common resource that should be governed together, that development was not ideal, and that we were not afraid of hard work, were key elements of broadcasting a new vision.

---

[3] Occupy Oakland was one local manifestation of the "Occupy Wall Street" movement that formed in 2011.

[4] While I use the singular to describe OTF as a group, it must be noted that OTF cannot really be seen as a single entity and has varied in size, participation, forms of action, and demographics over time. Two of the original initiators of the occupation remain involved, but over five years the group has had different people involved, to varying degrees, of varying backgrounds, and for varying periods of time. Given this, it is difficult to make generalizations about OTF's demographics. Overall, many of those involved have been university students, alumni, and neighborhood activists. Many, but not all, have been white.

[5] The residents disputed the claim that the project would have no major impacts and called for a more robust impact assessment.

[6] Following common research practice as well as the wishes of OTF participants and organizers involved in my research, names of interviewees remain anonymous.

During the occupation, OTF questioned land use norms at the Gill Tract, and also discussed and critiqued general trends in the privatization of public resources. They organized workshops and open meetings on various topics relating to the land's history, UC Berkeley's collaboration with biotechnology corporations, and food sovereignty alternatives. Meetings to continue the occupation's organization were run in an open-to-anyone, "general assembly" model, as had been typical of Occupy encampments.

OTF's symbolic resistance in banners, interviews with media, slogans, and ceremonies at public events stood against UC Berkeley's development plans and in favor of a community farm alternative. Local television coverage was uncharacteristically positive; coming on the heels of Occupy Wall Street, media interest in political activism was strong, and this helped situate OTF within broader movements for democracy and food activism. During the initial occupation, thousands of people visited and participated in on-farm activities, and some participants joined in core OTF organizing.

The University, however, promoted an opposing narrative. The administration spokesperson argued that OTF attempted to "unilaterally" decide what the land should be used for, and said that it was undermining the "democratic" consultative process that had already been completed regarding the development plans. Attempting to discourage and stigmatize the occupation, police were deployed to film participants and threaten anyone on the Gill Tract with arrest for trespassing.

The University claimed that OTF was illegitimate, and accused occupiers of trampling on the researchers' "academic freedom" by advocating for agroecological production and putting it into practice. However, these same researchers would have been kicked off the Gill Tract had development moved forward, so the University's efforts to "protect" them seemed disingenuous. Furthermore, though OTF mobilized narratives opposing biotechnology, and the occupation took place on land that would have been used to grow research crops in the coming summer season, the group made efforts to leave already-planted research crops alone, and even attempted to convince researchers (without success) to realign their efforts to join the campaign to save the Gill Tract for agricultural research and education purposes, despite differing positions on biotechnology.

After three weeks, UC Berkeley's riot police forcibly evicted the OTF encampment and made nine arrests. The University also destroyed many of the vegetables planted during the occupation. After this, OTF hosted a series of public forums in order to craft a set of community principles regarding future management of the Gill Tract. Over the course of the year following the camp's eviction, occupiers re-entered the land six times, harvested produce from the planted crops left undestroyed by UC Berkeley (about 1/10th of the original plantings), and distributed thousands of pounds of food, mainly to low-income residents of nearby cities.

In September of 2012, the dean of UC Berkeley's College of Natural Resources (CNR) announced that management authority over the northern portion of the Gill Tract—an area of ten acres—had been transferred from Capital Projects to his college. A referendum by Albany residents forced the city council to rescind approval of the development agreement due to an inadequate Environmental Impact Report. Subsequently, Whole Foods—the proposed development's anchor tenant, to be included on the south side—pulled out of the agreement, citing too many delays. At that point, the existing development project seemed dead.

This was a victory for OTF and allies. However, the southern portion of the Tract was still slated for development under management of Capital Projects, so OTF members continued to organize against these plans. OTF's strategy for contesting the development was to organize a boycott of Sprouts Market, the new potential tenant replacing Whole Foods. OTF also attempted multiple guerrilla plantings on the southern portion, which resulted in arrests and the plowing under of crops by UC Berkeley. The continued emphasis on direct action reflected the interests and politics of the predominating demographics in OTF. Although the group did attempt to build broader alliances, their overarching approach was not necessarily that of the wider Bay Area food justice community, which did not plan or participate much in these actions.[7]

In July of 2013, CNR offered a small section of the north side of the Gill Tract for a "community-based" agroecology project. This project was spearheaded by agroecology professor Miguel Altieri, and community groups (including members of OTF) planted test plots and gathered data on output in order to assess the efficacy of various agroecological approaches. As the north side project developed into a 1.5-acre area, christened the "Gill Tract Community Farm" (GTCF), some OTF members participated in the "collaborative governance" structure for the project, along with students, Albany residents, and CNR faculty.

In the battle over the ongoing threat of development, the idea of "community" management of the *entire* Gill Tract came up against the difficult reality that GTCF participants and Albany residents (that is, some of the most relevant communities connected to the land in question) did not hold unified positions on the development. Albany residents include both active members of OTF and the GTCF, as well as vocal supporters of

---

[7] Low-income fast-food workers united under the banner of "Fight for 15" [hourly wage] did collaborate sporadically on the Sprouts campaign.

development. Those supportive of development claimed legitimate rights to dispute OTF's actions and demands, and these residents often played important roles in media coverage and the rhetoric of UC Berkeley officials.

Nevertheless, the original OTF occupation was successful in changing conditions of community access to the Gill Tract, in large part due to wide-scale participation and support. Even considering observers' potential concern for the action's illegal nature, widespread support for the ideals of sustainable farming, community access, participatory government, and green space helped legitimize the occupation and turn observers into supporters. OTF made an essential contribution by creating spaces for discussion of these issues within the occupation itself, and also through media and wider alliance-building.

Part of OTF's effectiveness was its focus on contextualizing the fight for the Gill Tract; OTF compared the existing use of the land for private sector-serving research to its better social function as a public good. Additionally, the existing history of university professors, students, NGOs, and other community members engaging with the University for urban agroecology and community access helped to legitimize OTF. Without this history and context, it is quite possible that the occupation would have been less effective in eliciting support, and that the outcome of the occupation—a new agroecological educational farm and a politicized base of activists and aspiring farmers passionate about food sovereignty—might have been quite different.

Ambiguities in Commons, Legitimacy, and Democratization of Land Resources

Occupy The Farm showed how diverse communities—students, residents, food justice activists, urban gardeners, and political organizers from different places and backgrounds—could join together to prevent the privatization and enclosure of public resources through direct action as well as other educational and community-building tactics. But protecting a commons from enclosure is not the same as building and managing a commons as a community once it has been established. Moreover, both defensive and constructive "communing" are challenged by the complex social circumstances of publicly owned urban land in capitalist societies.

Successful commons require commoners, user boundaries, an agreed-upon process of decision-making, and at least some degree of community cohesion. As part of a land-grant university located in an urban area, the Gill Tract is land with many constituencies, from hyper local to across the state, who certainly do not all agree on the best and highest use of the land, nor how to manage it. These constituents include, at least, UC Berkeley staff, administrations, and researchers; residents of Albany who are both pro- and anti-development; UC Berkeley students and alumni; the indigenous communities who inhabited and managed the land before white settlers ever arrived; California food justice activists; environmentalists; urban agriculture advocates with an interest in agroecological research; and citizens concerned with biotechnology.

Moreover, participants of the early encampment shared with me in interviews, that—despite use of the "General Assembly" model of consensus—some people felt that key decisions were made by the original core organizers, rather than by the entire encampment. For instance, decisions to ban alcohol on the farm (for "image" purposes) and to only empower certain participants (perceived as more educated and thus more "eloquent") to represent OTF to journalists were, according to these interviewees, reflections of class differences among the campers/occupiers. Core organizers, however, maintained that these decisions were meant to be strategic, rather than exclusionary, and argued that complaints stemmed from some occupiers' commitment to a liberal, middle-class political ideal of "horizontal" decision-making, above other considerations.

While the successes of OTF in reclaiming a portion of the land and raising a discourse about access and food sovereignty are inspirational, the process as well as the outcomes of OTF are ambiguous; they reflect the limitations of democratic decision-making itself under existing power imbalances and social inequalities. This is why land commoning must be critically questioned, and why we must continually ask who benefits or is to be benefitted by such efforts.[8] As some of the brief examples above indicate, OTF couldn't address certain power inequalities with regards to the use and benefit of the Gill Tract, and they also failed to stop the development of the south side. While there are no failsafe strategies, and it is difficult to pinpoint cause and effect, it seems these failures stemmed in part from unequal power relations within the group itself and the dedication of the group (influenced strongly by its most long-time and active members, who are also white and educated) to direct action as a tactic—in addition to the demobilization and recuperation strategies of the University.

This brings up a challenge to OTF's attempts to "reclaim the commons:" it was tactically necessary for OTF to intervene (occupy) on behalf of a "community" left out of decisions about the Gill Tract in order to contest the University's undemocratic land use decisions. OTF never

---

[8] Importantly, such criticism must be leveled at least partly aside from questions of intention on the part of activists, since power and inequality are social, not individual, in origin.

claimed to be the only community relevant to the Tract, nor did occupiers claim exclusive rights to manage the land once it was "saved." In fact, OTF made clear that they occupied in order to provide an opening for relevant pro-food justice constituencies to lay claim to managing the land as a commons. Yet, there was no explicit elaboration of who the pertinent community was to this commons, and thus the door to claim decision-making power was left open for community members who, whether defined geographically or by institutional relationship to the Gill Tract, did not share OTF's positions or political views. Meanwhile, many poor people and people of color working locally for food justice did not take action to make greater claims to the Tract, while college students, OTF members, of members of pro-urban farming Albany residents did.

In addition, few GTCF participants have shown interest in or support for ongoing efforts to prevent development of the south side. The reticence of many Farm participants to engage in OTF's continued direct action attempts to occupy and encamp the south side (in 2015 and 2016) hints at the paradoxical demobilizing effect of victory: winning the concession of the north side farm gave erstwhile occupiers something "positive" and less risky to do to feel they were advancing agroecology and food justice/sovereignty, reducing their interest in the uncertain action of occupying land.

This is a frustrating outcome for those who want to prevent development on the entire Tract, and especially those who repeatedly risked arrest to create the conditions for the GTCF. CNR faculty participating in the management of the GTCF also argued that continued protests against the south side development would jeopardize the success of the north side collaboration, particularly by scaring off potential funders. The presence of the GTCF—itself a victory won by the original occupation—thus managed to hinder continuing efforts to prevent development on the south side.

All commons are challenged by "internal" stratification and marked by racial, ethnic, gender, and generational conflicts of interest (Borras and Franco 2012). No one has a predetermined right to represent the "public" in contentious issues of public good, and those from more marginalized segments of society tend to be less visible, vocal, or listened to in debates over particular public resources. In contention over public resources, expanding legitimacy of claims often requires meaningful representation of the interests of communities at the base of society—"the people"—and the way struggle is conducted over the resource has impacts on this degree of meaningfulness and thus the level of success in contention.

Since participation in many spheres of decision-making and action is shaped by existing social inequalities, representation can often end up rehashing the same old structures of power: the white and privileged attending meetings, making plans, accessing resources, and determining the social conceptions of commons. OTF, to some degree, was "guilty" of this, in that low-income people (and especially low-income people of color) were not the main drivers of the occupation or the most involved constituencies in the GTCF. Even more troubling, some people of color and women involved in OTF have expressed feeling marginalized by patriarchy, white supremacy, and classism in the group, exhibited in decisions and behaviors of key organizers.

The Role of Legitimacy

Legitimacy for the occupation came from three main forces: (1) narratives about the land that emphasized its historical role as a space for agricultural research, (2) community-driven struggles over the land that preceded the occupation itself (especially BACUA), and (3) social sectors committed to the wider issues the occupation addressed (such as the action's anti-GMO and anti-privatization narratives). To the extent that Occupy the Farm manifested itself as a righteous and necessary social intervention to support struggles based in this land, its adjacent geographic community, and the larger community with interest in the land, it held the perceived legitimacy necessary to garner significant support.

In the case of the State of California's public university system, all Californians should benefit, so all the state's residents have a "right" to make claims of opposition to privatization. Claims to more specific public benefits from a public resource, however, are less clear: would any Californian have a right to gain from UC land? Why one particular benefit rather than another?

In the case of the Gill Tract, an argument made against OTF was that "the community" of Albany deserved to benefit first and foremost. Insofar as Albany residents expressed preference for development, the legitimacy of OTF's claims are put in question. Indeed, the main argument from pro-development Albany city councilmembers was that the development would bring valuable tax revenues that UC Berkeley's ownership of the land (as a tax-exempt public institution) did not.

From a food justice perspective, legitimacy also requires that a group creates tangible changes for racial and economic justice. Some activist groups attempt to represent marginalized groups without their inclusion, or attempt to bring more marginalized constituencies into their groups after the fact, to bolster claims of diversity and inclusion. Such tokenism rarely leads to legitimate inclusion. What matters are the tangible impacts and normative implications of actions on communities of color and people from more marginalized social positions, generally. In this sense, OTF has exceled at foregrounding race and justice issues, but has been less effective at including food justice constituencies in its direct action organizing. The resulting GTCF has had a bit more success here, probably due to being a "safer," more stable and resourced space for participation.

What OTF has done is to act in solidarity with justice struggles of other non-white and marginalized communities, locally and internationally. OTF supported the creation and defense of the guerrilla garden in Oakland known as Afrikatown—a space explicitly dedicated to de-gentrification struggles and community building among Black and Indigenous people. Individuals within OTF have worked with and for local food justice organizations like Phat Beets Produce, Planting Justice, and Urban Tilth. In the case of the struggle for the Tract itself, in 2015, the group stepped back as the main organizers of anti-development action in order to support the "Indigenous Land Action Coalition," a group of organizers of indigenous ancestry who wanted to bring attention to the land's original inhabitants and commoners. OTF has also hosted international exchanges with militants from the Landless Workers' Movement of Brazil, who are well known for organizing land occupations to reclaim land for agroecology and food sovereignty.

These efforts notwithstanding, the Gill Tract land itself may not be serving these constituencies as much as they continue to serve more privileged members of society, namely students of UC Berkeley and residents of the relatively wealthier north East Bay. And while OTF has not been demographically homogenous over the course of its history, as a core group it remains led by white activists, and key leadership roles have largely remained with a smaller number of mostly white organizers.

I believe it is of crucial importance to recognize in this critique that anti-racism is a process, not a singular act, and no one should be "faulted" for failing to overcome white supremacy in a single instance of organizing. This is simply not something someone can accomplish or fail to do at any one moment. The importance of OTF's example is showing how (mostly white) antiracist political groups still face limits to achieving impacts for the most marginalized racial, ethnic, and social groups in society.

What does OTF Offer Marginalized Communities and the Greater Food Justice Movement?

The claims that Occupy the Farm made at the Gill Tract—particularly that government property is the peoples' right and should therefore serve those people rather than corporate interests—resonated with many people. Yet some members of marginalized groups (particularly indigenous groups, but also others like queer people and people of color) have never felt included in the "public" served by the state in the first place, so the idea of "reclaiming" a public sphere that has not previously served them can be strange. In settler colonial society, claims over stolen land are multi-layered and never straightforward.

Yet, the idea that people can act directly to reclaim land and move towards greater food justice is inspiring, and the story is certainly one that needs to be told. The occupation has elevated the story that "direct action gets the goods," by pushing the university to better enact its mandate to serve the public good, including better representation of the needs of marginalized groups. The occupation worked to achieve change in access and management. OTF—even if not as inclusive and representative as it might like to be—succeeded in opening up pathways towards a greater diversity of research and educational interests at the Gill Tract than existed before; this constitutes a meaningful, even if imperfect and partial, step towards food justice.

Another important implication is that food sovereignty requires the reclamation of the public sphere surrounding the (re)production of crops, farms, and agricultural knowledge; this need to reclaim public science, public education, and public space implicates urban folks in constructing food sovereignty as much as it requires rural people. There is hope in the reclamation of peasant identity and capacities, and in the politicization that comes with direct actions that create spaces for this reclamation. This construction of "agrarian citizenship" among urbanites is no doubt a slow process, requiring rebuilding among people who have been historically divorced from land and the difficult politics of commoning. This more urbanized form of agrarian citizenship offers promise, as well, in creating social, political, and agrarian connections across identities and geographies, from Black land liberation in the flatlands of Oakland to white antiracist activism in the student movement.

Another important lesson is that each site of struggle will succeed only inasmuch as it reflects previous trajectories of struggle: direct action cannot be expected to work plopped down on a community. Just the same, looking at the OTF case, we see that in any struggle over land we will find multiple forms of contestation between and within classes and individuals, including contestation over rights, legitimacy, and particular claims. These will be negotiated by actors and actor groups in each circumstance, and there simply are no easy answers to the question of how to make direct action to reclaim the commons "work" in advancing food justice and food sovereignty. There is no guaranteed way to organize a direct action successfully, or to build a truly inclusive and justice-building land commons.

The Frame of "Land Sovereignty"

The typical (and powerful) narrative of the global food sovereignty is of land access and control for peasants, who are assumed to form the production base for a sovereign food system globally (Bernstein 2014, 2). In the US and many other more industrialized societies, however, there are few obvious "peasants" who would benefit from such democratized land access (usually expected to come about from government-involved land reform).

Borras and Franco (2012) propose the concept of "land sovereignty" to frame land politics in a way that effectively encompasses a plurality of struggles over land. Land sovereignty is "the right of working peoples to have effective access to, use of, and control over land and the benefits of its use and occupation, where land is understood as resource, territory, and landscape" (ibid). Looking at the case of Occupy the Farm, it seems that land sovereignty offers a more compelling framework than either land reform or commons.

Land sovereignty addresses the conditions that affect real and sustained access to land, differentiating between land access and property rights, reminding us that the ability to derive benefit from land is not equivalent to ownership (Ribot and Peluso 2003, 6). This frame treats the role of governments critically, accepting that they both facilitate land dispossession and concentration on one hand, and offer potential opportunities for increased land access for non-elites on the other (Borras and Franco 2012, 7). Land sovereignty addresses land redistribution for economic justice, but also social justice more broadly, drawing attention to the unfortunate and sometimes-ignored intra-community inequalities that may exist regarding land access and use. This frame, then, can direct our view towards the difficulties of working class commoning, helping keep attention to the ways in which this class is itself stratified in many ways.

Future Directions for the Use of Direct Action for Food Justice

The OTF occupation achieved material gains and advanced the idea of community rights to public land and the benefits of its use. The gains included halting the north side development; the transfer of ten acres to CNR's management; and the food, education, and experiences from the resulting GTCF. The occupation made tangible progress on community access to the Gill Tract, while building a politicized agrarian citizenry and potentially inspiring others to consider direct action occupations as a viable tactic. The OTF action showed that land occupations could counter the dominant mainstream food production model (in this case the research agenda which supports it) and legitimize food justice/sovereignty alternatives, while leading to greater space to grow sustainable and accessible food.

Occupations might not achieve all of their food sovereignty or food justice goals, but they might help advance the idea of community and public rights to land and the benefits of its use, and may even result in tangible access, too. But over the long term, achieving land justice means changing overall norms of land use and structures of land ownership in society. This cannot be built simply by occasional and dispersed actions, but requires a long term and mass movement to change the way land rights are thought of, actualized, and supported—by citizens, governments, institutions, and others. Insofar as Occupy the Farm has helped build these movements, it has succeeded.

Note: For more information, please see www.takebackthetract.com. A documentary film on Occupy the Farm is available at www.occupythefarmfilm.com.

References

Bernstein, Henry. 2014. "Food sovereignty via the 'peasant way': a sceptical view." *Journal of Peasant Studies* 41(6): 1031-1063.

Borras, S.M. Jr. and Jennifer Franco. 2012. *A 'Land Sovereignty' Alternative? Towards a Peoples' Counter-Enclosure.* Amsterdam: Transnational Institute.

Jennings, Bruce H. 1997. "The Killing Fields: Science and Politics at Berkeley, California, USA." *Agriculture and Human Values* 14(3): 259-271.

Kloppenburg, Jack Ralph Jr. 2005. *First the Seed: The Political Economy of Plant Biotechnology (Science and Technology in Society).* Madison: University of Wisconsin Press, 2nd edition.

Ostrom, Elinor. 1990. *Governing the Commons: The Evolution of Institutions for Collective Action.* New York: Cambridge University Press.

Ribot, Jesse and Nancy Lee Peluso. 2003. "A Theory of Access." *Rural Sociology* 68(2): 153-181.

Wittman, Hannah. 2009. "Reworking the metabolic rift: La Vía Campesina, agrarian citizenship, and food sovereignty." *The Journal of Peasant Studies* 36(4): 805–826.

CHAPTER 14

National Land for the People and the Struggle for Agrarian Reform in California

Cliff Welch[1]

George and Maia Ballis wanted to get everyone to take one of their "seminar in reality" tours of California's Central Valley. "If we could figure out a way to get everybody to take the tour," George wrote in 1982, "we would win this fight no matter how much money the biggies spent" (Ballis 1982, 15). Ballis, a small-farm defender since the 1950s, used the reality tour to encourage participants to question the US agribusiness model. He wanted to win their support for a policy that prevented farms over 160-acres from receiving irrigation water from something known as the Central Valley Project (CVP).

Work began on the CVP in 1937. Gradually, 20 dams and reservoirs, pumping stations, and hundreds of miles of canals were built from Mount Shasta in northern California to Bakersfield in southern California. A massive undertaking that took decades to construct, the project currently moves around 7 million acre-feet[2] of water a year from the wet areas of the north and east to the dry areas of the south and western parts of California's 400-mile long central basin. The largest public works project in US history, CVP dams store around 13 million acre-feet of water, helping to control floods, generate electricity, supply drinking water, and irrigate more than 3 million acres of farmland (USBR 2013).

This last CVP statistic is the cornerstone of California's world leadership

[1] The author thanks Justine MacKesson Williams and Maia Ballis for their helpful comments and Brazil's Coordination for the Improvement of Higher Education Personnel (CAPES) for Senior Fellowship grant BEX 3964/13-4, supporting his research in California.

[2] An acre-foot is a unit of measure representing the quantity of water necessary to flood an acre of land at a depth of 12-inches, which is equivalent to a volume of 43,560 cubic feet.

in agricultural production. It has allowed the state's agribusiness leaders to create "the most prosperous agricultural region of the advanced industrial nations" (Walker 2004, 3). It also inspired the Ballises to activism, provoking them to do all they could to break-up "the biggies" of California's corporate agro-industries. As they saw it, the rapacious power of these agribusiness corporations could be controlled if the federal government enforced a 160-the size of farms eligible to receive CVP irrigation water. A 1902 federal law mandated such acreage limits on all farms irrigated by United States Bureau of Reclamation (USBR) water projects in the 17 western states. From the perspective of the Ballises, enforcing the act would transform American society by destroying vast estates; containing agribusiness lobbies; empowering farmworkers and landless farmers; discouraging monoculture; limiting the use of chemicals; preserving aquifers; and strengthening public health through the production of healthier food.

The 1902 Reclamation Act

Congress established the 160-acre limit in the 1902 Reclamation Act, signed into law by President Theodore Roosevelt. The act embodied the commitments of a decade-long campaign by moralists and social reformers to institutionalize agrarian values in the use of tax money. If taxpayer money were to be spent to "reclaim" arid western lands through the costly redistribution of its water resources, debated one South Dakota congressman, the benefits should be reserved "exclusively for the protection of the settler and actual homebuilder, and every possible safeguard... made against speculative ownership and the concentration of land and water privileges into large holdings" (Hundley 2001, 118).

On its own terms, the 160-acre limitation intermingled several dimensions of interventions. The first dimension aimed to prevent land concentration and strengthen rural occupation. In the case of federally funded water projects, the 1902 act stated:

> No right to the use of water for land in private ownership shall be sold for a tract exceeding one hundred sixty acres to any landowner and no such sale shall be made to any landowner unless he be an actual bona fide resident on such land, or occupant thereof residing in the neighborhood of said land (US Reclamation Act 1902).

Publicly owned land was to be given away at no charge. Privately owned land holdings larger than 160-acres—called "excess lands"—had to be sold off in units no larger than 160 acres in order to receive irrigation water. By requiring beneficiaries to live on or near their farms, legislators strived to avoid absentee ownership with its tendency to encourage land concentration and social stratification.

A second major dimension was that of providing water and its byproducts—like hydroelectric energy—nearly free of charge to family farmers and local authorities. Whatever expenses were involved were to be subsidized through long and lax pay-off terms. In addition, the newly settled family farmers could count on rural extension services from state or federal agencies. The first commissioner of the US Reclamation Service, established to implement the 1902 law, commented that his agency's duty was "not so much to irrigate the land as it is to make homes. . . whereby the man with a family can get enough land to support that family" (F. H. Newell in Frampton 1979/1980, 92).

Supporters of the act saw in it, "a chance for 'the moral regeneration of the nation'," wrote the historian Norris Hundley, Jr. (2001, 116). He described it as "a counterpoise in American society to the rampant individualism that, in states like California, had led to monopolistic land and water holdings and thousands of landless agricultural laborers." Salvationist ends like these animated the Reclamation Act and had profound roots in both Christian notions of the "promised land" and secular intellectual circles stemming from enlightenment thinkers like John Locke and Thomas Jefferson. President Abraham Lincoln appealed to both when he opened the west to settlers with the Homestead Act of 1862. The distribution of public lands to needy and willing workers—*land reform*—became a capitalist development policy in the United States, especially when it was tied to granting large tracts of land to railroad company investors like California's Leland Stanford, president of the Central Pacific (later Southern Pacific) Railroad Company.

The social import of such "irrigation crusaders" only became more present as the act was amended in 1912, 1914, and 1926. Although the law faced opposition, a majority of legislators consistently strengthened its reformist qualities. The point of the 160-acre limit, a Nevada congressman commented, was "not only to prevent the creation of monopoly in the lands now belonging to the Government, but to break up existing land monopoly in the West" (Newlands in Koppes 1978, 610). To close loopholes, they placed a ten-year limit on excess land sales, and specified that prices had to reflect the value of the land before the availability of irrigation water. To help small farmers, Congress also relaxed repayment terms. Indeed, project planners counted on energy sales to the private sector to pay nearly all construction and maintenance costs. Farmers had 40 years to pay their debts, did not need to start making payments until the 11th year of occupancy, and were charged no interest. Numerous institutions, including labor unions, churches, veterans' organizations, and farmer groups like the California Grange supported the belief that public appropriations should benefit all people equally, not just a few big companies.

At least two tendencies undermined the transformative aspirations of the amended act, creating a situation that required advocates like Ballis to push for enforcement. Perhaps the most important was the resistance of landowners and agribusiness interests. Whereas many idealizers —the irrigationists—imagined the West as a "virgin land" waiting to be designed by its conquerors, most of the space had long been disputed. In the case of California, the government had already granted large tracts of the Central Valley to Stanford and his railroad companies. Other historic beneficiaries included owners of The Los Angeles Times and owners of transnational agribusinesses, like the Del Monte canning company (Burbach and Flynn 1980). A 1945 study revealed that just four percent of landowners in three San Joaquin Valley counties controlled more than half of all irrigable land (Taylor 1949, 243). These firms and landlords lobbied tirelessly to gain exemption from the 160-acre limit in order to retain their privileges and benefit from public water and energy subsidies.

Another influence was the US economy's rapid growth following World War II. Most returning soldiers, many of them from the countryside, sought work in the newly booming industrial sector rather than agriculture. The shift toward cities strengthened the tendency of ambitious politicians and bureaucrats to ignore the distributive features of reclamation law. While a diversity of politicians, bureaucrats, and civil society organizations defended the 160-acre limit into the 1980s, the experience of partnership between big business and big government in confronting the Great Depression and WWII enthroned such relationships. Politicians sought the support of wealthy landowners, and the new commissioner of the USBR, Michael Straus, sought to consolidate the leadership of his agency in public works. "The growth emphasis meant that the Bureau of Reclamation placed more importance on increasing the capacity of dam and irrigation works; how the products were distributed became secondary" (Koppes 1978, 621).

While Straus—who led the agency from 1946 to 1953—testified in support of the 160-acre limit and other redistributive provisions of reclamation law, he devised two strategies to help landowners. He called them "technical compliance" and "accelerated payment," and established directives to instruct landowners how to skirt the law's objectives (Koppes 1978, 624-28). Through "technical compliance," landholdings could be increased by attributing every 160-acre parcel to individual members of a corporate board of directors. For those who were married, both spouses could be claimed as title-holders, doubling the limit to 320 acres. Gradually, those with "technical" titles expanded to include other relatives, managers, and friends.

Through "accelerated payments," landowners were encouraged to believe they could free themselves from reclamation regulations. According to Straus, landlords could evade the 160-acre limitation if they paid-off the cost of supplying water to a farm through a bureau project within the allowable 10-year period for selling off "excess-lands." Thus, by the 1950s, the agency created to enforce the 160-acre limit actually worked to undermine it, presenting itself publicly as dedicated to small family farming, while surreptitiously gutting policies specifically designed to break-up land monopolies and redistribute the land, water, and power to needy families. The post-war mantra of economic development and a rapidly growing economy helped mask the subterfuge.

The Central Valley Project

Due to semi-arid climatic conditions, California's 42,000 square-mile Central Valley required a massive intervention to harness its agricultural potential, a "reclaiming" conceived without consideration for its potential environmental impact. By the 1930s, when the California legislature approved the first viable plans for irrigating the region, the valley's powerful cluster of landlords showed little interest in supporting projects requiring Bureau of Reclamation participation. They feared being forced to break-up their estates.

But since the state lacked adequate resources to build the project independently, legislators asked voters to approve federal involvement in 1935. In the context of the Great Depression, the Roosevelt administration favored the 160-acre rule to generate jobs and weaken the influence of conservative landlords. As the project proceeded, diverse efforts to escape the limit were attempted, including involvement of the Army Corps of Engineers—which excluded some water districts from Reclamation Act norms—and funding for the California Water Project, a proposed state-run system with no acreage limitations that received voter approval in 1960. Thereafter, the state constructed a massive aqueduct carrying water some 400 miles down the dry west side of the San Joaquin valley and pumping it 2,000 feet uphill at the Tehachapi Pass, in order to bring water to thirsty Los Angeles and its sprawling suburbs (Arax & Wartzman 2003, 350-51). The aqueduct was to be fed by the San Luis unit.

As a reclamation bureau project, the San Luis unit played an emblematic role in the history of the CVP, and in George Ballis's political awareness. Junior congressman Bernie F. Sisk became the project's main advocate in the House of Representatives in the late 1950s. An apparently liberal Democrat, Sisk accepted funding from Central Valley agribusiness leaders and responded to their demands by sponsoring legislation to appropriate $500 million for building the unit.

In 1959, Sisk defended the legislation in Congress, testifying that if the San Luis unit were built, "the present population of the area will almost quadruple. There will be 27,000 farm residents, 30,700 rural non-farm residents, and 29,800 city dwellers; in all, 87,500 people sharing the productivity and the bounty of fertile lands blossoming with an ample supply of San Luis water" (Sisk in Carter 2009, 12). Sisk further claimed that the 160-acre limit would force the number of farms in the irrigated area to increase from "1,050 ownerships. . . [to] 6,100 farms, nearly a sixfold increase." The Reclamation Law would "assure fair prices in the breaking up of farms to family-size units."

Sisk's representations helped win funding in 1960, and his cooperation with big farmers helped him get re-elected until he retired in January 1979. However, nothing Sisk claimed came true. Indeed, the number of farms actually decreased to 216 in 1979, with most in the 2,000- to 3,000-acre range, while giant agribusiness firms like J.G. Boswell's Boston Ranch[3] retained over 26,000 acres, Harris Farms more than 18,000 acres, and Southern Pacific over 100,000 acres (Frampton, 1979, 90).

The progress of the San Luis unit depended on a number of "circumventions" that increasingly came to be structurally embedded in the CVP. The economist Paul S. Taylor, a tireless defender of the Reclamation Act, revealed an ever more complicated pattern of policy decisions designed to make "excess lands" disappear (Taylor 1964). One strategy involved convincing lawmakers that "recordable contracts" anticipating the sale of property over 160-acres did not need to be concluded before congress allocated funding for construction, contrary to the procedures written into the law and its amendments. This enabled the USBR to remove negotiations with landowners from public view, where backroom "technical compliance" deals could be struck.

Agrarian Reform in California

Ballis' grasp of California politics grew with the advancing San Luis unit. Much of his work hinged on exposing "technical compliance" and the diverse unjust subterfuges involved in it. In fact, it was in the context of the

---

[3] Due to its extraordinary influence in California and beyond during much of the 20th century, the Boswell family was the subject of a penetrating study by journalists Mark Arax and Rick Wartzman (2003).

San Luis project that he first rehearsed many of the tactics that would define National Land for People—his project for agrarian reform—in the 1970s. In the 1950s, George raised questions about Sisk's dependency on big farm campaign contributions. Published in Fresno's *Valley Labor Citizen*, where he worked as editor-in-chief, Ballis's editorials provoked Taylor to send him a packet of information about the 160-acre limit and the CVP. Eventually, the economist taught him "not only the details of the federal irrigation program and its abuses, but the historic and worldwide framework of land reform" (Ballis 1982, 5).

Taylor's land reform expertise led the United Nations (UN) to hire him to evaluate the relationship between land tenure and community development in Latin America (Taylor Papers, Folder 32-27). After the Cuban Revolution of 1959, land reform became a central part of the Alliance for Progress. To participate in the aid program, nations had to pass land reform laws intended to build up a rural middle class by transforming both small *minifundio* (land said to be incapable of producing a surplus) and large *latifundio* (land maintained by owners for status rather than productive purposes) into mid-sized operations.

Despite discourses of socio-economic improvement, most national histories unfolded in ways that eliminated large numbers of minifundio, forcing millions of peasants to move to urban slums, while expanding latifundio, through the distribution of minifundo among the cronies of governing elites. Some latifundio received subsidies to enhance their productive capacity and efficiency through mechanization and the application of chemical inputs, influencing the growth of agroindustry (Petras & LaPorte 1971). In other words, land reform in Latin America came to mean land grabbing, land monopolization, and increased social stratification (Burbach & Flynn 1979). As we have seen, promise and practice also diverged sharply in the Central Valley, where Sisk's congressional district— one of the richest—ranked worst in the country in terms of human development (Burd-Sharps & Lewis, 2011).

Informed by Taylor, Ballis became increasingly involved in trying to correct this divergence and achieve the agrarian dream, that persistent longing in American culture, "that only agriculture and landownership could ensure independence and virtue, thereby providing the basis for a republican democracy" (Guthman 2004, 10). Ballis led a group of young Democrats in Fresno in producing a series of landownership maps of the San Joaquin Valley. They called the series their "obscene slide show" because it documented illegal land concentration in the valley. Ballis used it to lobby in congress to amend the bill Sisk supported.

In 1962, the "seminars in reality" began. From the mid-1960s to the mid-1970s, Ballis regularly set out in a rented bus with 30 to 60 people who sought to understand how agrarian reform could be implemented in the Central Valley. Participants signed petitions to authorities to enforce the 160-acre limit. Demands for the tour grew as the 1960s unfolded and a counter-culture took shape, especially in the San Francisco Bay Area, lacing together environmental concerns; the anti-Vietnam war movement; criticism of US imperialism; the civil rights struggle; fear of corporate power; and demands for pesticide-free, unprocessed "health food." Ballis both fed-off these influences and contributed to them.

In 1972, Ballis and Taylor took part in organizing the National Coalition for Land Reform by preparing a ballot initiative to support agrarian reform in California (Taylor Papers, Folder 32-15). The proposal suggested an acreage limit on farms receiving water from the CVP. To wrangle support, Governor G. "Pat" Brown promised to limit farm size once the project was built. But Brown's chief water advisor was an attorney for large corporate farmers, so Brown never fulfilled his promise. The National Coalition's ballot initiative never got on the ballot either, but the coalition held a national conference on land reform attended by 400 people, published a broadsheet magazine called *People & Land,* and produced a book called *The People's Land* (Barnes 1975). In other words, while the idea of agrarian reform in California may seem a fantasy today, it was the objective of a fairly broad-based social movement just two generations ago.

National Land for People

Based in Fresno, the National Land for People (NLP) was incorporated as a non-profit in 1974. It was *national* because its main cause was to agitate, sue, and lobby for implementation of the federal Reclamation Act. The NLP also understood its work as part of the international land reform movement, which it interpreted as providing *land* and other resources for *people*, especially through the break-up of large federally irrigated agricultural estates by enforcing contractual sales at dry land prices (excluding the value of federal water).

Had the NLP succeeded, California would have undergone an historic transformation, beginning with dramatic changes to the Central Valley landscape and ending with political renovation. It must be remembered that the factory farms that lawyer and social critic Carey McWilliams (1966 [1935]) railed against in the 1930s still operated in the valley on the basis of 19th century social relations. Valley landlords depended on hundreds of thousands of migrant farmworkers to get the job done. Machine harvesting was most advanced in cotton, totally displacing workers by 1970, but still highly controversial in the harvesting of tomato, grape, and other valley crops. Machines not only put people out of work, they also increased land concentration due to economies of scale. Very costly, they functioned most efficiently on large fields, which also promoted monoculture and aerial spraying of deadly pesticides (De Janvry et al. 1981). These agricultural practices also encouraged wasteful flood irrigation. Forcing the sale of excess lands under the Reclamation Act would have disrupted all of these practices and processes, with international ramifications as yet to be imagined.[4]

Instead, it was the Reclamation Act that somersaulted when it underwent a process of revision during the first years that Ronald Reagan, a former California governor long allied with big growers, was president. James Watt served as Reagan's interior secretary and, according to *The King of California*, the Central Valley entrepreneur J. G. Boswell "persuaded" Watt "to tear out the teeth of the eighty-year-old federal reclamation law all in the name of keeping Boswell territory in one piece" (7-8). Of course, the process was complicated, but the result derailed the NLP and George Ballis.

Research in the NLP records reveals their deep suspicion of capitalist power, corrupt politicians, and an imperial presidency. They also show that a large number of organizations and people around the country believed agrarian reform was fundamental to setting the US and the world on a healthy course. Allies included Ralph Nader in Washington, DC, and the Haight-Ashbury Food Conspiracy, part of San Francisco's counterculture food scene (Curl 2012).

From beginning to end, George Ballis acted as executive director of the NLP. Born in 1925 in a small farming town in Minnesota, he first learned about the world beyond the 100-mile radius of his home as a Marine Corps mechanic in the Pacific Theater of World War II. After the war, he studied at the University of Minnesota, married and in 1953, moved to Fresno to work on the *Valley Labor Citizen*. Eventually, his advocacy of United Farm Workers (UFW) organizing and the 160-acre limit provoked the Central Labor Council, responsible for newspaper, to demand his resignation. Around 1970, he divorced his first wife and became involved with Maia Sorter, who applied her graphic artist skills to charting illegal land sales and producing more "obscene slides" and

---

[4] Of course, imagining a world without industrial agriculture is at least as old as Alexander Chayanov (1986 [1920], xliv-xlvi) and as recent as the on-going Local Food movement.

the NLP monthly newsletter. "It was just such a rich time of exploration and possibility," commented Maia (Ballis 2014). Together, they built the NLP as a lobby, advocacy group, and community-farm alliance that ran a food co-op and organized a network of farm suppliers. These diverse elements made-up what George and Maia described as their "spiral strategy" of organizing (Ballis 1982, 34).

Through this multi-level approach, the NLP sought to create a development model for a re-imagined Central Valley. Implementation of the 160-acre limit was the strategy for bringing a flood of small-farm properties to the market. To prepare, they collected information on farmworkers and others who might want to farm their own land and generated guides to small-scale farming. The main public thrust included gathering information to feed the publication of newspaper articles and production of film documentaries; they also included public speaking appearances, membership growth, and petition drives. To be prepared for winning the battle, the NLP also worked to support existing small farms, to recruit farmers like Berge Bulbulian, an Armenian grape grower with a 150-acre farm on the Valley's eastside, and outreach to former farmworkers like UFW organizer Jessie de la Cruz, who belonged to a small, cooperative farm. The board of the NLP was headed by Bulbulian and included representatives not only of Armenian growers and Mexican farmworkers, but also of African-American and Asian farmers.

Yet another loop in the spiral was that of farm conversion from conventional to alternative agricultural methods. During the "seminars in reality," the bus stopped for a view of the Harris Farms feedlot, where 100,000 cattle awaited their deaths, engorging on drug-laden feed. There, George "made the case for vegetarianism," noting not only the cruelty of the confinement system but its inefficacy and insalubrity for both cows and consumers. For the Ballises, the personal was political. George recalls saying, "The reforming out of our land and our food system begins the first time we DON'T go to the McDonald's, or the first time we pick a tomato we have grown" (Ballis 1982, 30).

Another turn of the spiral was the fight to preserve the law in congress and its enforcement through the courts. Most of their efforts focused on the westside of the Valley, where CVP water started to be delivered in the 1960s. Accordingly, the 1970s marked the outer limit of the ten-year tolerance period for excess-land sales. The two battlegrounds—Congress and the courts—required the NLP to have a lawyer. They found an excellent attorney in Mary Louise Frampton, who gathered significant evidence to document violations of the reclamation law by Westlands Water District property owners.

In 1976, the NLP advanced a test case by mobilizing members to buy "excess land." Even though the ten-year limit had passed, they found no "for sale" signs on the Westlands District. Landlords used "technical compliance" and other tactics to evade the law by transferring lots to associates and family. Bureau of Reclamation involvement made it a federal case, and the NLP sued the federal government for violating the will of Congress. Ballis wrote of the trial:

> On one side of the court, Frampton, rosy-cheeked, looking like that all-American girl next door, with her brother George, equally clean cut. Back of them, Jessie de la Cruz, leader of a small farmer's co-op and secretary of the NLP. Eddie Nolan, African American director of a successful black and Latino farmer's co-op and NLP board member; and myself. On the other side of the court, 12 very prosperous looking older attorneys. Back of these attorneys, several of the biggies, including Jack Harris [of Harris Farms], looking the part of the plantation owner (Ballis 1982, 32).

This time, David beat Goliath. The interior department was ordered to stop all excess land sales until new rules and regulations were written in compliance with the Reclamation Act.

The decision came down in the midst of the presidential campaigns that elected Jimmy Carter. The court victory moved much of the debate from the courts to the chambers of the interior department and corridors of congress, but little changed until Carter's inauguration in 1977. His interior secretary, Cecil Andrus, proved sympathetic to the NLP position, and set about writing regulations. Hearings were held around the west, but their promulgation was blocked by an injunction obtained by the Farm Bureau, the powerful big-agriculture lobby aligned with the Republican Party.

In this context, congress sought to amend the act. During the negotiations, Ballis and the National Farmers Union (NFU), a family farm lobby aligned with the Democratic Party, accepted the idea of coupling a "15-mile residency" requirement with a "640-acre limit on the amount of land which could be irrigated with federal water by any one farm operation" (Ballis 1982, 32). Late in 1977, Taylor got word of the concession and warned Ballis that any negotiation of the 160-acre limit would betray the Reclamation Act (Taylor Papers, Folder 2-1). Indeed, revising the law allowed its enemies to stall a vote until Carter lost his re-election bid to Ronald Reagan. With Reagan in power, Ballis found himself and the NLP undermined at every turn. Instead of issuing rules to control excess land sales, Watt worked with allies in Congress to pass the Reclamation Reform Act in 1982. It raised the 160-acre limit six fold to 960 acres, eliminated the residency requirement and left "market forces" to decide excess-land prices.

Lessons for Today

After the reform act passed, Ballis finished an autobiographical essay. "A week after Congress finally buried the 160," he wrote, "the main message seems to be that we humans are incapable of sustaining a good society" (Ballis 1982, 41-42). Soon after this, he and Maia took "national" out of the NLP's name and added the word "food" to create the "People, Food & Land Foundation." In 1983, they established a land trust in the Sierra Nevada and moved to a 40-acre farm they called Sun Mountain to try and foster an alternative community.

George concluded that it was folly to have lobbied for legislation while "the biggies" were spending more than $250,000 a month to defeat their efforts (Ballis 1982, 37-38). He noted the electoral defeat of his allies in congress and challenged the legislature's "authority, legal or moral, to give the West to a few rich people." He evidenced a rural class divide somewhat equivalent to the contemporary "99%" argument. Almost "96 percent of existing reclamation farms are in compliance with the policies proposed by Land for People," he wrote. "The remaining 4 percent of a total of 1,837 farms in the entire 17 western states, operate nearly 40 percent of reclamation land. These are the beneficiaries of the new legislation" (39).

Many of the key contradictions that plagued the NLP continued to be debated three decades later by newer groups formed around land access and small farm viability questions, such as the Community Alliance with Family Farmers (CAFF) and National Family Farm Coalition (NFFC) in the US, the Landless Workers' Movement in Brazil, and La Vía Campesina internationally. In California, CAFF started out in 1978 defending farmworkers who had been displaced by machines, confronting "the biggies" of agro-industry, and continues lobbying the California legislature to develop and amend laws to help small-scale, ecologically sustainable agriculture thrive. The NFFC promotes the "local food" movement nationwide, fights against subsidies for agro-industry and, in 2016, sponsored an international conference on "people's agrarian reform." In more than 100 countries worldwide, direct-action peasant organizations like the MST, affiliates of La Vía Campesina, engage in land and resource access struggles. Thus, fighting for public policy that helps family farmers hardly ended when George and Maia retreated to Sun Mountain.

They had decided there was no "constituency" for what the NLP advocated. George worried that all "smallies" aspired to become "biggies," but it is probably more realistic to conclude that after years of struggle, land reform in the Central Valley seemed too much like a pipe dream. For many farmers, such drawn-out struggles as the NLP's failed to be practical, an important value for those who make their living from the soil. But the persistent organizing in resistance to industrial agriculture demonstrates that dreams die-hard and hopes live on, challenging Ballis's suspicions that all small farmers want to become "biggies." The persistence of farming as a *way of life* rather than a *road to riches* remains relevant in the 21st century and the NLP's stalwart struggle is one more chapter that proves the point.

Another lesson of the NLP story is the attention it gave to public policy and the state. The progressive movement in turn-of-the-century US politics produced the Reclamation Act. In striking contrast to contemporary neoliberal ideology, which calls for reduced government action, the progressives believe in the responsibility and capacity of the state to construct a commonwealth. Implementation of agrarian reform in the region in the manner defined by the NLP would have rid the valley of *latifundia*, just as US agrarian reform was meant to do in Latin America at the time. Here, as there, such a policy probably would have resulted in more egalitarian, prosperous, and democratic political economies. But here, as there, those in power fought to protect and expand systems that reinforced their privileges.

Powerful landlords like Stanford and Boswell agreed with George Ballis when he wrote, "land equals power, self-respect, dignity, muscle, confidence, a measure of independence." They surely disagreed when he added, "To the extent that our workable land is widely controlled in workable pieces, we have some semblance of a decent society. To the extent that it is narrowly held, we have tyranny, dependence and the welfare state" (Ballis 1982, 18).[5]

---

[5] In 2010, having just turned 85, George passed away. In 2014, Maia left Sun Mountain and returned to live in Fresno.

References

Arax, Mark and Rick Wartzman. 2003. *The King of California: J. G. Boswell and the Making of a Secret American Empire*. New York: Public Affairs.

Ballis, George. 1982. "Ballis testimony drafts on land reform, Reform the Land, Reform Our Lives." Unpublished manuscript. Found in the National Land for People Collection, Special Collections Research Center, California State University – Fresno. Box 19, Folder 17.

Ballis, Maia. 2014. Interview conceded to author. Fresno, CA, November 4.

Barnes, Peter, ed., 1975. *The People's Land: A Reader on Land Reform in the United States*. Emmaus, PA: Rodale Press.

Burbach, Roger; and Patricia Flynn. 1979. "Objetivos agroindustriales de América Latina." *Investigación Económica* 38(147): 49-98.

Burd-Sharps, Sarah and Kristen Lewis. 2011. *A Portrait of California: California Human Development Report 2011*. New York: American Human Development Project (SSRC).

Carter, Lloyd G. 2009. "Reaping Riches in a Wretched Region: Subsidized Industrial Farming and Its Link to Perpetual Poverty." *Golden Gate University Environmental Law Journal* 3(1): 5-41.

Chayanov, Alexander Vasilevich. 1986 [1920]. "Journey of My Brother Alexei to the Land of Peasant Utopia" [under the pseudo Ivan Kremnev] in Kerblay, Basile, "A. V. Chayanov: Life, Career, Works" in Thorner, Daniel; Kerblay, Basile and Smith, R. E. F. eds. *The Theory of Peasant Economy*. Madison: The University of Wisconsin Press, xxv-lxxv.

Curl, John. 2012. *For all the People: Uncovering the Hidden History of Cooperation, Cooperative Movements, and Communalism in America*. 2nd ed., Oakland: PM Press.

De Janvry, Alain; Phillip LeVeen; and David Runsten. 1981. "The Political Economy of Technological Change: Mechanization of Tomato Harvesting in California." Department of Agricultural and Resource Economies, University of California, Berkeley. 1-32.

Frampton, Mary Louise. 1979/1980. "The Enforcement of Federal Reclamation Law in the Westlands Water District: A Broken Promise." *University of California Davis Law Review* 13: 89-122.

Guthman, Julie. 2004. *Agrarian Dreams: The Paradox of Organic Farming in California*. Berkeley: University of California Press.

Hundley, Jr., Norris. 2001. *The Great Thirst: Californians and Water. A History*. Rev. ed. Los Angeles: University of California Press.

Koppes, Clayton. R. 1978. "Public Water, Private Land: Origins of the Acreage Limitation Controversy, 1933-1953." *Pacific Historical Review* 47(4): 607-636.

McWilliams, Carey. 1966 [1935]. *Factories in the field: the story of migratory farm labor in California*. Berkeley: University of California Press.

Petras, James and LaPorte, Robert Jr. 1971. *Cultivating Revolution: The United States and Agrarian Reform in Latin America*. New York: Random House.

Sun Mountain. Accessed March 16, 2016. http://www.sunmt.org/intro.html.

Taylor, Paul S. 1949. "Central Valley Project: Water and Land." *The Western Political Quarterly* 2(2): 228-253.

_____. 1964. "Excess Land Law: Calculated Circumvention." *California Law Review* 52(5): 978-1014.

Taylor, Paul Schuster. Guide to the Paul Schuster Taylor Papers, 1660-1997. BANC MSS 84/35 c. Bancroft Library. University of California, Berkeley, CA.

USBR-United States Bureau of Reclamation. 2013. "Central Valley Project." Accessed March 14, 2016. https://www.usbr.gov/mp/cvp/.

Walker, Richard A. 2004. *The Conquest of Bread: 150 Years of Agribusiness in California*. New York: The New Press.

CHAPTER 15

The Future Is Here: First Nations & Black Sovereignties in a New Era of Land Justice

Richael Faithful

We are going to Mars because whatever is wrong with us will not get right with us so we journey forth, carrying the same baggage / But every now and then leaving one little bitty thing behind. / One day looking for prejudice to slip, / One day looking for hatred to tumble by the wayside, / Maybe one day the Jewish community will be at rest, the Christian community will be content, the Muslim community will be at peace / And all the rest of us will get great meals at holy days and learn new songs and sing in harmony. / We are going to Mars because it gives us a reason to change. — Nikki Giovanni (2016)

I can hear the sizzle of newborn stars, and know anything of meaning, of the fierce magic emerging here. I am witness to flexible eternity, the evolving past, and I know we will live forever, as dust or breath in the face of stars, in the shifting pattern of winds. — Joy Harjo (Harjo and Strom 1989, 56)

The search for a land of one's own remains an active part of the Black American imagination. Black Americans have long-dreamed of knowing a place other than Earth, whether through Garvey's Back-to-Africa Movement or in Nikki Giovanni's Afrofuturist lyric. We have deeply longed for a place that did not rely on our collective exploitation, forcible removal from our ancestral homeland, and systematic traumatization on the land to exist. Now, more than ever, we have opened ourselves to the possibility that such a place may be sitting amongst the cosmos—every being's original home. A departure to Mars, from this point-of-view, would not mark an escape as much as a liberational leap toward self-determination.

Where the fire of Black imagination for another home begins to glint is where the spark of First Peoples' memories of home starts to alight. Nearly three decades ago, author and activist Vine Deloria Jr. explained that although tribes no longer physically occupied or legally owned their ancestral lands, "they did not abandon the spiritual possession that has been a part of them" (Deloria and Lytle 1984, 11). The present places where many tribes or Indigenous people dwell are far from the land of their ancestors. White settler displacement and genocide have physically separated many Indigenous people from their homes. Yet, in the way sacred connections to homelands remain unbroken for African-descendants, the commitment of First Nation Peoples to sovereign survival continues.

This chapter works to weave together two sovereignty struggles: Indigenous and Black folks' land justice movements. History reveals that these fights are parallel (and admittedly, at times, in conflict) because of colonial violence. Yet, there is much positive history to build upon that extends from free societies, from maroon communities[1] to sanctuary activities, such as those of the Lumbee tribe, which welcomed runaway slaves. Plus, as we slowly enter into an age of post-colonial politics, any serious conversation about land justice must be intersectional, given the complex histories that surround land power and access related to genocide and chattel slavery.

Within this conversation, there must also be an analysis of how capitalism's tactical scarcity impacts Indigenous and Black folks who are making claims for resources that were systematically taken from them. The many contexts in which Indigenous and Black folks find their sovereign movements are similar, and in important ways meet at ideological intersections. Therefore, this chapter speaks a language of interdependence—futures that are laced together, much like pasts. I argue that Indigenous and Black folks share common goals for land justice during a political moment when many communities are desperately grasping for a better quality of life, particularly those harmed by imperialist ambitions, though in their uniquely intricate ways.

The first section of this chapter details a brief legal history of Indigenous land dispossession, and current efforts to regain land access and control. It explains through the voices of Indigenous scholars that sovereignty,

---

[1] Maroon communities formed, over the course of more than four centuries, among runaway slaves across the Americas, including in the southeast and southwest United States (Price 1973).

as a political and legal concept, is the core to tribal nation-building and autonomy.

The second section tells of a related yearning held by more and more Black folks to improve their lives by "returning to the land." Although Blacks were not original inhabitants of land on what became the North American continent, their historic connection to land that they were forced to work—but from which they could not own or derive fair economic benefit—remains strong. Their agrarian desires shape a driving force to return to more indigenized lifestyles—growing fresh food, community-centered living, and restoring relationships to nature—as an alternative to urban displacement, economic exploitation, and other systemic problems.

The third section considers these movements against the backdrop of the shifting landscape of international human rights, and notes the ways in which Indigenous and Black folks have used international interventions to leverage their land justice struggles. It provides an overview of an emerging international landscape that rejects colonial conceptions of justice in favor of post-colonial demands for justice, through the theory of Indian economist Amartya Sen.

Finally, this chapter discusses specific considerations for First Nations and Blacks as they influence their land justice futures, pointing out opportunities for mutual support and solidarity moving forward.

It is important to have a shared understanding of sovereignty in a conversation about land justice futures. Sovereignty is commonly defined today as "supreme power over a body politic," as "freedom from external control or controlling influence" (Merriam-Webster 2016). It is the guiding principle of post-colonial reorganization across the world, of which reparative justice—the return of land to people, people to land, and access to resources—is a critical part. In this context, it refers to the right of a people to autonomous self-determination. It is among the most relevant moral debates being revived in the United States today. The concept of land justice, which should guarantee concessions from colonialism's beneficiaries to those who have been injured by it, is necessarily part of restoring sovereign power.

The ability to control opportunities for sustainable living and economic viability is a key aspect of sovereignty linked to the material necessity of land. Basic economic and social rights are gaining international support in a moment when European economic theories that suppress them are facing repudiation. Indian economist Amartya Sen is among numerous intellectuals who are challenging colonial theories of labor and distribution. In his seminal work, *The Idea of Justice*, he critiques rationalists' economic justice theories, advances his own substantive freedom model, advocating for the credibility of a human rights framework, particularly for the South Asian subcontinent that is his ancestral home.

These international discussions on sovereignties weave into and inform conversations about justice among Black Americans and North American Indigenous tribes. In these spaces, a tapestry of political resistance, restorative demands, and new economic thought is weaving together new futures, within which the politics of land play a central role. So, the transformative opportunity before us is to share in solidarity efforts toward building multiple sovereignties that change haunted pasts into hopeful presents.

Indigenous Dispossession and Land Liberation

The continent upon which the United States was founded is still known as Indian Country. Indigenous tribes are sovereign nations whose power to self-govern is both pre- and extra-constitutional. Tribal sovereignty existed before and outside of the US Constitution. Yet, the historical occupation of land by white settlers limits tribes' legal sovereignty. Thus, fundamental access to and control over lands and the natural resources found within them remain definitive elements of First Nations' struggle for justice and autonomy under imperialist US law (Wilkins and Lomawaima 2001, 5).

US law—through the Federal Trust Doctrine— has been the most significant contributor to tribal land divestment, even more so than land sales or war. Many tribes permitted the US government to hold their remaining lands in trust under treaty agreements. Trusteeship, originally claimed to be restricted in scope to certain areas agreed upon by treaty and under specific circumstances, ballooned into prevailing US law as government officials and courts adopted the rationale that tribes were too incompetent to govern their own lands (Deloria 1988, 31).

The lynchpin Supreme Court ruling favoring trusteeship was *Cherokee Nation v. State of Georgia* (30 U.S. 1) in 1831. The majority opinion reasoned that tribes were neither nations nor states, but "domestic dependent nations." The invention of this concept subjected tribes to an absolute discretionary power from the US Congress, which effectively stripped their sovereign power and autonomy. Two more pivotal cases during early US history, *Johnson v. McIntosh* (21 U.S. 543) in 1823 and *Worcester v. Georgia* in 1832 (31 U.S. 515) (Deloria 1988, 47), calcified colonial control. These three cases, known as the Marshall Trilogy, named after Chief Justice John Marshall, codified white settlers' chauvinisms into jurisprudence, and it is still considered relevant legal precedent today.

Naturally, many voices continue to resist the label of "dependent nation." Lumbee legal author and strong sovereignty advocate, Robert A.

Williams Jr., suggested that Indigenous nations across the world should build their judicial capacities to fight this label and exercise legal power over their lands, people, and affairs. In a recent appeal to tribal leaders he argued:

> We know that the real keys are practical self-rule. Well, think of what a tribal court does for you. It takes your tribal law and custom, its traditions, your constitution, the codes, the statues that you enact and apply them every day in a transparent, rational, non-political, non-partisan way so that everybody on the reservation—Indian and non-Indian—feels they are treated as equals with equal dignity and respect as human beings according to our tribal customs and traditions... You need a legal framework for nation building (Williams 2011).

Williams believes that nation-building is the most effective resistance against US intrusion. He encourages more strategic use and expansion of First Nations' laws and legal structures to counter colonialist US law. More robust tribal courts and stronger exercise of jurisdictions, he argues, can push back against tribal sovereignty encroachments, such as usurping rightful land access. If First Nations have the capacity to control the decisions about land on which they currently dwell, then they are positioned to enlarge their overall sovereign powers in the future.

Some legal voices concerning sovereignty have made more direct demands. Robert Odawi Porter, former Seneca Nation president and legal scholar, called upon President Barack Obama's administration to assist tribes in achieving "land liberation." Land liberation, in his view, mandates two steps: the return of trust land to tribal sovereigns and restored sovereignty to control returned land (Porter 2009).

The land liberation vision contains many meanings. One meaning is land restoration—reinstating original land claims and access that were taken from tribes and tribal members. Land restoration, which is the return of tribal land titles from federal government trusts, would allow tribes to independently execute their own land-related laws and policies that open opportunities for a range of sovereign powers, including renewable energy production and gaming (casino) development. Porter argues, among many other First Nation voices, that the absence of tribal ownership over land not only limits tribal sovereignty, but also prevents tribes from achieving economic sustainability. He believes that the return of First Nation land is a pre-requisite for sovereign nationhood.

Underlying First Nation struggles for land sovereignties, beyond that of reparative justice, are the means to create sustainable economic futures.

The meaningfulness of land titles is diminished without the full sovereign power to regulate related activity. The issue of "produced water" from hydraulic fracturing (fracking) on tribal land is one example. Federal regulations overseeing environmental standards related to fracking contain a "livestock loophole" that permits the beneficial use of fracking wastewater. Some tribes accept wastewater for their members and livestock with the expectation that the federal government will monitor pollution levels, while other tribes have more restrictions based on concerns about harmful fracking discharges.

In 2012, the Wind River Reservation caught national attention when a reporter captured images of a "foam" and "sheen" on standing pools of black water while cattle grazed nearby. The reporter was warned by fracking workers to step away from the discharge points and told that she might experience "respiratory distress or death from hydrogen sulfide fumes." Federal officials then conducted tests of the water and documented the high toxicity of the water. But as tribal leaders pointed out, this evidence of toxicity had been occurring "for several decades without attracting much interest" until the reporter brought the issue into the publics' eyes (Whitney-Williams and Hoffman 2015, 454).

Law professors Heather Whitney-Williams and Hillary M. Hoffmann observe that when federal regulators act as water quality regulators and land trustees for tribes, their roles present a clear conflict of interest—one that principles of trust law would otherwise prohibit (2015, 491). Concurrent legal authority with the US government fundamentally undermines tribes' ability to regulate land use with tangible impact on tribal health, safety, and business interests. Environmental regulation is an exemplar of the paternalist failures of federal trusteeship and demonstrates that economically sustainable futures are almost impossible under US imperialist control.

Ultimately, tribal sovereignties require returned lands and abilities to govern the people who reside, and conduct activity, on them. Sovereign power is also a critical element of nation-building. First Nations' local control fosters a governance integrity and adaptability that federal oversight can never achieve. There are powerful possibilities to not merely mount new resistance within a post-colonialist period but to regain sovereignties within the rise of a human rights era.

Back To the Land

The rise of a human rights era bears a promise of sovereign power to other dispossessed peoples as well, such as Black folks in the US. It is a time during which Blacks may be able to pick up cracked dreams of mobility and ease evinced from the Great Migration after emancipation. As the imaginings of a better life in northern cities recede, existential questions about futures free from violence and insecurity are surfacing among many in Black communities. At this juncture, decisions about ways to realize economic and social opportunities need to be made.

Faced with these immense challenges, more and more Black folks, younger and older, are going "back to the land." There's better living in the areas where there is more land, more space, and more affordability. Going "back to the land," as some folks see it, offers not only an improved quality of life, but also more influence over their personal affairs and a stronger sense of community. Returning to the South, or to other land-rich areas, carries opportunities for sovereignty that outweigh risks of mistreatment. It also, however, raises ethical and practical concerns, namely how to return and to which and whose lands.

An increasing number of Black folks are attempting to restore their relationships with land, despite a painful estrangement embedded in the cultural psyche (Glave 2010, 4). While some folks are returning to rural lands, others are building urban farms. As an example, in June 2016, Zachari Curtis, owner of Good Sense Farm & Apiary, which produces mushrooms and honey, opened a new 7,200-square-foot space along one of the busiest thoroughfares in Washington, DC. Curtis, who was born and raised in the city, explained, "'[T]he goal is to show people what an urban mushroom farm can look like and give them a place to gather'" (Simmons 2016).

Good Sense is a small business model for Black-owned urban farms across the country which, beyond growing organic food, aims to re-connect food, land, and nature to city-folk. "'It's not about how many hikes you've been on or national parks you've visited. People come to me with different sets of experience with wilderness based on their level of privilege. . . I'm trying to acknowledge that if you're excited about food, you're a wilderness lover'" (Simmons 2016).

Substantial barriers still exist for Blacks to access land in either urban (see Yakini and Ahmadi, both in this volume) or rural areas (see Davy et al, this volume). The legacy of systematic land dispossession through legal maneuvering and communal violence still strongly resounds. Histories of land divestment paired with massive wealth inequities mean that there may no longer be homes with land for folks to return to or available resources with which to acquire new land on the market.

As described elsewhere in this volume, groups like the Black Belt Justice Center and Black Family Land Trust (BFLT) are investing in strategies that help preserve and create new Black land ownership. In BFLT's view of land ownership, Blacks must see land as an asset, not a burden. They advocate for an "African American Land Ethic" to honor stewards of the land that came before them and to hold faith in stewards of the land that will come. BFLT, along with many others, are supporting re-orientation toward land for future sustainability.

Good Sense Farm and BFLT both operate through collective resource-sharing, also known as cooperative economics. Good Sense Farm, for instance, co-founded the Community Farming Alliance (CFA), a producers' cooperative for farmers and other food system workers of color seeking to nurture mutual aid to one another (Melville 2015). CFA maintains a community supported agriculture program twice a year, and joins together to sell food at local farmers' markets. These kinds of efforts are tried-and-true in the Black community.

As historian Jessica Gordon Nembhard explains, and other authors in this volume elaborate, "African Americans have a long, rich history of cooperative ownership, especially in reaction to market failures and economic racial discrimination" (2014, 1). Nembhard has meticulously documented the prolific yet hidden histories of Black co-ops, especially in the rural south. Connecting economic sustainability to sovereignty, she describes how co-ops created such economic independence from white community members that they were able to take part in racial justice organizing without fear of job loss throughout the earlier decades of the twentieth century (2014, 48). In her view, the cooperative movement among Black Americans helps to support economic independence and community well-being (2014, 214).

Returning to the land, however, carries ethical implications in regard to First Nations' parallel struggle for land liberation. In a future in which tribes regain land titles and sovereign powers, positive relationships among tribes, tribe member-landowners, and Black prospective landowners will be highly context-dependent, meaning that they will depend on careful consideration and negotiation around matters of equity, necessity, and sustainability. There will be opportunities to navigate future contractual use, land sale, or co-ownership models between Black prospective landowners and First Nations. And of course, there will be transfers and re-negotiations of current land use agreements when titles are passed from the US government to tribes.

Black folks returning to the land must recognize the reality that they are part of a complex web of land ownership in which they inherit ethical burdens created by white colonialism. This political moment offers opportunities to share in sovereignty struggles driven by traditional cooperative economic models, and sustainable stewardship traditions, supported by Blacks and First Nations alike.

Indigenous and Black folks stand to gain a lot from building on collaborative land histories. Negative histories are present as well, from which deep lessons about the costs of exploitation and conflict form. Importantly, over the coming decades, there are opportunities to diverge from the re-investment in white, neoliberal-capitalist scarcity politics that have hurt Black, Brown, and Indigenous people across the world. Efforts to reinforce land justice visions and avoid competition among groups harmed by colonialism are helped by a new global human rights landscape.

Land Justice as a Fundamental Human Right

It is hard to envision land justice futures without the political landscape that has re-energized conversations about land liberation across the globe. Over the last few decades, international politics have shifted as human rights have ascended. Human rights are "rights inherent to all human beings regardless of nationality, residence, sex, religion, race, or any other status" (United Nations Human Rights Office of the High Commissioner). The proposition of human rights at international and national levels is growing in force amidst current post-colonial power transitions. Many observers, including political thinkers, have engaged these changes by re-examining widely-regarded theories of justice.

Whereas conventional western theories have often propped up legal and political structures that disconnect Indigenous, Black, and Brown people from land and resources, newer approaches provide support for sovereignty struggles. Amartya Sen, a prominent Indian economist, is among a cohort of thinkers who are redefining justice principles away from European-derived traditions that associate justice with abstract concepts of happiness or fairness.

Sen's *The Idea of Justice*, published in 2009, both contributes to, and departs from, the hallmark of progressive economic justice thought seen in John Rawls' seminal 1971 work, *A Theory of Justice*. Rawls argued against Enlightenment theories that defined justice through a lens of individual autonomy—the belief that justice means freedom from interference by others or government, also known as negative rights. Rawls, instead, believed that justice was more than negative rights. He believed that the *process* of establishing just institutions was of paramount importance; thus, to create a fair society he urged that rational individuals must form institutions without knowledge of their personal outcomes. In Rawls' view, this concept, known as the "veil of ignorance," is the vehicle to shaping a just society.

While Sen is in agreement with Rawls' orientation that justice goes beyond individuals' abilities to do whatever they please, he critiques Rawls and most other historical conceptions of justice by pointing out:

> [T]he question to ask in this context is whether the analysis of justice must be so confined to getting the basic institutions and general rules right. Should we not also have to examine what emerges in the society, including the kind of lives that people can actually lead, given the institutions and rules, but also other influences, including actual behaviour, that would inescapably affect human lives (Sen 2009, 9-10)?

Here, Sen asks: what about the outcomes? His implication is that even if a process, in theory, seems fair, it may not be fair in reality. In other words, he wants to bring empiricism to this area of economic philosophy. Further, he insists that the measure of this reality ought to be the impact on real lives—not theoretical experiments or intellectual replicas.

Sen's point is that actual lives and the opportunities that we possess to make choices both matter. He rejects ahistorical perspectives preferred by European theorists whose contemporaries and descendants greatly benefited from individualistic notions of happiness. Sen's perspective is that we can examine the real ways in which collective bodies, lands, and livelihoods, at the center of sovereign existence, have been impacted by processes and institutions. This person-centered vision, which has the potential to be invoked by land liberation and back-to-land visions, supplants the political motivations behind sovereignty struggles.

Sen's vision of economic justice contains a twenty-first century texture that Rawls and other theories do not have. In many ways, his view of justice resonates with an intersectional analysis—a Black feminist lens developed by Kimberlé Crenshaw (1991)—which highlights the plural and overlapping nature of various social categories. Sen explains that there are "multiple dimensions in which equality matters, which is not reducible to equality in one space only, be that economic advantage, resources, utilities, achieved quality of life or capabilities" (2009, 293).

As post-colonial societies emerge from under their most oppressive conditions, they are introducing basic human rights or positive rights—the entitlement to a degree of well-being—to global understandings of justice. They are insisting that groups hurt by colonialism, including Black folks in the US and Indigenous nations, have the right to control their land and its (clean) resources, to suitable housing, and to medical care, to start. In doing so, they are rejecting European-influenced theories, which merely express what individuals should not do to others, and making powerful claims to "moral rights" that contain underlying freedoms which affirm not only an individual or group's rights and liberties, but the interests and rights of others (Sen 2009, 364-368).

Sen's analysis imposes realities onto economic justice theories with which European thinkers will need to grapple. *The Idea of Justice* makes a significant pronouncement for the future: we are no longer in a time when a "single homogenous virtue" can defend immoral choices that affect arrangements of power (2009, 396). His views on justice, at the very least, force conversations within white intellectual traditions that have been used to validate violations of sovereignty within their own languages of impartial rationality.

A return to sovereignty is a global banner for occupied lands and former colonies. The notion of human rights, as a political sovereignty project, radically departs from hegemonic approaches to rights. The creation of this space has allowed international forums to become gateways toward sovereign power. First Nations and Black Americans are among many groups that have petitioned the international community for redress as governments have failed to adequately respond.

The Indigenous rights movement, for instance, has strategically fought for sovereignty through mechanisms they helped create, such as the 2007 United Nations Declaration on the Rights of Indigenous Peoples, which contains statements regarding the right to self-determination (Article 3); the right to self-government (Article 4); the right to not be forcibly removed from land (Article 10); the right to land resources that they have traditionally owned (Article 26); the right to maintain a spiritual relationship with traditionally owned or occupied lands (Article 25); and the right to determine how to develop and use land (Article 32).

Black Americans, too, rely on international bodies to recognize restitution still owed by the United States and the regime of violence under which they still live. In February 2016, the United Nations Working Group of Experts on People of African Descent engaged in a fact-finding mission, issuing a series of recommendations, including reparations for African-American descendants of slavery and acknowledgment that the trans-Atlantic slave trade was a crime against humanity (Holland 2016). The group easily traced systemic abuse from slavery and the antebellum era into the present day. The group's chair, Mireille Fanon Mendes-France, even observed, "[Contemporary] police killings and the trauma it creates are reminiscent of racial terror lynchings in the past" (Holland 2016).

The generational value of fundamental human rights makes reparative justice—and therefore, land justice—more viable than ever. As the era in which colonialist powers, namely the United States and Europe, could unilaterally steer international law has passed, we enter a new period of "substantive pluralism," in which, as law professor William W. Burke-White describes, rising powers are "articulating distinct preferences within the existing system that challenge aspects of the transatlantic vision of international law, often through a reassertion of the role of the state" (Burke-White 2015, 5). Amidst major international power shifts, human rights movements have begun to demand accountability for States to pay their debts—historically and institutionally. Struggles for sovereignties—vis-à-vis international platforms—hold unique openings to heal past wounds and to create positive, affirming futures if they can create in solidarity together.

Struggles for Sovereignties, Lands, and Futures

It is easy to view struggles for sovereignties within the territory known as the United States as distinctively singular, and therefore to discount international post-colonialist theory. No experience of a group or nation is like any other, and each context deserves its own nuanced analysis about its particular future. Yet, when the terror of colonialism is measured, there are patterns of its imprints that cannot be denied. Worse, without acknowledgment, these imprints grow stronger in impact and memory, which merely serve the lingering powers that still seek to control. The most optimistic futures are steeped in shared struggle and collective action.

Economic viability is a shared incentive from which to act toward sovereign futures. Everybody needs to eat, and some folks are eating much more than they need, and very well compared to others. Attorney Antonio Moore pointed out that during apartheid in South Africa, the median Black family held about seven percent of the typical white family's wealth. In the contemporary US, the median Black American family holds only 1.5 percent of the median white American family wealth (Moore 2016). Indigenous peoples' median wealth was equal to only 8.7 percent of the median wealth of all Americans in 2001 (Austin 2013). The fact is that wealth is organized and concentrated by race, ethnicity, and citizenship, centuries after white settlers arrived.

Although the sources of systemic inequality are linked to unique histories, Indigenous and Black folks have aligning motives to dismantle rigged economic systems and promote redistribution policies. They are in need of leadership that reflects their collective interests—not just members of their nations or communities, but individuals with transformative values and courageous politics who are willing to remove imperialist and caste systems. This shift is slowly occurring in the United States, among First Nations, and across the world.

Conversations about sovereign futures must be broadly-envisioned. There are at least three ways for land justice sovereignty struggles to move forward in solidarity:

Anticipate plural land ownership and use. In a land justice vision with finite space and resources, more groups of people will need to negotiate and navigate relationships around living on land and decision-making about its resources. These groups will have to accomplish these tasks within a legal system inadequate to meet their goals, and will likely return to old approaches or invent creative ones to realize a layered, pluralist co-existence. Land possession and title is a capitalist, colonialist legal principle incorporated into US law. Land justice advocates, leaders, and administrators should assume that land reinvestment will mean plural ownership and use among Nations, families, cooperatives, and other communal entities. This poses special challenges in more densely populated areas, such as cities that have been built on stolen land. However, the current opportunities are vast to incubate innovations for plural, anti-capitalist land ownership and use mechanisms at very local levels.

Honor complex, sacred relationships to land. Land is more than a commodity; it is part of a sacred Earth on which all life depends. Many groups of people linked to their Indigenous culture view humans within a web of relationships with all of nature, honor land as the living being, and respect their connections to Her. Future visions of sovereignty must include spiritual connections as part of the new systems of land residency and relationships. That is, different tribes must be able to acknowledge spiritual ties to homelands; descendants of enslaved Africans must be able to reconnect and heal with land from which many are still estranged; Black Indigenous people must be positively embraced as legacies of common places between Indigenous and Black folks; and everyone must be able to share in the ethical stewardship of land.

Integrate universal, sovereignty movement-building. Land justice conversations and proposals need to be grounded in a global perspective. Strategies should strive to support sovereignty-centered human rights movements because these struggles directly influence one another from the position of imperialism. If sovereignty advocates, especially from the West, can not only use international systems to amplify their work, but also contribute toward the infrastructure of these systems, many sovereign futures around the globe will be better off.

Twenty-first century land politics guarantee to be challenging. As tensions over the socio-political control of land and the resources within it rise, we are seeing significant shifts away from white, colonialist power structures. The best hope for a sustainable future is through investments into shared sovereignty struggles for First Nations and Black Americans. The economic and emotional values of land will only increase over time. If groups who have survived colonial conquests can help each other achieve sovereign futures, there will be a stronger likelihood that a more equitable co-existence will be realized. The future is here.

References

Austin, Algernon. 2013. "Native Americans and Jobs: The Challenge and The Promise." Economic Policy Institute Briefing Paper #370. December 17.

Burke-White, Williams W. 2015. "Power Shifts in International Law: Structural Realignment and Substantive Pluralism." *Harvard International Law Journal* 56(1):5.

Crenshaw, Kimberle. 1991. "Mapping the Margins: Intersectionality, Identity Politics, and Violence Against Women of Color" *Stanford Law Review* 43(6):1241-1299.

Deloria Jr, Vine and Clifford M. Lytle. 1984. *The Nations Within: The Past and Future of American Indian Sovereignty.* Austin: University of Texas Press.

Deloria Jr., Vine. 1988. *Custer Died for Your Sins: An Indian Manifesto.* Norman: University of Oklahoma Press.

Giovanni, Nikki. 2016. "Soul Food, Sex, and Space." On Being Program. March 17, 2016. www.onbeing.org/programs/nikki-giovanni-soul-food-sex-and-space/.

Glave, Dianne D. 2010. *Rooted In The Earth: Reclaiming the African American Environmental Heritage.* Chicago: Chicago Review Press.

Harjo, Joy and Stephen Strom. 1989. *Secrets from the Center of the World.* Tucson: Sun Tracks and The University of Arizona Press.

Holland, Jesse J. 2016. "U.N. Group Says U.S. Should Consider Reparations." *U.S. News & World Report*, January 29.

Melville, Wes. 2015. "The Story Behind the Community Farming Alliance: An Interview with Zachari Curtis." Petworth Community Market, October 27.

Merriam-Webseter Dictionary. 2016. "Sovereignty." Accessed July 6. http://www.merriam-webster.com/dictionary/sovereignty.

Moore, Antonio. 2016. "Our Real Racial Wealth Gap Story." *Inequality.org, A Project of the Institute for Policy Studies*, January 22.

Nembhard, Jessica Gordon. 2014. *Collective Courage: A History of African American Cooperative Economic Thought and Practice.* University Park, Pennsylvania: Penn State University Press.

Porter, Rob. 2009. "Beyond Land-into-Trust: Creative Land Ownership Options for Tribes." Presentation at D.C. Indian Law Conference. November 13.

Price, Richard, ed. 1973. *Maroon Societies: Rebel Slave Communities in the Americas.* Doubleday: Anchor Books Edition.

Sen, Amartya. 2009. *The Idea of Justice.* Cambridge Massachusetts: The Belknap Press of Harvard University Press.

Simmons, Holley. 2016. "A mushroom farm and community space is heading to Park View." *Washington Post*, June 1.

United Nations. 2007. "Declaration on the Rights of Indigenous Peoples."

Whitney-Williams, Heather and Hillary M. Hoffman. 2015. "Fracking in Indian Country: The Federal Trust Relationship, Tribal Sovereignty, and the Beneficial Use of Produced Water." *Yale Journal on Regulation* 32(2).

Wilkins, David E. and K. Tsianina Lomawaima. 2001. *Uneven Ground: American Indian Sovereignty and Federal Law.* Norman: University of Oklahoma Press.

Williams, Robert A. Jr. 2011. "Law and Sovereignty: Putting Tribal Powers to Work." Presentation at Emerging Leaders Seminar, Native Nations Institute for Leadership, Management, and Policy, University of Arizona. Tucson, Arizona. March 23.

CONCLUSION:

Together Toward Land Justice

Eric Holt-Giménez and Justine M. Williams

L and justice is the idea that people and communities that have been historically oppressed have a right to land and territory. It recognizes the central role of land in culture, in society, and in relations of power, as well as its restorative, protective, and healing potential. As a pillar in people's struggle for the right to fresh, healthy food, land justice is the agrarian link to food justice. Land justice is a call for a new kind of agrarian reform.

Why agrarian reform?

Only one hundred individuals own over 34 million acres in the US—about one and half percent of all the nation's land. This is an area larger than the states of Delaware, Maryland, Hawaii, and West Virginia, combined (*The Land Report* 2015). Every time rural land values drop (usually due to agricultural oversupply), billionaires buy up more of it. The steady concentration of land ownership projects the political power of these individuals deep into the agrarian sphere. Their influence on agriculture, conservation, and climate change, biodiversity, and ultimately, agricultural land access for hundreds of thousands of farmers, is incalculable.[1]

Still, the concentration of the best national lands in the hands of a financial aristocracy is just the tip of the iceberg. Hidden from view, thousands of land transactions per second are taking place, steadily concentrating the value of land in global financial markets, far from the countryside and the people who work it. The concentration of land and land value has been accompanied by the expansion of highly capitalized mega-farms. The growth of large farms goes hand in hand with the steady disappearance of medium-sized, family farms.

---

[1] Media moguls John Malone and Ted Turner are the nation's largest landholders, with over 2 million acres each. Much of the land belonging to the top 100 is dedicated to ranching, hunting, fishing, ecotourism, and conservation.

At the same time, new farms—small, and often barely viable—are springing up like weeds, breaking through the asphalt of a dysfunctional food system, supplying local markets and bringing better diets to under-served communities. Aligning closely with the global food sovereignty move-ment, these farmers are building a new culture of civic agriculture, or what *La Vía Campesina* calls "agrarian citizenship" (Obach and Tobin 2014, Wittman 2009). Women and people of color are highly represented in this growing smallholder sector that, despite its vibrancy, has a precarious hold and lim-ited access to land. After many decades of dormancy, the re-appearance of agrarian demands in the US follows the struggle for survival of medium-scale farms and the rise of small farms. Agrarian demands today are closely associ-ated with historic demands for racial, labor, and gender justice.

The challenge for land justice is not just how to confront the issues of concentrated private property and the financialization of agricultural land, or how to forge an agroecologically sound and economically equitable form of agriculture, but how to confront capitalism. Our skewed system of land tenure reflects a regressive political-economic system, itself embedded in a continuing legacy of dispossession, concentration and exploitation. Just as we can't isolate food justice from land justice, we can't isolate land from the need for deep political and economic transformation. The question is: *what is the role of land within a process of transformative, social change?*

As this book makes clear, land is a social relation. Whether by private property, or a commons, or by spiritual or normative agreements, land is an integral part of the culture and the organization of society. Nothing of land is homogenous, monolithic, or pre-determined. Like society, land use and land access are complex, contested, and dynamic. Land in the US today is integral to the power of elites. But it is just as integral to resistance.

This book addresses the role of land justice by raising the Agrarian Question in the United States: how does agrarian capitalism evolve, who wins, who loses, and what social alliances can resist, contest, and propose alternatives? But the book also goes beyond the industry/agriculture di-chotomy of the classic agrarian question, bringing in the entire food sys-tem. Contributions are written not just by scholars, but by farmers, la-borers, and human rights activists. Their collective vision is based on an appreciation that land is a means to both prosperity and exploitation; and on a stubborn hope that land can be a means for liberation.

The private ownership of all land in the US began with a capitalist process of accumulation by dispossession, in which settlers took the land of indigenous peoples and exploited the labor and knowledge of enslaved Africans to establish the new nation's place as a global power (Harvey 2003). The insights of Black Agrarianism not only describe the violent ways in which capitalism and agriculture have shaped property, they show the tenacity of ancient agrarian cultures as reservoirs of knowledge, hope, resistance, and continued generational and institutional renewal.

Gender is central to the experience of agrarian resistance. While often the subject of development strategies in the Global South, women are less likely to be discussed when considering the land question in the US. This omission stems, in part, from the fact that when this nation was founded—and in many states throughout the nineteenth century—women were prevented from both owning and managing property. This restricted their access to farmland for many generations. Today, women farmers must overcome ongoing masculine expectations and productivist paradigms to make their own decisions about how their land is farmed. Alice Walker's concept of "womanism" opens the possibility for a creative use of land and artistry to produce food, medicine, nourishment, and collective healing, highlighting the ongoing struggles of rural women, and revealing the ways women of color build agrarian power to fight patriarchy and racism.

The concept of land justice would be incomplete without including the role of labor. The enormous subsidy that underpaid farmworkers provide the food system is captured in the labor process and embodied in cheap food. The value of exploited, overwhelmingly immigrant labor also accrues on the *land*—land that can be used as collateral for loans, or that can be financialized and traded on global markets. But the distance between family farmers and landless farmworkers is fluid, often with less than a generation of separation between the labor camp and the farmhouse. The depressed value of farm labor affects the labor of small farmers as much as it does the labor of farmworkers. Both would benefit from a food system that truly valued their work. Family farmers and farmworkers also share pride in farm work and a love for the land. Many immigrant farmworkers in the US were farmers themselves, and would jump at the opportunity to farm again. Though many farmers openly lament the passing of the family farm, there is no shortage of people with the skill and the desire to work the land—if the pathway was made available.

Under neoliberal capitalism, land has gone from being a means to a barrier to farming. The pressure of financialization, real estate development, and urban expansion into rural areas makes it nearly impossible for young farmers to afford land—particularly those who farm fresh produce and need to be close to urban markets. Competition in these saturated markets is fierce, and the cosmetically dazzling fruits and vegetables found in farmers markets across the country come with high production costs. Even when land is rented, it is difficult to make a living by farming on a small scale. Community Supported Agriculture agreements can address the chronic lack of production credit and help stabilize the market for these farmers, but the impermanence of rental contracts makes it impossible to make the capital investments in soil, biodiversity, and labor needed for agroecological farming. While land trusts can help with access, there simply isn't enough philanthropic money to go around to meet the land needs of aspiring farmers. Land banks—that also need philanthropic support—are largely focused on undervalued urban housing, not farmland.

Much of the farmland in the US is rented, and most smallholders around the world do not own the land they work. But farmers in the Global South are frequently embedded in dense village and extended family networks that help them cope with the hard work and poverty that plagues peasant agriculture. Unfortunately, market niches accessed by new farmers in the US do not come with village or extended family networks. Living a landless peasant's life within a developed country brings all the work and none of the security these farmers need in order to raise a family, stay healthy, educate their children, and retire before their backs give out. Their love of farming is essential, but it is not enough. If these farmers are going to have a chance, not only will they need equitable land access (through government land banks and trusts, preferential loans, leased easements, etc.), but society will have to ensure farming's *social wage* by guaranteeing the health, education, and welfare of the people who produce our food.

In order to create a food system that is healthy and equitable, we must tackle the land question, and the larger, agrarian question. We need to not only push for equal rights under the current land regime, but— as the title of this book suggests—to re-imagine and rethink the kind of agrarian citizenship we need for a new society.

As chapters in this book attest, this is not the first time in our country's recent history that a call has been made for agrarian reforms. During the 1960s and 1970s, Black liberation and economic justice activists in the South, farmers in the Midwest and the water activists in the West all worked to advance democratic agrarian models for economic independence and self-determination. The lack of a large enough social base to create political will among politicians hampered these movements. Today, broad-based coalitions could build this power by expanding the concept of agrarian struggle to encompass the entire food system, and by building an alliance between farmworkers, farmers, food workers, and consumers up and down the food value chain.[2]

---

[2] See Appendix A for an account from members of the US Food Sovereignty Alliance on the steps they have taken during the first years of formation to address land, resources, and reform.

Notably missing from this book have been the standard white settler narratives, in which the courage and hard work of European colonizers are credited for building the agrarian foundation of this nation. This is not an oversight. The white settler story has been told and retold—with the predictable embellishments and omissions—since before the signature ink was dry on the Declaration of Independence. It's important to engage with the stories this country tells about itself. However, critically reprising the US's agrarian mythology would have taken up most of this book and focused our attention on many of the very social pathologies we seek to look beyond. Instead, the chapters in this book come from the perspective of those whose lives are systematically invalidated in the accounts of national agrarian greatness. The voices in this book don't come from the "margins," but from the core of what it means to produce real food and to live with the land in the United States. Amplifying these calls for justice addresses the structures of injustice that affect everyone.

The US agrarian transition operated with a narrative of dissolution that on one hand employed genocide, force and the dispossession of the means of existence, and on the other forced the cultural assimilation of native peoples (Goldstein 2014a). Similarly, the erasure of the agrarian histories of farmers and farmworkers of color from the US's agrarian mythology assimilates all agrarian experience into the triumphal ethos of large-scale, industrial production. With the recent rise of indigenous and agrarian movements, the US agrarian origin myth is unraveling. In the face of increasing acts of dispossession, monopolization, and marginalization, Indigenous peoples, farmers and farmworkers of color, and smallholder farmers have refused to assimilate into the corporate food regime.

At the time of this writing, Native people and their allies have gathered by the thousands in camps at Standing Rock, North Dakota, sharing songs, dance, and prayer to protect water from the relentless onslaught of extractive industries. The sharing of culture at Standing Rock not only contradicts centuries of forced assimilation, it re-introduces indigenous leadership into the broad-based struggles for land, water, and territory. This international gathering—unprecedented in the US—builds on longstanding, territorial relationships that cut across ethnicities. In the words of indigenous author Hartman Deetz, "The cowboy and Indian alliance isn't new; it's always been people against profit. . . The more you strip things down, the more you have to look at the commonality between us. Differences disappear very fast. The [Dakota Access Pipeline] project puts at risk our very future... When you talk about threatening people's water, it becomes very hard to break people apart" (Deetz in Salmasi 2016).

In many indigenous cultures, to join a ceremonial dance, song, or prayer, is to make cause with a people. To dance together is to commit—to friendship, work, the hunt… or to battle (Deetz 2016). The ceremony is a demonstration of faith, hope, and solidarity in which people come together, and in doing so, affirm that not everything can be assimilated.

The voices in this book invite us to join a circle of liberation. They invite us to hope and dream, and to see that—contrary to the dominant capitalist narrative—agrarian struggles in the US have not been irretrievably assimilated into the corporate food regime. To join their call for land justice is to commit to ending injustice in all aspects of society.

What is the role of land justice in social change? Ultimately, it may be to bring us together on that irreducible terrain of hope from which all other struggles for food, livelihoods, water, and environment emerge: the land.

References

Deetz, Hartman. 2016 "NO DAPL & Native Organizing." Panel discussion, UC Berkeley Law. Berkeley, November 16.

Goldstein, Alyosha, ed. 2014a. "Toward a Genealogy of the US Colonial Present." In *Formations of United States Colonialism*. Durham: Duke University Press Books.

———. 2014b. "Finance and Foreclosure in the Colonial Present." *Radical History Review* 2014 (118): 42–63.

Harvey, David. 2003. *The New Imperialism*. New York: Oxford University Press.

Obach, Brian K., and Kathleen Tobin. 2014. "Civic Agriculture and Community Engagement." *Agriculture and Human Values*, 31(2):307–322.

Salmasi, Neeka. 2016. "Standing Rock and Iowa Pipeline Resistance: A Report-Back." November 7. https://foodfirst.org/standing-rock-and-iowa-pipeline-resistance-a-report-back/.

The Land Report. 2015. "2015 Land Report 100." October 15. http://www.landreport.com/2015/10/2015-land-report-100/.

Wittman, Hannah. 2009. "Reworking the metabolic rift: La Vía Campesina, agrarian citizenship, and food sovereignty." *The Journal of Peasant Studies* 36 (4): 805–826.

ABOUT THE AUTHORS AND CONTRIBUTORS

Cover Artist

Jonathan Green is a nationally acclaimed and award professional artist who graduated from the School of the Art Institute of Chicago in 1982. His 38 year track record of creating art, and the extensive listing of his inclusions in national and international museum collections and exhibitions have led to his being considered by numerous art critics and reviewers as one of our nation's outstanding American artists and highly recognized visual master for capturing the positive aspects of American and African American southern culture, history, and traditions.

Prefaces

Winona LaDuke is an internationally renowned activist working on issues of sustainable development and food systems. As Executive Director of Honor the Earth (co-founded with the Indigo Girls), she works nationally and internationally on issues of climate change, renewable energy, and environmental justice alongside Indigenous communities. In her own community, she is the founder of White Earth Land Recovery Project, one of the largest reservation-based non-profit organizations in the country. She is a graduate of Harvard and Antioch Universities, the author of six books, and a two time vice presidential candidate with Ralph Nader. In 2007, she was inducted into the National Women's Hall of Fame.

LaDonna Redmond is a long-time community activist. When she couldn't find a healthful food source in her Chicago neighborhood, she decided to rebuild the food system. She has worked successfully to get Chicago Public Schools to evaluate junk food, launched urban agriculture projects, started a community grocery store, and worked on federal farm policies to expand access to healthy food in low-income communities. She is a 2003 WK Kellogg Food and Society Policy Fellow, was named a Responsibility Pioneer by Times Magazine in 2009, and is a Green for All Fellow. In 2013, she launched the Campaign for Food Justice Now (CFJN). She is also a diversity and community manager for Seward Community Co-op, host of two weekly radio shows, and curator of SOUL food monologue. (photo credit: Matthew Glidden).

George Naylor has raised corn and soybeans on his family farm near Churdan, Iowa, since 1976, choosing to never raise GMO crops. He is a member of the boards of the Center for Food Safety and the Non-GMO Project, past president of the National Family Farm Coalition, a former member of the board of the Iowa chapter of the Sierra Club, and is active in Iowa Citizens for Community Improvement. Agroecological farming and Food Sovereignty, concepts promoted by the international farmer and peasant movement, La Via Campesina, are two of George's passions.

Editors

Justine M. Williams was born and raised in North Carolina, where her interest in social justice, ecology, and farming began. For the past decade, she has worked toward food and farming justice from there, D.C., and California. She holds an MA a PhD in anthropology from the University of North Carolina, Chapel Hill, where her research has focused on how people become committed to alternative futures and/or resistance. Since 2010, she has conducted research on the social dynamics of agroecology and permaculture in Cuba.

Eric Holt-Giménez, Ph.D. is the executive director of Food First/Institute for Food and Development Policy. A political economist and agroecologist, Eric grew up working on farms in Northern California and worked for over 30 years in international agricultural development. He has published many magazine and academic articles on agroecology, development, food justice and food sovereignty and is author/editor of several books including: *Food Movements Unite! Strategies to transform the food system* and *Campesino a Campesino: Voices from Latin America's Farmer to Farmer Movement for Sustainable Agriculture*. Eric has a Ph.D. in Environmental Studies from the University of California, Santa Cruz and a M.Sc. in International Agricultural Development from the University of California, Davis.

Section One

Monica White, Ph.D. is an assistant professor of Environmental Justice at the University of Wisconsin-Madison. Her research investigates communities of color and grassroots organizations that are engaged in the development of sustainable, community food systems as a strategy to respond to issues of hunger and food inaccessibility. She is the author of the forthcoming book *Freedom Farmers: Agricultural Resistance and the Black Freedom Movement.* She is President of the Board of Directors of the Detroit Black Community Food Security Network (DBCFSN), and on the advisory board of the Southeastern African American Farmers Organic Network (SAAFON).

Owusu Bandele, Ph.D. is professor emeritus at the Southern University Agricultural Center (SUAREC) and co-founder of the Southeastern African American Farmers Organic Network (SAAFON). Dr. Bandele has conducted organic production workshops throughout the Southeast and the Caribbean. Through his work with SAAFON and SUAREC he has provided organic training that led to organic certification of over 40 farmers in the Southeast, most of whom were African Americans. During the 1990s, Bandele and his wife, Efuru, established the Food For Thought Farm in Louisiana, which was a certified operation. Dr. Bandele has also served on the National Organic Standards Board.

Gail Myers, Ph.D. is a cultural anthropologist, community organizer, educator, and avid gardener. She founded Farms to Grow, Inc. and the Freedom Farmers Market in Oakland, CA. Dr. Myers lectures and consults frequently with community based, universities, and national organizations, as well as local, state, and federal agencies. She educates communities about the rich historical traditions of Black farmers and traditional food ways. Dr. Myers has received numerous awards and recognitions including from the California State Senate and the Ohio State House of Representatives. She continues a wide spectrum of grassroots organizing and coalition building through her work with Farms to Grow,

Inc. Her upcoming documentary film, "Rhythms of the Land," is currently in post-production. www.rhythmsoftheland.com.

Dánia C. Davy, Esq. serves as Deputy Director of the Black Belt Justice Center where she leads the Acres of Ancestry Oral History Project, provides agri-business legal services and advocates for increasing diversity in the legal marijuana industry. She began her legal career as a Skadden Fellow at the North Carolina Association of Black Lawyers Land Loss Prevention Project where she provided estate planning and foreclosure defense legal services for underrepresented farmland owners, served on the inaugural North Carolina Sustainable Local Food Advisory Council and directed her first documentary—"Our Land, Our Lives: The North Carolina Black Farmers Experience." Dánia's interests include health and wealth equity, agri-business development & sustainability.

Edward "Jerry" Pennick retired from the Federation of Southern Cooperatives/Land Assistance Fund after serving for 39 years as its Director of Land Assistance and Policy Coordinator for African American farmers, landowners, and rural communities. He currently works part—time as Rural Policy Coordinator for Tuskegee University's School of Agriculture. He is also a rural development consultant.

Savonala Horne, Esq. is the Executive Director of the North Carolina Association of Black Lawyers Land Loss Prevention Project. As a state, regional and national non-governmental organization leader, Savonala has been instrumental in addressing the needs of small and socially-disadvantaged farmers. Horne serves on national sustainable agriculture and small farms boards, including the National Family Farm Coalition, the Rural Coalition and the Black Family Land Trust.

Tracy Lloyd McCurty, Esq. is a mother, activist, and attorney with over ten years of experience working on a range of legal issues disparately impacting the African Diaspora community. However, her most cherished work has been in service of multigenerational African American farm families and cooperatives living on the land in the rural South. Tracy is the Co-Founder and Executive Director of the Black Belt

Justice Center, a legal and advocacy nonprofit dedicated to the preservation and regeneration of African American farmlands and land-based livelihoods through effective legal representation, advocacy, and community education. Greatly influenced by the visionary blueprints of the Emergency Land Fund and the New Communities Community Land Trust, Inc., Tracy is dedicated to the advancement of community-controlled financing as well as communal forms of land ownership.

Blain Snipstal is an ecological farmer at Black Dirt Farm on the Eastern shore of Maryland. He is a part of the Black Dirt Farm Collective that facilitates and organizes trainings, gatherings, and workshops on topics ranging from agroecology to Afro-ecology, forestry to popular and political education throughout the Chesapeake Bay region (the North-South). Black Dirt Farm is a member of SAAFON, where Blain sits on the board of the organization.

Leah Penniman is an educator, farmer, and food justice activist from Soul Fire Farm in Grafton, NY. She is committed to dismantling the oppressive structures that misguide our food system, reconnecting marginalized communities to land, and upholding our responsibility to steward the land that nourishes us. She is a core member of the Freedom Food Alliance, which cultivates life-giving food for apartheid neighborhoods and of Ayiti Resurrect, which coordinates reforestation projects in Haiti, her ancestral homeland. She holds an MA in Science Education and BA in Environmental Studies and International Development from Clark University. She has been farming since 1996 and teaching since 2002.

Section Two

Angie Carter currently lives in Iowa and teaches sociology at Augustana College in Rock Island, IL. She is an environmental sociologist studying intersections of community, inequality, and social change. She thanks the Women, Food and Agriculture Network, Iowa Farmers Union, and Practical Farmers of Iowa for their leadership and for welcoming her as she learned more about gender-based inequality in agriculture.

Kirtrina M. Baxter, MA is a dedicated mother, drummer, urban farmer, food justice activist, and community organizer. As an afroecologist, she has a passion for preserving and creating cultural agrarian traditions through art, cooking, and nutrition; growing food; seed keeping; and collective organizing. Kirtrina is currently the community organizer for the Garden Justice Legal Initiative—a program of the Public Interest Law Center of Philadelphia. She works with gardeners around the city, assisting them in gaining access to land and other resources. In this capacity, she also organizes Soil Generation, a diverse body of urban agriculture advocates and food justice activists who work within a racial and economic justice framework to help inform policy and provide community education and support to gardeners in the city.

Dara Cooper is an activist and organizer collaborating with other food justice activists nationally to organize the National Black Food and Justice Alliance, a coalition of Black-led organizations working towards cultivating and advancing Black leadership; building Black self-determination; building Black institutions; and organizing for food sovereignty, land, and justice. Prior to this work, Dara served as director of the NYC Food and Fitness Partnership (NYC FFP). Prior to NYC FFP she led the launch and expansion of Fresh Moves (Chicago), an award-winning mobile produce market with community health programming, which quickly became a nationally recognized model for healthy food distribution and community based self-determination and empowerment. Dara is also a National Alliance Against Racist Political Repression Human Rights Awardee; a member of Black Farmers Urban Gardeners and the Malcolm X Grassroots Movement; and a board member of Cooperation Jackson.

Aleya Fraser is a Baltimore native who now lives and works on the agriculture-rich Eastern Shore of Maryland. She has worn many hats: educator, scientist, researcher, organizer, farmer, and event planner. She obtained her B.S. in Physiology and Neurobiology from the University of Maryland, College Park; taught middle school science; and worked various jobs in the medical field before beginning her journey into working with land. Her farming experience includes managing an urban farm in Baltimore (Five Seeds Farm & Apiary) and co-managing a larger farm on rural land in Preston, MD (Black Dirt Farm Collective) using agroecological practices. Working with farmers and the land is the crux of all her passions, and she uses it as a platform for social justice, inter- and intra-personal transformation, education, and scientific discovery. And she thinks farming is fun!

Shakara Tyler is a mother, returning-generation farmer, educator, and organizer-scholar. Her personal journey of loving, healing, and decolonizing is intimately wedded with working and learning with the land. She is committed to working with communities to explore the pedagogies of reconnecting to land and using land-based activism as a tool for building community self-determination. As part of her academic studies, she explores decolonial pedagogies in the food justice and food sovereignty movements within the communal praxis of black agrarianism.

Section Three

Caitlin Hachmyer founded Red H Farm, a diversified vegetable operation in Sebastopol, CA, in 2009. With an undergraduate degree in Anthropology and Conservation Resource Studies from the University of California, Berkeley and a graduate degree in Urban and Environmental Policy and Planning from Tufts University, her work on the ground is complimented by research, writing, teaching, and activism. In addition to building a biodiverse, agroecological farm landscape, she is a contract researcher and writer for the Institute for Food and Development Policy/Food First, a member of the Sonoma County Food Systems Alliance, a lead instructor at the Permaculture Skills Center's Farm School, adjunct faculty at Sonoma State University, an advisory board member at Petaluma Bounty, and the founder of the project Foundations and the Future: Celebrating Women's Leadership in the Food Movement. In 2016 she was acknowledged by the Food and Agriculture Organization of the United Nation's through their Agroecology Knowledge Hub and by American Farmland Trust's Profiles in Stewardship project.

Devon G. Peña, Ph.D. is the founder and president of The Acequia Institute and Professor of American Ethnic Studies and Anthropology at the University of Washington. A lifelong activist in the environmental and food justice movements, Dr. Peña manages a 181 acre Acequia farm in San Pablo, CO where the Institute operates an agroecology and permaculture farm school and grassroots extension service. He is an award winning research scholar with several books, two edited encyclopedias, and hundreds of other publications. His most recent book is *Mexican-Origin Foods, Foodways, and Social Movements: Decolonial Perspectives* (University of Arkansas Press 2017).

Hartman Deetz is a Wampanoag of the Mashpee community. Born in Massachusetts, he moved to Berkeley, California at age 2. Beginning at age 12, Deetz became a bicoastal child after his father's return to Mashpee. Deetz spent ten years living and working within the community for tribal cultural education programs. Deetz returned to college and in 2016 earned his BA in cultural education and sustaining marginalized communities from Goddard College in Vermont. Deetz currently lives in Richmond, California where he continues to be active in native environmental rights with the San Francisco chapter of Idle No More.

Section Four

David Bacon is a writer and photographer, and former union organizer. He is the author of several books on labor, migration, and the global economy including *The Children of NAFTA, Communities Without Borders, Illegal People*, and *The Right to Stay Home*. His new book, *In the Fields of the North* will be published this winter by Colegia Frontera Norte. His photographs and stories can be found at http://dbacon.igc.org and http://davidbaconrealitycheck.blogspot.com

Rosalinda Guillén is a widely recognized farm justice leader and Executive Director of Community to Community Development (C2C), a Bellingham-based, women-led grassroots organization that promotes food justice, immigration reform, and farmworker rights in Northwest Washington State. C2C is also a leading organization in the US Food Sovereignty Alliance, the National Dignity Campaign Network, North Sound Immigrant Justice Alliance, Grassroots Global Justice Alliance, the Agricultural Justice Project, and the National Domestic Fair Trade Alliance. Rosalinda has worked with Cesar Chavez's United Farm Workers of America (UFW) where she was the lead legislative and political officer for four years, and also served as the elected National Vice President of the Union.

Andrew Ofstehage is a Ph.D. candidate in anthropology at the University of North Carolina at Chapel Hill. He grew up on a South Dakota corn and soybean farm, learned to operate a combine and tractor, and then studied to be an agronomist. He turned to ethnographic research of agrarian change to better understand the social world of agriculture and studied the socio-ecological impacts of commodification of quinoa in the southern Altiplano of Bolivia before re-focusing his research on American farmers. His dissertation research is a study of transnational farming and the emerging assemblage of Brazilian Cerrado, US farmers, soy, and the political ecology of Soylandia.

Section Five

Brahm Ahmadi is a social entrepreneur working to build healthier and more equitable inner city communities. In 2003, he co-founded People's Grocery, a nonprofit organization that has attracted national attention for its projects in food enterprise, urban agriculture, and nutrition education. In 2010, Brahm founded People's Community Market to create a fresh food retail business model that fosters health and social interaction in low-income communities. He's also piloting a model for catalyzing the general public to invest in mission-driven companies and local communities. Brahm holds a BA in Sociology from the University of California and an MBA from the Presidio Graduate School. He was a "Food and Community Fellow" at the Institute for Agriculture and Trade Policy (2011-2013). Brahm was born in Tehran, Iran, grew up in Los Angeles, and now lives in Oakland, CA.

Malik Kenyatta Yakini is a founder and the executive director of the Detroit Black Community Food Security Network (DBCFSN). DBCFSN operates a seven-acre urban farm and is spearheading the opening of a co-op grocery store in Detroit's North End. Yakini views the "good food revolution" as part of the larger movement for freedom, justice and equality. He has an intense interest in contributing to the development of an international food sovereignty movement that embraces Black communities in the Americas, the Caribbean, and Africa.

Section Six

Antonio Roman-Alcalá is an organizer, writer, and educator based in the San Francisco Bay Area. He is a co-founder of multiple urban farms and grassroots alliances, a documentary filmmaker, and blogger at antidogmatist.com. He currently works promoting agroecology in the US through scholarly, advocacy, and grassroots initiatives.

Clifford Andrew "Cliff" Welch teaches history at the Federal University of São Paulo (UNIFESP) in Brazil. He was born in San Francisco and researched the history of the NLP (National Land for People) while serving as a history department Research Associate at the University of California - Santa Cruz, funded by grant BEX 3964/13-4 from Brazil's Coordination for the Improvement of Higher Education Personnel (CAPES).

Richael Faithful is a Black folk healer, creative writer, and lawyer based in Washington, DC Faithful is the author of numerous legal articles and creative non-fiction essays which discuss the intersections of identities, spiritualities and politics, and currently serves as a contributing editor with the *National Lawyers' Guild Review*.

The US Food Sovereignty Alliance: Developing a National Strategy for Land and Resource Reform

Tristan Quinn-Thibodeau, Stephen Bartlett, Lisa Griffith, and Kathy Ozer

The US Food Sovereignty Alliance (USFSA) was formed in 2010 by a group of activists and organizations out of various networks and working groups, with the goal to advance food sovereignty in the US by strengthening the leadership of frontline organizations and building connections with the global struggle for food sovereignty. USFSA member organizations—which now total more than 30 "grassroots" and "grassroots support organizations"—discussed the common issues facing their communities, and we found that all were struggling to regain control over land, water, and fisheries. As discussed throughout this book, farmers and fishermen report being squeezed off their land and out of their boats; African-American and Latino farmers recount ongoing discrimination; beginning farmers cannot access land; and urban communities are challenged in their efforts to build food justice through gentrification and real estate speculation.

The USFSA formed the Land and Resource Grabs and Reform Team to resist these enclosures and to push for reform. Our initial team strategy was to build momentum for a national movement by offering a network of support to the communities that are "born into struggle." We reached out to organizations in the midst of current land and resource conflicts, and asked them to define the kind of support they needed from the USFSA.

The team held many calls to learn about land struggles and to offer support to on-the-ground campaigns. For instance, we joined a social media campaign to stop the Detroit City Council's sale of public land to a private developer (see Yakini, this volume) and built international solidarity with the Black Honduran Fraternal Organization by working to raise US awareness of their struggles against land takeovers. However, our collective soon realized that "fighting fires" would not be enough. The USFSA needed to do more to develop a national strategy and space for action so that we could support grassroots leadership without leaning on them to take on more work.

After the USFSA's Second Membership Assembly in 2013, the collective decided to plan a National Day of Action. We invited organizations representing four core frontline constituencies—farm workers, family farmers, small-scale fishermen, and urban communities fighting for community land to grow healthy food—to join the mobilization with actions of their own: Community 2 Community Development, a farmworker-led food justice and sovereignty organization, and *Familias Unidas por la Justicia,* a farmworker union, organized a People's Movement Assembly in Portland, Oregon; the National Family Farm Coalition brought family farmers and fishermen to the People's Climate March in New York; the Commercial Fishermen of Bristol Bay organized a petition drive to stop the government from building a mine that would damage Alaskan fisheries; and Occupy the Farm in Berkeley and Albany, California organized an occupation to protest the University's plan to sell public, urban farmland. Because these activities actually spanned September 17 (the anniversary of Occupy Wall Street) to October 16 (World Food Sovereignty Day), we renamed them the National *Days* of Action in Defense of Land and the Commons. We also created popular education materials on the injustice of land distribution to share at these actions and on social media.

After the mobilization, team members and participants shared experiences and analyzed impact. We made two decisions about our strategy for future mobilizations. First, we needed to put more time and capacity into making media and communications more effective. The team agreed to recruit more organizations and to create better social media and web platforms. We created social media template materials for groups to use. Second, we agreed that we needed to both deepen the political implications of our analysis, and simplify our message for public audiences. Because *privatization* was driving land and resource grabs, we reframed our efforts as taking back "the commons," because resources like land and fisheries belong to everyone. We named the 2015 mobilization the "Month of Community Power to Reclaim the Commons," and developed new popular education materials to highlight how centralized land control connects to poverty and oppression.

In October 2015, nine community-based organizations led actions as part of the Month of Community Power to Reclaim the Commons: Occupy the Farm organized a day to plant seeds and renew commitment to reclaim public farmland; the Northwest Atlantic Marine Alliance organized a day of protest against fisheries privatization in Plymouth, MA; Southwest Workers Union and Soil Generation organized urban gardening community trainings in Austin, TX and Philadelphia, PA, respectively; the Beach Flats Community Garden led a march to defend the garden from development in Santa Cruz, CA; and various farmers and fishermen groups coordinated an educational exhibit about land and water issues at Farm Aid in Chicago, IL.

The processes of organizing the 2014 National Days of Action and 2015 Month of Community Power have led to the creation of much needed infrastructure for communications, messaging, and strategy. Making this available at a national level for grassroots organizations to use is important because struggles over land and resources are never just local; grabs are reinforced by national and even international policy. Without a national platform, it is difficult for local groups to mobilize the mass movement needed to return land and water back to the people.

In early 2016, members of the USFSA attended the International Conference on People's Agrarian Reform, hosted by La Vía Campesina in Marabá, Brazil. We learned that "People's Agrarian Reform" is a program for all of society that ensures that everyone has access to healthy food and secure livelihoods by ensuring that food producers are fully supported; it is not just about providing land and support to farmers, but is an alliance between the rural and urban people centered around healthy food and care for the land and water. We saw that this was the kind of platform that communities demanded, so we organized a learning call and adopted People's Agrarian Reform as the theme of the 2016 Day of Action. One of the core actions of this Day of Action was a learning call and the launch of a US campaign by the USFSA and its allies to stop land grabbing and speculation by the pension fund TIAA, the largest institutional investor of farmland in the world and one of the leaders in the financialization of farmland. For us, farmland is not a commodity, but an important resource for all of society.

Halting foreclosures of farms, raising wages and creating pathways to land ownership for farm workers, rejecting national privatization policies to manage the fisheries, and reversing gentrification in our cities are the frontline issues we most regularly battle. But we also have to create new alternatives that de-commodify land and resources and return privatized lands to the people from whom they were stolen.

There are many challenges facing the movements for food sovereignty—communities have increasing needs and there are never enough resources to address them—but one of the biggest challenges may be the urgent timeframe we are facing. In the next 15 years, it is estimated that 400 million acres of US farmland will transfer ownership as many farmers retire. If this land is governed by the free market instead of the democratic will of the people, it will be lost to exploitative profit-making and industrial agriculture. To ensure that society supports all people and cares for the land and the water, we need food sovereignty, and that means we need to commit to each other now to take collective action to defend the earth, repair historical injustices, and protect our future.

INDEX

ABOUT FOOD FIRST

The Institute for Food and Development Policy, also known as Food First, is a nonprofit research and education-for-action center dedicated to investigating and exposing the root causes of hunger in a world of plenty. Over 41 years of research has shown that hunger is caused by injustice—not scarcity. Resources and decision-making are in the hands of a privileged few, depriving the majority of land, dignified work, and healthy food.

Founded in 1975 by Frances Moore-Lappé, author of the best-selling book, Diet for a Small Planet, and food policy analyst Dr. Joseph Collins, Food First has published over 60 books. Hailed by the New York Times as "one of the most established food think tanks in the country," Food First's groundbreaking work continues to shape local, national, and international polices and debates about hunger and its root causes. Learn more at www.foodfirst.org.

Become a Member!

We invite you to join Food First. As a member, you will receive a 20 percent discount on all Food First books. You will also receive our quarterly publications, newsletter, and backgrounders, providing information for action on current food and land struggles in the United States and around the world. All contributions are tax deductible. Please visit our website for details at www.foodfirst.org, or contact us at foodfirst@foodfirst.org or (510) 654-4400.

RECOMMENDED READING
FROM FOOD FIRST

Available from www.foodfirst.org

Fertile Ground: Scaling Agroecology from the Ground Up
Edited by Steve Brescia
Agroecology is our best option for creating an agrifood system capable of nurturing people, societies, and the planet. But it is still not widespread. Fertile Ground, edited by Groundswell International's Executive Director Steve Brescia, offers nine case studies authored by agroecologists from Africa, Latin America, the Caribbean, North America, and Europe, that demonstrate how the endogenous practice of agroecology can be "scaled" so that it is known by more farmers, practiced more deeply, and integrated in planning and policy.
March 2017, Paperback, $14.95

World Hunger: 10 Myths
Frances Moore Lappé and Joseph Collins
Brimming with little-known but life-changing examples of solutions to hunger worldwide, this controversial, myth-busting book argues that sustainable agriculture can feed the world, that we can end nutritional deprivation affecting one-quarter of the world's people, and that most in the Global North have more in common with the world's hungry people than they thought. For novices and scholars alike, World Hunger: 10 Myths is an accessible, solutions-based book that will change how people think about the world and inspire a whole new generation of hunger-fighters.
May 2015, Paperback, $18.00

Food First: Selected Writings From 40 Years of Movement Building
Edited by Tanya M. Kerssen and Teresa K. Miller
This book looks back on forty years of writings from Food First/Institute for Food and Development Policy on the occasion of its fortieth anniversary. The book highlights the breadth and depth of the organization's published works, addressing issues such as hunger, international trade, US foreign policy, the Green Revolution, agroecology, land reform, food and farm workers' rights, climate justice, and food sovereignty.
September 2015, Paperback, $20.00

CPSIA information can be obtained
at www.ICGtesting.com
Printed in the USA
JSHW051449151221
21288JS00007B/162

9 780935 028041